THE PENNYPINCHER
HOUSEHOLD HANDBOOK

DAVID & CHARLES
Newton Abbot   London   North Pomfret (Vt)

**British Library Cataloguing in
Publication Data**

The pennypincher household handbook.
   1. Home economics – Handbooks,
      manuals, etc.
   I. Wadey, Rosemary
   640   TX145

   ISBN 0-7153-7844-9

Printed in Great Britain
by Redwood Burn Ltd, Trowbridge & Esher
for David & Charles (Publishers) Limited
Brunel House Newton Abbot Devon

Published in the United States of America
by David & Charles Inc
North Pomfret Vermont 05053 USA

CONTENTS

Baking Breads

Preserving and Pickling

Easy Vegetable Growing

Making Your Children's Clothes

Everyday Home Repairs

BAKING BREADS

Rosemary Wadey

Basic Rules in Yeast Cooking

Freshly baked bread has a tantalizing and persistent aroma. Many people are rather scared of coping with yeast cooking although they long to produce their own bread and enjoy both the smell and satisfaction of 'baking their own'.

The baker's skill is age-old and has been handed down through the generations, but yeast cookery is really very simple provided that you follow a few simple rules and don't try to hurry. With a little practice, excellent home-made bread can be achieved.

The point to remember is that yeast is a living plant, unlike other raising agents, and in order to make it grow it needs gentle warmth, food and liquid. Given these conditions, the yeast grows rapidly and gives off a harmless and tasteless gas called carbon dioxide. These air bubbles of gas cause the dough to rise and the trapped air bubbles are then baked into the bread to give light airiness to the loaf. The yeast also produces alcohol when it is rising which gives the characteristic smell and taste to freshly baked bread.

Yeast

There are two types of yeast which can be used in breadmaking and both are readily available. Fresh yeast is often sold in health food shops and in many baker's shops which sell their own bread. Dried yeast is sold in supermarkets and chemists.

Fresh baker's yeast resembles putty and has a smell rather like wine. It will keep for up to a month in a refrigerator when stored in a loosely tied polythene bag, or for four to five days in a cool place. It will freeze for up to a year, but package it in small usable amounts, ie 15g (½oz) or 25g (1oz), and wrap first in cling-film and then foil.

Dried yeast will keep for up to six months if stored in an airtight container. It looks like small granules of compacted fresh yeast. Instructions for activating the yeast and quantities required are given on the tin or packet. It should either be reconstituted in warm liquid with a little sugar added and be left in a warm place until frothy (which usually takes 10–20 minutes) or it should be mixed into a flour, sugar and milk or water batter, which should be left in a warm place until frothy—about 20–30 minutes. This method is more often used for richer breads.

Basic Rules in Yeast Cooking

Flour

A strong, plain flour, called bread flour by bakers, gives the best results in breadmaking, because it has a higher gluten content than ordinary plain flour, allowing more absorption of water and thus giving a greater volume and lighter bread. A soft flour absorbs more fat but less water, thus giving a smaller volume and closer, shorter texture ; but this type of flour is sometimes used for rich, fancy breads. If strong flour is not available, use an ordinary plain flour (never self-raising flour). The result will not be as successful but the recipe will still work. There are also speciality flours which are used to make certain types of bread : rye flours, stone-ground and compost-grown flours, etc. These can be incorporated into breads but they are often more expensive.

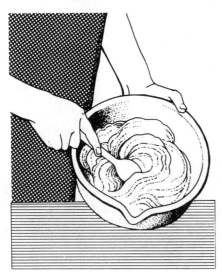

Liquid

This should be added all at once to the dough to mix it evenly. Extra flour can be easily kneaded in if the dough is too sticky, but it is not as easy to knead in extra water. The liquid is usually water or milk or a mixture of the two. Part of the liquid is used to dissolve the yeast and then the resulting yeast liquid and remaining liquid are added at the same time.

Fat

A small amount added to plain mixtures helps keep the bread moist, but it is not essential. It is usually rubbed into the dry ingredients and can be in the form of lard, butter or margarine. With richer mixtures, more fat is required and it is often melted, or sometimes softened, and added with the other liquid ingredients ; sometimes it can be rubbed in. It can also be put on to the dough in flakes or spread in a softened form and then folded up and rolled out several times as with flaky pastry. This gives extra crispness and lightness by trapping the air in two ways, as is necessary in croissants and Danish pastries. Oil can be used in place of fat in some recipes.

Warmth

All yeast mixtures need warmth and, for the best results, the bowl, flour and the liquid should all be warmed before starting. Liquid needs to be between 37–43°C (98–110°F). Too much heat, or water that is too hot will quickly kill the yeast, so take care not to put a rising dough in a hot place—it just needs to be warm.

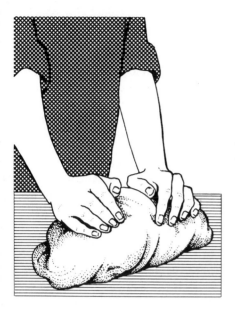

Kneading

Dough must be kneaded to strengthen
and develop it in order to give a good
rise. Knead by folding the dough
towards you, then push down and
away from you with the palm of your
hand. Give the dough a quarter turn
and continue the kneading process,
developing a rocking action. Continue
for about 10 minutes until the dough
feels firm and elastic and no longer
sticks to your fingers. An electric mixer
can be used if the instruction book says
that the mixer is suitable for kneading
dough. Use a dough hook and switch
on for 3–4 minutes on a low speed.
Follow instructions for the maximum
amount the mixer can handle.
Overloading will damage the machine.

Rising

All yeast doughs must rise at least once
before baking. After kneading, the
dough should be shaped into a ball and
put into a large covered container
which has been lightly greased, eg a
large oiled polythene bag, a lightly
greased saucepan or a plastic storage
container, etc. There must be enough
space for the dough to double in size
at the least.

Rising times vary with the
temperature but the dough needs time
to rise to double in size and should
spring back when lightly pressed with a
floured finger. On average, it takes
$\frac{3}{4}$–1 hour in a warm place ; 2 hours at
room temperature ; up to 12 hours in a
cold room or larder, or up to 24 hours
in a refrigerator. (Remember to allow
refrigerated dough to return to room
temperature before proceeding.) A
longer, slow rise does give a stronger
dough and better bread, but the type
of rising should be chosen to fit in with
the daily routine. Surplus dough can be
stored in a polythene bag or container
for up to two days in a refrigerator.

After the dough has been shaped, it
is ready to be put to rise for a second
time. Put the tin or baking sheet which
holds the dough inside a large, oiled
polythene bag or cover it with a sheet
of oiled polythene to prevent a skin
forming on it while it rises to double its
size again. Remove the polythene
before baking.

Baking

Use a hot oven, 190–230°C (375–
450°F) mark 5–8. The richer, fruity
mixtures are usually cooked at the
lower temperature scale, with lighter
breads, etc, at the hotter. A pan of hot
water placed in the bottom of the oven
gives the steamy atmosphere needed
to bake the very best breads. Dark tins,
if available, bake better bread.

Basic White Bread

The basic white loaf can be made into a variety of shapes and sizes and the following recipe can be used to make a basic dough from which other fancy breads can be made. This method of making bread can be used as a basis for all types of yeast cookery.

Ingredients

700g (1½lb) strong plain white flour
10ml (2 level tsp) salt
15g (½oz) lard
15g (½oz) fresh yeast or 7.5ml (1½ level tsp) dried yeast and 5ml (1 level tsp) caster sugar
400ml (¾pt) warm water 43°C (110°F)

Grease a 900g (2lb) loaf tin or two 450g (1lb) loaf tins or 2–3 baking sheets if you are making rolls.

Sieve the flour and salt into a bowl and then rub in the lard. Blend the fresh yeast with the water. If using dried yeast, dissolve the sugar in the water, sprinkle the yeast over the top and leave in a warm place until frothy—about 10 minutes. Add the yeast liquid to the dry ingredients all at once and mix, using a wooden spoon or fork, to form a firm dough. Add a little extra flour if necessary until the dough leaves the sides of the bowl clean. The dough should be firm but not stiff. Turn out on to a lightly floured surface and knead thoroughly until the dough is smooth and elastic and not at all sticky. To do this, hold the dough in front of you and then push it down and away from you using the palm of your hand, fold it over towards you, give a quarter turn and continue in this way for about 10 minutes. Shape it into a ball. Place the dough in a large, lightly oiled polythene bag, loosely tied at the top. This will prevent a skin forming. Put it to rise until it has doubled in size and will spring back when lightly pressed with a floured finger. For a quick rise 45–60 minutes will suffice in a warm place—about 23°C (75°F)—such as above the cooker or in an airing

cupboard. For a slower rise, about two hours will do at average room temperature. For an overnight rise, leave the dough for up to 12 hours in a cold larder or room, or up to 24 hours in a refrigerator.

All types of rising give good results, but a slow rise will give the best results. However, use whichever fits in best with your routine. Remember that refrigerated dough must be allowed to return to room temperature before proceeding. This takes about 1 hour.

Remove the risen dough from the polythene bag and turn it on to a lightly floured surface, flatten it with the knuckles to knock out the air bubbles then knead it to make it firm and ready for shaping. This takes about 2 minutes. The process is called 'knocking back'. Use flour very sparingly as too much kneaded into the dough at this stage will spoil the colour of the crust. The dough is now ready for shaping, proving and baking.

To make one large loaf, stretch the dough into an oblong shape the same width as the tin and then fold it into three and turn it over so that the seam is underneath. Smooth over the top, tuck in the ends and place it in the greased 900g (2lb) tin. For two smaller loaves, divide the dough in half and shape each piece as for the large loaf and then place in the greased 450g (1lb) loaf tins. For rolls, divide the dough into 50g (2oz) pieces and shape into rolls (see p 20). Place them well apart on greased baking sheets. Put the tins or baking sheets inside large, oiled polythene bags and put to rise again in a warm place until the dough reaches the top of the tin. This will take about 45–60 minutes. Cooler

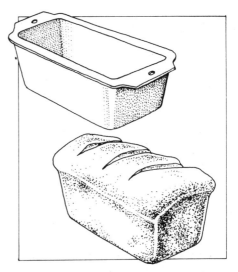

rising will take longer. Leave rolls until doubled in size. Remove the polythene and place the loaf tins on a baking sheet. Bake in a very hot oven, 230 °C (450 °F) mark 8, for about 40 minutes for a large loaf, about 30 minutes for smaller loaves, and 15–20 minutes for rolls. They will be well risen and golden brown. When ready, the loaves shrink slightly from the side of the tin and the base sounds hollow when tapped. Turn on to a wire rack and leave to cool.

Note The dough can be mixed and kneaded in a large electric mixer using a dough hook. But check in the instruction book on the amount of dough recommended to be made in your particular machine before you start. Overloading will cause damage. Allow about 3–4 minutes for kneading, until smooth and elastic. This bread freezes well and can be made in larger batches, if preferred.

Shaping Loaves

Once the dough is made, there are numerous ways to shape it before baking. The traditional tin loaves are easy and successful, but you can have great fun working dough into simple or exotic shapes which can be baked in a variety of tins or on baking sheets. All the following shapes can be made using the basic white bread dough.

Coburg loaf

Cottage Loaf

This traditional crusty loaf is often used as a baker's individual emblem. It is most attractive and can be made into various sized loaves or rolls.

Divide the basic white bread dough in half to make two smaller loaves or use it all for a large loaf. Remove one-third of the dough for the topknot. Shape the remainder into a bun shape and place on a greased baking sheet. Shape the smaller piece into a ball, damp the base and put it on top of the large bun. Secure by pushing your first finger and thumb right through the centre of the loaf to the base, keeping the topknot central. Brush with egg wash (see p 18), cover loosely with

Cottage loaf

oiled polythene and put to rise in a warm place until doubled in size. Remove polythene and bake in a very hot oven, 230°C (450°F) mark 8, for 30–40 minutes. For a notched cottage loaf, after proving, cut the loaf vertically with downward sweeps, using a large, sharp knife and then bake.

Coburg Loaf

Divide the basic white bread dough into two pieces and shape each piece into a round ball. To do this, roll the dough in a circular movement with the palm of your hand, gradually easing the pressure to give a smooth, round ball. Place on a baking sheet and brush all over with milk or egg wash. Mark a cross on top of the loaves using a sharp knife. Place in an oiled polythene bag and put to rise in a warm place until doubled in size then remove polythene and brush again with milk or egg wash. Bake at 230°C (450°F) mark 8 for 30–40 minutes, until golden brown. Cool on a wire rack.

Bloomer

This is a long, baton-shaped, crusty loaf with slashes all along the top. Use all the basic white bread dough for a large loaf or divide it in half for two smaller loaves. Shape each piece into an even thickness baton by rolling backwards and forwards with the palms of both hands. Tuck the ends underneath and place on a greased baking sheet. Brush with egg wash or milk, cover with a sheet of oiled polythene and put to rise in a warm place until doubled in size. Make several slashes along the top of the loaf using a sharp knife. Bake in a very hot oven, 230°C (450°F) mark 8, for 30–40 minutes, until golden brown and crusty. Cool on a wire rack. The loaves can be sprinkled with poppy seeds before baking.

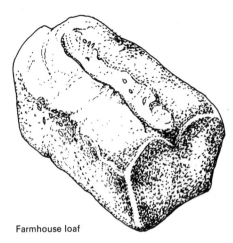

Farmhouse loaf

Farmhouse Loaf

This is an unglazed loaf which can be either baked in a tin or on a tray. It has a deep slash along the length of the loaf which opens out during baking.

Shape the dough to fit one large 900g (2lb) or two small 450g (1lb) tins and then, when proved, make a cut along the length of the loaf using a sharp knife. If you prefer a loaf baked without a tin, shape the dough into a bloomer shape, put on a greased baking sheet, cover with oiled polythene and put to rise. Before baking, make a cut along the top as for the loaves in tins. Bake in a very hot oven, 230°C (450°F) mark 8, for 30–40 minutes. To crisp up the loaves baked in tins, return them to the oven without the tins when they are cooked. Cool on a wire rack.

Bloomer

Shaping Loaves

French Stick

The traditional French stick is put to rise in a cloth-lined basket, but any long, narrow container or dish can be used after lining it with a well floured cloth.

Roll half the basic white bread dough out carefully, using the palms of both hands, to give a sausage shape about 35cm (14in) long. Place in the prepared container and put to rise in a warm place until it has doubled in size. Carefully turn the loaf out on to a long greased baking sheet and remove the cloth. Make diagonal cuts into the dough at 4in (10cm) intervals holding the blade of the knife horizontally. Bake in a very hot oven, 230°C (450°F) mark 8, on the centre shelf, with a bowl of boiling water on the shelf below, for 20–30 minutes. Shorter loaves can be made if preferred. For a Vienna loaf, make into thick sausage shapes with tapered ends 23–25cm (9–10in) long. Prove, slash and bake as for French sticks.

Crescent Loaf

An attractive rolled up loaf which takes a little practice to perfect. Use half the basic white bread dough and roll out to an oval shape on a well floured surface. Leave to rest for 5 minutes then roll up tightly, pulling on the edge nearest to you all the time until it forms a sausage shape. Bend into a crescent shape and place on a greased baking sheet. Cover with oiled polythene and put to rise in a warm place until the dough has doubled in size. Brush with egg wash and bake in a very hot oven, 230°C

(450°F) mark 8. for 25–30 minutes, until well browned. Cool on a wire rack.

Plaited Loaf

This method of shaping can be used to make large or small plaits or rolls. Take the required amount of white bread dough and divide into three equal pieces. Roll the three pieces out to long, thin sausage shapes of equal length. Place the three strands next to each other perpendicular to you and, starting in the middle and working towards you, plait them evenly, pinching the ends tightly together. Turn the plait completely over with the plaited end away from you. Plait the remaining pieces towards you to complete the plait, and secure the ends. Place on a greased baking sheet and brush with egg wash. Cover with oiled polythene and put to rise until doubled in size. Brush again with egg wash and either leave the loaf plain or sprinkle it with poppy seeds or sesame seeds. Bake in a very hot oven, 230°C (450°F) mark 8, for 20–35 minutes, depending on size. Rolls will take 10–15 minutes. Cool on a wire rack.

Egg Wash

Beat 1 egg with 15ml (1 tbsp) water and a pinch of salt until evenly mixed.

(*Opposite, from the top*) French stick ; Crescent loaf ; Plaited loaf ; Brushing loaf with egg wash

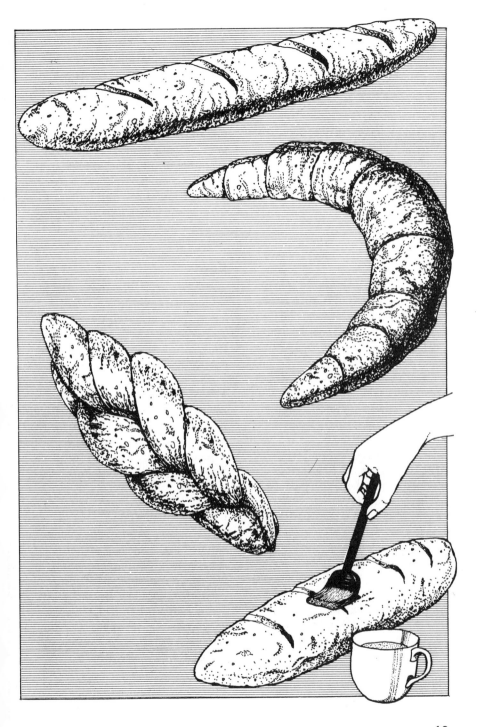

Shaping Rolls

Most doughs can be made into rolls as well as loaves. Rich, fruited doughs are best shaped into straightforward round buns, but the plainer doughs can be twisted, tied and cut into most exotic-looking rolls. The size of the rolls is up to you and dependent on the specific purpose for which they are required—but they are usually shaped from 50–75g (2–3oz) pieces of risen dough.

For soft-sided rolls—the type you pull apart—put the pieces of dough about 2cm (¾in) apart on the baking sheet, but for crusty rolls leave plenty of space around each one so that they do not touch while baking. Crustiness is helped by brushing the tops with salted water before baking.

Cover all rolls, after shaping and placing on a greased baking sheet, with a piece of oiled polythene or put the whole baking sheet into a large oiled polythene bag and put to rise in a warm place until doubled in size. This usually takes 15–30 minutes. Remove the polythene and either brush the tops with egg wash (see p 18), milk or salted water, or leave unglazed. The tops can be left plain or be sprinkled with poppy seeds, sesame seeds or, for brown rolls, cracked wheat or crushed cornflakes. Bake rolls in a very hot oven 230°C (450°F) mark 8, for 10–20 minutes, depending on size, until well risen and browned. Cool on a wire rack.

Rolls freeze well when packaged in thick-gauge polythene bags, so you can save time by baking a large batch and freezing the surplus.

Traditional Round Rolls

Divide the dough into the required sized pieces and shape each piece into a ball by rolling it round and round, on a very lightly floured surface, with the palm of your hand. Press down hard at first and gradually ease the pressure until the ball is formed. You can also shape dough into a ball by folding the edges of it into the centre until smooth, even and round, and then turning it over to keep the smooth side upwards. Place on greased baking sheets, put to rise and bake.

Knots

Roll each piece of dough into a long sausage shape with the palms of both hands and then quickly tie into a knot. With practice, double and other fancy knots can be made. Place on greased baking sheets, put to rise and bake.

Twists

Divide each piece of dough in half and shape each piece into a long, thin sausage. Twist these two pieces together, securing the ends and place on greased baking sheets. Put to rise and bake.

Cottage Loaves

Divide the dough into pieces of the required size, then break off one-third of each piece. Roll the shapes into balls and place the large balls on a greased baking sheet. Brush the tops lightly with water and put the small balls on top. Secure by pushing your first finger right through the centre to the base. Put to rise and bake.

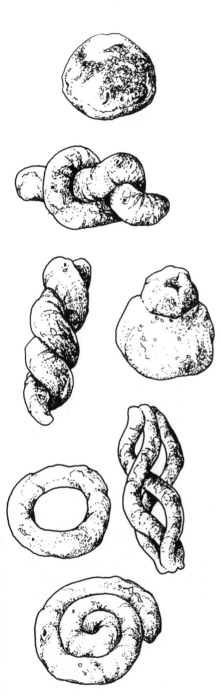

Plaits

Divide each piece of dough into three pieces and roll each out to a long, thin sausage. Plait these strands together evenly and secure the ends. The method for plaiting loaves (see p 22) gives a better shaped plait but it is not as easy to do if you are using small amounts of dough. Slightly larger pieces of dough will give a better plaited roll. Place on greased baking sheets, put to rise and bake.

Rings

Roll the pieces of dough into long, thin rolls and form into a ring. Damp the ends and mould them together securely. For twisted rings first twist two long strands of dough together and then form into a circle and mould the ends together. Place on greased baking sheets, put to rise and bake.

Coils

Roll the pieces of dough into long, thin sausage shapes. Starting at the centre, roll the sausage round and round to give a coil, tucking the ends underneath. For figure of eight coils, roll half of the dough sausage in one direction and the other half in the other direction. Place on greased baking sheets, put to rise and bake.

Enriched White Bread

This bread is made by the sponge batter method, which is especially good when using dried yeast because it does not have to be reconstituted first. It has a shorter texture than plain white bread because of the extra ingredients. Methods for making two kinds of loaves using this dough are given.

Ingredients

450g (1lb) strong plain white flour
5ml (1 level tsp) caster sugar
25g (1oz) fresh yeast or 15ml (1 level tbsp) dried yeast
250ml (8fl oz) warm milk, 143°C (110°F)
5ml (1 level tsp) salt
50g (2oz) margarine
1 egg, beaten

Glaze

1 egg, beaten
5ml (1 level tsp) caster sugar
15ml (1tbsp) water
Poppy seeds (optional)

Put 150g (5oz) sieved flour into a bowl with the sugar, yeast (either fresh or dried) and the milk. Put aside in a warm place for about 20 minutes until it is frothy and the yeast dissolved. Sieve the remaining flour with the salt into a bowl and rub in the margarine until the mixture resembles fine breadcrumbs. Add the beaten egg and the flour mixture to the yeast batter and mix well to give a fairly soft dough which will leave the sides of the bowl clean.

Turn the dough on to a lightly floured surface and knead (see p 13) until it is smooth and no longer sticky.

This should take about 10 minutes by hand or 3–4 minutes if you are using an electric mixer (no extra flour should be necessary). Form the dough into a ball and place in a lightly oiled polythene bag, tie loosely and put to rise in a warm place until doubled in size. See p 13 for alternate rising times.

Remove the dough from the polythene bag on to a sparsely floured surface and knead lightly. Divide the dough into two pieces ready for shaping into plaits.

Three Strand Plait

Divide each piece of dough into three, then roll each piece into a strand of about 30cm (12in). Lay the three strands side-by-side on a flat surface. Beginning in the middle, plait the three strands towards you, pinching the ends together. Turn the plait completely over so that the unplaited strands are perpendicular to you ; then plait these to complete the loaf, pinching the ends together. Place on a greased baking sheet.

Crown Loaf

Grease one 22.5cm (9in) or two 15cm (6in) round sandwich tins. Divide all the dough into twelve equal-sized pieces and roll each piece into a ball. Place these in a circle round the edge of the large tin with three or four in the middle or, if you are using the smaller tins, five round the edge of each one, with one ball in the centre.
For each loaf continue as follows:
Combine the beaten egg, sugar and water for the glaze and brush all over the plait or crowns. Sprinkle with poppy seeds or sesame seeds, if liked.

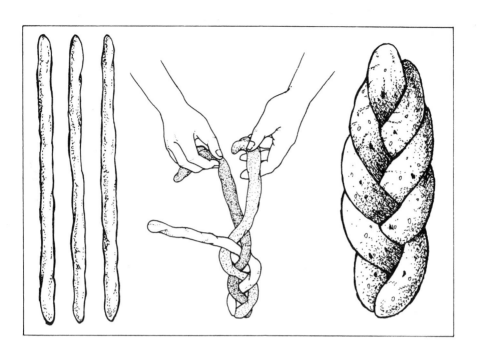

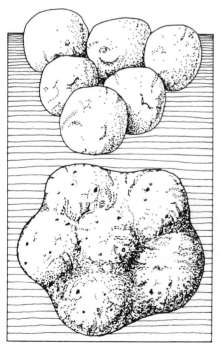

Put to rise inside a lightly oiled polythene bag in a warm place until the dough has doubled in size.

Bake in a moderately hot oven, 190°C (375°F) mark 5, for 45–50 minutes for the plaits, 50–60 minutes for the large crown, or 35–40 minutes for the small crowns, until they are lightly browned and hollow sounding when tapped on the base. Cool on a wire rack.

This dough can also be used for making rolls (see p 20 for shaping and baking).

Short-time White Bread

This recipe cuts out the initial rising stage of breadmaking and replaces it with a 5–10 minute rest period. The ascorbic acid (Vitamin C) used is available from larger chemists in 25, 50 or 100mg tablet form and it is crushed and added to the dry ingredients in the liquid. Fresh yeast only should be used in this recipe.

Ingredients

700g (1½lb) strong plain white flour
10ml (2 level tsp) salt
5ml (1 level tsp) caster sugar
25g (1oz) lard or margarine
25g (1oz) fresh yeast
400ml (14fl oz) warm water 43°C
  (110°F)
25mg ascorbic acid, crushed

Sieve the flour, salt and sugar into a bowl. Rub in the lard or margarine. Blend the yeast in the water and then add the crushed ascorbic acid. Add the yeast liquid to the dry ingredients all at once and mix to form a firm dough which will leave the sides of the bowl clean. Add a little extra flour, if necessary. Turn the dough on to a lightly floured surface and knead thoroughly until smooth, firm and elastic—this should take about 10 minutes by hand or 3–4 minutes if you are using an electric mixer. Form into a ball, put into a lightly oiled polythene bag and tie loosely. Leave to rest for 5 minutes. Remove the dough from the bag and knead lightly ready for shaping.

For a large loaf, shape to fit a greased 900g (2lb) loaf tin. Stretch the dough into an oblong shape the same width as the tin, fold into three, then turn it

over so that the seam is underneath. Smooth the top, tuck in the ends and place in the tin.

For two smaller loaves, shape as above to fit 2 greased 450g (1lb) loaf tins. For other shaped loaves, see p 16.

This dough can also be used to make eighteen to twenty plain or shaped rolls (see p 20) : put on to greased baking sheets about 2.5cm (1in) apart. Place the tins inside an oiled polythene bag or cover the rolls with a sheet of polythene and put to rise until doubled in size. The dough should spring back when lightly pressed with a floured finger. Rising should take 45–60 minutes at room temperature for loaves and up to 30 minutes for rolls. Remove the polythene and either leave plain, dust with flour or brush lightly with milk or beaten egg. Bake in a very hot oven, 230°C (450°F)

mark 8, for 30–35 minutes for the large loaf, 25–30 minutes for the smaller loaves, and 15–20 minutes for rolls, until well risen and golden brown. Turn out on to a wire rack to cool. For a crisper crust return the loaf to the oven for 4–5 minutes without the tin.

Garlic Bread

The above recipe is ideal for garlic bread if the loaves are shaped into batons or sticks. Beat 100–150g (4–6oz) butter until smooth and add several crushed cloves of garlic to taste. Cut the bread into slanting slices 2.5cm (1in) thick, but try not to sever the slices right through the loaf (the ideal is to leave the bread intact all the way along the bottom). Put the bread on to a piece of foil large enough to enclose it. Then spread the butter paste down into each slice on both sides. Wrap the foil round the bread and put in a medium to hot oven for about 15 minutes. After ten minutes open the foil parcel a little to make the bread a crisp golden brown.

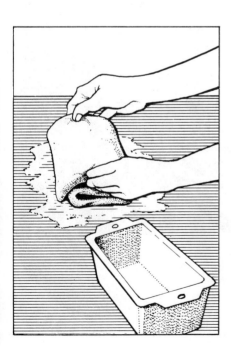

Wholemeal Bread

This bread can be made with any of the plain brown-bread flours whether stone-ground or compost grown, etc.

Ingredients

50g (2oz) fresh yeast or 30ml (2 level
    tbsp) dried yeast and 5ml (1 level
    tsp) caster sugar
900ml (1½pt) warm water
1.4kg (3lb) plain wholemeal flour
30ml (2 level tbsp) caster sugar
10–20ml (2–4 level tsp) salt
25g (1oz) lard

Blend the fresh yeast with one-third of the water. For dried yeast, dissolve the 5ml (1 tsp) sugar in one-third of the water, sprinkle over the dried yeast and leave in a warm place until frothy— about 10 minutes.

    Mix the flour, sugar and salt together in a bowl and rub in the lard. Stir the

yeast liquid into the dry ingredients with sufficient of the remaining water to form a firm dough which leaves the sides of the bowl clean.

Turn out on to a lightly floured surface and knead the dough until firm, smooth, elastic and no longer sticky. This should take about 10 minutes by hand or 3–4 minutes if you are using an electric mixer and dough hook. (This amount of dough will be too large to be kneaded all at once in a mixer, so do it in two halves to prevent overloading.) Shape the dough into a ball and put it into a lightly oiled poylthene bag. Tie the bag loosely and put it to rise in a warm place until the dough has doubled in size—this should take about 1 hour (see p 13 for alternate rising times).

Turn the dough out on to a lightly floured surface, knock back and knead again until smooth. Divide into two or four pieces and shape to fit two greased 900g (2lb) loaf tins or four 450g (1 lb) tins (see p 16 for method of shaping). Brush the tops of the loaves with salted water and put each one in a warm place to rise in a lightly greased polythene bag, until the dough reaches the top of the tins—about 1 hour. Bake in a very hot oven, 230°C (450°F) mark 8, for 30–40 minutes, depending on the size of the loaves, until well risen, with the base sounding hollow when turned out and tapped. Cool on a wire rack.

Alternate Shapings

Shape each quarter of the dough into a round cob and place on greased baking sheets. Either dust with flour or brush with salted water and sprinkle with cracked wheat. Put to rise and bake as above.

Shape all the dough into a large, round cob or halve the dough and form into two smaller cobs and place on greased baking sheets. Using a sharp knife, score each cob deeply into four quarters and sprinkle with cracked wheat or flour. Put to rise as above. Before baking, again mark into quarters and bake for 30–45 minutes depending on size. Cool on a wire rack and break into quarters to serve.

Divide the dough into two or four pieces, then divide each piece again into four. Shape into rolls. Place side-by-side in the appropriate sized greased loaf tins. Put to rise and bake as above.

Note Any of the shapings described on p 16 for loaves or p 20 for rolls can be used for this dough. For crusty brown bread or rolls, brush the tops with salt water after shaping. Cracked wheat or crushed cornflakes can be sprinkled over the top.

Light Brown Bread

This loaf has only a small proportion of brown flour, but it does give colour and flavour to a light loaf with a floury top. It also keeps fresh for longer than pure wholemeal breads.

Ingredients

450g (1lb) strong plain white flour
7.5ml (1½ level tsp) salt
225g (½lb) plain wholemeal flour
25g (1oz) lard or margarine
25g (1oz) fresh yeast or 15ml (1 level
    tbsp) dried yeast and 5ml (1 level
    tsp) caster sugar
450g (¾pt) warm water 43°C (110°F)

Sieve the white flour and salt into a bowl. Add the wholemeal flour and mix thoroughly. Rub the lard into the dry ingredients. Blend the fresh yeast in half of the water. If using dried yeast, dissolve the 5ml (1 tsp) sugar in half of the water, sprinkle the dried yeast over the top and leave in a warm place until frothy—about 10 minutes. Add the yeast liquid and remaining water to the dry ingredients and mix to form a fairly firm dough which leaves the sides of the bowl clean. Turn out on to a floured surface and knead the dough until smooth, elastic and no longer sticky. This should take about 10 minutes by hand or 3–4 minutes if you are using an electric mixer.

Shape the dough into a ball, place in an oiled polythene bag and secure the top. Put to rise in a warm place for about 1 hour or until it has doubled in size and it springs back when pressed lightly with a floured finger. Other rising times to remember are 2 hours at room temperature, up to 12 hours in a cold larder or up to 24 hours in a refrigerator. Remember to allow refrigerated dough to return to room temperature before shaping. This takes about 1 hour.

Remove the dough from the polythene, knock back and knead for about 2 minutes until smooth and ready for shaping. This dough can be used for one large loaf using a greased 900g (2lb) loaf tin, for two smaller loaves using two 450g (1lb) tins, for any of the loaf shapes described on pp 16–19, or for any of the rolls described on p 20. It is also good for making into flat bap rolls (see p 36) which should be dusted with flour before baking.

Coiled Loaf

Grease a deep pie tin about 17.5cm (7in) in diameter. Use half the dough and roll this into a long, thin sausage about 4cm (1½in) thick. Starting at the outside edge of the tin, wind the sausage of dough in to the centre of the tin with the centre being raised up higher than the outside. Loaves and rolls can be dusted with flour or brushed with salt water, milk or beaten egg before proving, and can be sprinkled with cracked wheat or crushed cornflakes if liked.

Variations

Herby Bread

At the knocking-back stage, knead in 45–60ml (3–4tbsp) chopped mixed herbs and a little powdered garlic, if liked. Continue as for basic light brown bread for loaves or rolls.

Yeast Extract Loaf

Stretch out the knocked-back dough ready to fold to fit the tins, then spread evenly over it 15–30ml (1–2 tbsp) yeast extract. Fold up and place in the prepared tin. Continue as for basic light brown bread.

Quick Brown Bread

This is an easy recipe which requires only one rise. The texture is a little closer than traditional home-baked bread and it may not stay fresh quite as long, but it is well worth making for the amount of time it saves.

Ingredients

15g ($\frac{1}{2}$oz) fresh yeast or 10ml (2 level tsp) dried yeast and 5ml (1 level tsp) caster sugar
Approx 300ml (approx $\frac{1}{2}$pt) warm water 43°C (110°F)
450g (1lb) plain wholemeal flour or 225g ($\frac{1}{2}$lb) each plain wholemeal flour and strong plain white flour
5ml (1 level tsp) caster sugar
7.5ml (1$\frac{1}{2}$ level tsp) salt
25g (1oz) lard

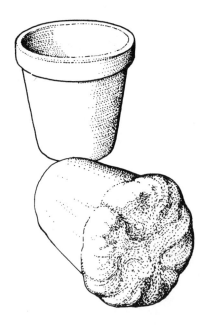

Blend the fresh yeast with the water. For dried yeast, dissolve the 5ml (1tsp) sugar in half the water, sprinkle the dried yeast over the top and leave in a warm place until frothy—about 10 minutes. Mix together the flour(s), sugar and salt in a bowl and rub in the lard.

Add the yeast liquid and remaining water to the dry ingredients and mix to a fairly soft dough, adding more warm water if necessary. Turn the dough on to a lightly floured surface and knead (see p 13) until smooth, elastic and no longer sticky—about 10 minutes by hand or 3–4 minutes if you are using an electric mixer. Divide the dough into two equal pieces. Shape the dough to fit two 450g (1lb) greased loaf tins or shape into two round cobs and place on a greased baking sheet.

Alternatively, you can make flower-pot loaves. Use two clean 10–12cm (4–5in) terracotta flower-pots and grease well. Bake the empty pots in a hot oven for about 20 minutes, and repeat this several times before filling them with dough; this will prevent the loaves from sticking. Shape each piece of dough to half-fill a flower-pot. Brush the tops with salt water and sprinkle with cracked wheat or crushed cornflakes.

Place the tins in oiled polythene bags and put to rise in a warm place for about 1 hour or until doubled in size. The dough should spring back when pressed with a floured finger. (For alternate rising times see p 13.) Remove the tins from the polythene and bake in a very hot oven, 230°C (450°F) mark 8, for 15 minutes. Reduce the temperature to fairly hot, 200°C (400°F) mark 6, for a further 30–40 minutes for loaves, or 20–30 minutes for cobs. Cook flower-pots in a very hot oven for about 40 minutes. Turn out and cool on a wire rack.

Quick Brown Rolls

The dough from the above recipe can also be used for shaping into rolls :

Divide the dough into twelve pieces and roll into rounds. Place on greased or floured baking sheets. Leave plain or mark with a cross.

You can also shape into twelve finger rolls and put them on to greased or floured baking sheets. For soft-sided rolls, place $\frac{3}{4}$cm ($\frac{1}{4}$in) apart and dredge with flour ; for crusty rolls, place well apart and brush with salt water.
A third method is to flatten the dough to 1.5cm ($\frac{1}{2}$in) thickness and cut it into rounds using a 6cm ($2\frac{1}{2}$in) cutter. Place on greased or floured baking sheets.

Cover the rolls with oiled polythene and put to rise in a warm place until doubled in size. Bake in a very hot oven, 230°C (450°F) mark 8, for 20–25 minutes, until well risen and browned. Cool on a wire rack. Do not pull the soft-sided rolls apart until cold.

Variation

Apricot Nut Bread

Using the above recipe and half brown and half white flour, add the grated rind of 1 lemon, 100g (4oz) chopped shelled nuts and 225g (8oz) chopped dried apricots to the rubbed in ingredients before adding the yeast liquid. Continue as above, shape to fit two 450g (1lb) greased loaf tins. Prove and bake as above. Brush the hot cooked loaf with a wet pastry brush dipped in honey or syrup.

Milk Bread and Rolls

This bread can be made using either all milk or half milk and half water. Using milk only gives a close textured loaf with a softer crust.

Ingredients

15g (½oz) fresh yeast or 7.5ml (1½ level tsp) dried yeast and 5ml (1 level tsp) caster sugar
Approx 400ml (approx ¾pt) warm milk or milk and water mixed, 43°C (110°F)
700g (1½lb) strong plain white flour
10ml (2 level tsp) salt
50g (2oz) lard or margarine

Blend the fresh yeast with the milk. For dried yeast, dissolve the sugar in 150ml (¼pt) milk, then sprinkle the dried yeast over the top and leave until frothy. This takes about 10 minutes in a warm place.

Sieve the flour and salt into a bowl and rub in the fat. Add the yeast liquid and remaining milk and mix to a fairly soft dough, adding a little more warm milk, if necessary. Turn out on to a floured surface and knead until smooth and elastic—about 10 minutes by hand or 3–4 minutes if you are using an electric mixer. Shape into a ball and place in a lightly oiled polythene bag. Tie the top loosely and put to rise until doubled in size. The dough should spring back when pressed lightly with a floured finger. Allow 45–60 minutes in a warm place, 2 hours at average room temperature, up to 12 hours in a cold larder or up to 24 hours in a refrigerator. (Refrigerated dough must be allowed to return to room temperature before shaping. This takes about 1 hour.) Remove the dough from the polythene, knock back and knead until smooth and ready for shaping.

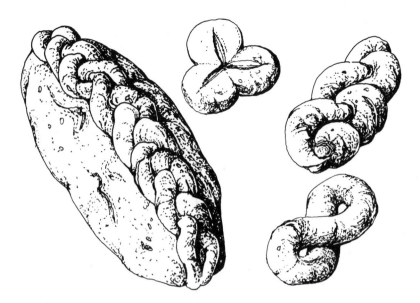

Loaves

Shape the dough to fit a greased 900g (2lb) loaf tin or two 450g (1lb) tins or make into any of the shapes described on pp 16–19.

Decorated Baton

Break off a quarter of the dough and divide this small amount into two equal pieces. Shape the remaining dough into a fat baton shape, slightly tapering at the ends, and place on a greased baking sheet. Roll each of the small pieces of dough into long sausages and twist lightly together. Brush the top of the baton with water and lay the twist on top, folding the ends under the loaf. Sprinkle lightly with poppy seeds, if liked.

Put the loaves inside an oiled polythene bag and put to rise for about 1 hour at room temperature. Brush the loaves with beaten egg or milk, or dust with flour. Bake in a hot oven, 220°C (425°F) mark 7, for 30–40 minutes.

Rolls

Divide the dough into 50g (2oz) pieces and shape into rolls. Place on greased baking sheets. Popular shapes for rolls are twists, plaits, cottage loaves, knots, rings, figures of eight, etc (see pp 20–21 for methods of shaping).

Cover the rolls with a sheet of oiled polythene and put to rise until the dough doubles in size, about 15–20 minutes at room temperature. They can be brushed with beaten egg or milk, or dusted with flour before baking, if liked. Cook in a hot oven, 220°C (425°F) mark 7, for 15–20 minutes. Cool on a wire rack.

Note This bread freezes well.

33

Rye Bread

Many people like rye bread and want to make their own version. It does, however, take longer than most breads as it requires a starter (or sour) dough. This needs to be made up and left for 12–24 hours before you can actually make the bread. However, the finished loaf is worth the trouble.

Ingredients

Starter Dough

150g (5oz) coarse rye flour
150g (5oz) fine rye flour
150ml ($\frac{1}{4}$pt) sour milk
5ml (1 level tsp) caster sugar.

Second Dough

125ml (scant $\frac{1}{4}$pt) warm water, 43°C (110°F)
15ml (1tbsp) black treacle
25g (1oz) fresh yeast or 15ml (1 level tbsp) dried yeast
300g (10oz) strong plain white flour
15g ($\frac{1}{2}$oz) salt

Starch Glaze

10ml (2 level tsp) cornflour
Approx 100ml (approx 4fl oz) water

Make the starter dough by mixing all the ingredients together in a bowl. Leave them overnight or up to 24 hours in a covered bowl in a cool place. The next day mix the warm water and treacle together in a large bowl and either crumble in the fresh yeast or sprinkle in the dried yeast together with 30ml (2tbsp) of flour. Leave the mixture in a warm place until frothy— about 10 minutes. Sieve the rest of the flour together with the salt into a bowl

and add to the yeast batter together with the starter dough. Mix the whole to give a firm but slightly sticky dough. Turn on to a floured surface and knead well for about 5–10 minutes until smooth and firm. Shape into a ball, place in an oiled polythene bag and put to rise in a warm place for 1–1$\frac{1}{2}$ hours or until doubled in size.

Turn out on to a floured surface, knock back the dough and knead until smooth. Divide into two pieces and shape either into a cob (a round ball) or into a baton (a thick fat sausage shape) and place on greased baking sheets. Cover with a sheet of oiled polythene and put to rise in a warm place until the dough has doubled in size and springs back when pressed lightly with a floured finger.

Make the starch glaze by blending the cornflour in a little cold water and adding sufficient boiling water. Stir continuously until the glaze clears. It should give about 100ml (4fl oz). Cool the glaze.

Remove the polythene and brush the loaves with the cooled starch glaze. Preheat the oven to very hot, 230°C (450°F) mark 8. Reduce to fairly hot,

200°C (400°F) mark 6, and put the loaves in the centre of the oven and bake for 30 minutes. Reduce the heat to 150°C (300°F) mark 2, and brush the loaves again with glaze. Bake for a further 30 minutes, glaze again and return to the oven for 1–2 minutes. Remove to a wire rack to cool.

Note For a coarser-textured loaf, use half fine rye flour and half strong white flour in place of all white flour in the second dough.

Rye Crispbread

Ingrédients

450g (1lb) risen rye bread dough (see p 34)
50g (2oz) lard or 30ml (2 tbsp) oil
10ml (2 level tsp) salt
15ml (1 tbsp) coarse rye or crushed cornflakes

Place the dough in a bowl and add either the lard, cut into small pieces, or the oil, the salt and rye or cornflakes. Knead and squeeze all the ingredients together until evenly blended. Roll the dough out thinly on a floured surface and place on greased baking sheets. Cut the dough into squares or rectangles using either a pastry wheel or a sharp knife. Cover with a sheet of oiled polythene and put to rise in a warm place until puffy. Bake in a fairly hot oven, 200°C (400°F) mark 6, for about 15 minutes, then turn off the heat and crisp off in the cooling oven. Remove to a wire rack and leave to cool. Store in an airtight container.

Floury Baps, Morning Rolls and Bridge Rolls

Floury Baps and Morning Rolls

Baps are the traditional flat loaves of Scotland. The small baps are known as morning rolls and were at one time served exclusively at breakfast. The rolls are particularly good when served warm.

Ingredients

15g (½oz) fresh yeast or 10ml (2 level
    tsp) dried yeast and 2.5ml (½ level
    tsp) caster sugar
300ml (½pt) warm milk and water
    mixed, 43°C (110°F)
450g (1lb) strong plain white flour
5ml (1 level tsp) salt
50g (2oz) lard or white vegetable fat

Blend the fresh yeast with the warm liquid. If you are using dried yeast, dissolve the 2.5ml (½tsp) caster sugar in half the warm liquid, add the dried yeast, sprinkling it over the top and leave in a warm place until frothy— about 10 minutes.

Sieve the flour and salt into a bowl, then rub in the fat. Stir the yeast liquid and the remaining liquid all at once into the dry ingredients and mix to form a softish dough, adding a little extra flour if necessary to leave the sides of the bowl clean. Turn out on to a lightly floured surface and knead the dough until smooth and elastic. This will take about 5 minutes by hand or 2–3 minutes if you are using an electric mixer. Shape the dough into a ball and place in a lightly oiled polythene bag. Tie loosely and put to rise in a warm

place until doubled in size (see p 13 for alternate rising times). Turn the dough out on to a lightly floured surface, knock back and knead until smooth and firm.

Use half the dough to make the large bap; shape into a ball and, using a floured rolling-pin, roll out into a round about 2cm (¾in) thick. Place on a floured baking sheet and dredge the

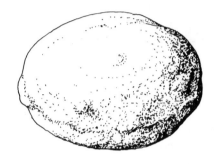

top with flour. Divide the remaining dough into five or six pieces; roll each piece into a ball and then roll out to an oval about 1.5cm (½in) thick. Place on the floured baking sheet and dredge with flour.

Cover lightly with a sheet of oiled polythene and put to rise at room temperature for about 45 minutes or until doubled in size. Remove the polythene and press the bap and rolls gently in the centre with three fingers to prevent blisters forming during cooking. Bake in the centre of a fairly hot oven, 200°C (400°F) mark 6, for 20–30 minutes for the bap and 15–20 minutes for the rolls until they turn a pale golden brown. Cool on a wire rack. This recipe makes two large baps or twelve morning rolls, or one bap and six morning rolls.

Note Small brown baps can be made using the light brown bread recipe on p 20. This bread and the rolls freeze well.

Bridge Rolls

These are the traditional rolls used for parties, buffets, etc either to be filled and left whole or to be cut in half and served as two open rolls.

Ingredients

15g (½oz) fresh yeast or 7.5ml (1½ level tsp) dried yeast and 5ml (1 level tsp) caster sugar
100ml (4fl oz) warm milk, 43°C (110°F)
225g (8oz) plain white flour
5ml (1 level tsp) salt
50g (2oz) butter or margarine
1 egg, beaten
1 beaten egg to glaze

Blend the fresh yeast with the warm milk. For dried yeast dissolve the sugar in the milk, sprinkle the dried yeast over the top and leave in a warm place until frothy—about 10 minutes. Sieve the flour and salt into a bowl and rub in the fat until the mixture resembles fine breadcrumbs. Add the yeast liquid and beaten egg to the dry ingredients and

mix to form a fairly soft dough, adding a little extra milk or flour, if necessary. Beat the mixture well, then turn on to a floured surface and knead well until smooth and elastic. Place in a lightly greased polythene bag or replace in the bowl and cover securely with oiled polythene and put to rise until doubled in size. This should take about 1 hour in a warm place (see p 13 for alternate rising times). Turn the dough out on to a floured surface and knead lightly until smooth and ready for shaping. The rolls can be made into various sizes, so divide the dough into the required amounts, ie 25g (1oz), 40g (1½oz), 50g (2oz), or larger or smaller if so required. Shape each piece of dough into a roll or finger shape with slightly tapering ends by pressing down and rolling backwards and forwards with the palm of either one hand or two, depending on the size of the roll, until the required shape and size is achieved. Place on greased baking sheets in rows fairly close together. They will expand to just touch during baking. For soft-sided rolls, place the dough shapes ¾cm (¼in) apart so that they really stick together during baking. Cover with a sheet of oiled polythene and put to rise for 15–20 minutes or until doubled in size. The rolls can be brushed with beaten egg before baking to give the traditional glazed top of bridge rolls. Bake in a hot oven, 220°C (425°F) mark 8, for 10–20 minutes depending on size, until golden brown. Slide them on to a wire rack and leave them joined together until cold.

Note These rolls freeze well. For larger quantities of bridge rolls, double the quantities of the ingredients.

Cheese Bread

A delicious flavoured loaf with a cheesy crust. It is ideal for something a little different for sandwiches, picnics and toasted dishes.

Ingredients

450g (1lb) strong plain white flour
10ml (2 level tsp) salt
5ml (1 level tsp) dry mustard
Ground pepper to taste
100–150g (4–6oz) Cheddar cheese, finely grated
15g ($\frac{1}{2}$oz) fresh yeast or 10ml (2 level tsp) dried yeast and 5ml (1 level tsp) caster sugar
300ml ($\frac{1}{2}$pt) warm water, 43°C (110°F)

In a large bowl sieve together the flour, salt, mustard and pepper. Mix in most of the cheese, reserving a little to sprinkle on top of the loaves. Blend the fresh yeast with the warm liquid. For dried yeast, dissolve the sugar in the liquid then sprinkle the dried yeast over the top and leave in a warm place until frothy—about 10 minutes. Add the yeast liquid to the dry ingredients and mix to form a firm dough, adding a little extra flour, if necessary, to leave the sides of the bowl clean.

Turn out on to a lightly floured surface and knead until smooth and elastic and no longer sticky—about 10 minutes by hand or 3–4 minutes if you are using an electric mixer. Shape into a ball and put into a lightly oiled polythene bag. Put to rise in a warm place for about 1 hour or until doubled in size. The dough should spring back when lightly pressed with a floured finger (see p 13 for alternate rising times).

Turn the dough out on to a lightly floured surface, knock back and knead until smooth and ready for shaping. Either shape to fit a greased 900g (2lb) loaf tin or two 450g (1lb) loaf tins, or shape into one or more of the loaves described on pp 16–19. The dough can also be used to make twelve to fourteen rolls (for shaping see p 20).

Put the loaves inside a large oiled polythene bag and put to rise in a warm place until the dough reaches the top of the tins—about 45 minutes. Cover the rolls with oiled polythene and put to rise until they have doubled in size. Remove the polythene, sprinkle the remaining grated cheese over the loaves or rolls and bake in a moderately hot oven 190°C (375°F) mark 5, allowing about 45 minutes for loaves or 20 minutes for rolls. Take care not to overbake or overbrown. Cool on a wire rack.

Variations

Cheese and Celery Bread

Mix 25g (1oz) grated cheese with 5ml (1 level tsp) celery salt and sprinkle over the loaf before baking.

Cheese and Herb Loaf

At the knock back stage of making the bread, knead 45–60ml (3–4 tbsp) freshly chopped herbs (or half the quantity if using dried herbs) into the dough. Use either mixed herbs or one particular herb of your choice. Continue as for cheese bread.

Note. This bread freezes well.

Orange Bread

This bread has a very pleasant, if unusual, flavour. It is especially good when eaten with cream cheese, chocolate spread or marmalade, and also toasts well. It is made from the hulls of oranges after the juice has been squeezed out, so it makes use of something usually thrown away.

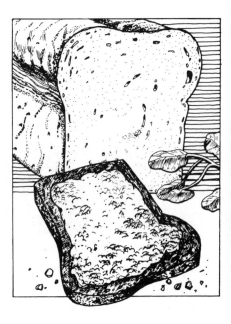

Ingredients

450g (1lb) strong plain white flour
10ml (2 level tsp) salt
25g (1oz) caster sugar
25g (1oz) fresh yeast or 15ml (1 level tbsp) dried yeast and 5ml (1 level tsp) caster sugar
150ml ($\frac{1}{4}$pt) warm water, 43°C (110°F)
1 egg, beaten
3 medium or 2 large shells (ie halves) of orange

Orange pulp

Either mince or very finely chop the peel shells from oranges which have had the juice squeezed out or, if preferred, use one whole orange minced.

Sieve the flour and salt into a bowl and mix in the sugar. Dissolve the fresh yeast in the water or, for dried yeast, dissolve 5ml (1tsp) sugar in the water, sprinkle the dried yeast over the top and leave in a warm place until frothy—about 10 minutes. Add the yeast liquid to the dry ingredients together with the egg and orange pulp and mix to form a softish dough, adding a little extra flour if necessary.

Turn on to a floured surface and knead until smooth and firm—about 10 minutes by hand or 3–4 minutes if you are using an electric mixer. Shape into a ball, place in a lightly oiled polythene bag and tie the end. Put to rise in a warm place for about 1 hour or until doubled in size and the dough springs back when pressed lightly with a floured finger (see p 13 for alternate rising times). Turn the dough out on to a lightly floured surface, knock back and knead lightly until smooth—about 2 minutes.

Either shape to fit a greased 900g (2lb) loaf tin for a large loaf or, for small loaves, use two 450g (1lb) loaf tins. For a farmhouse-shaped loaf, score right along the top of the loaf crust. Put the tins inside an oiled polythene bag and put to rise in a warm place until the dough reaches the top of the tins. Remove the polythene and bake in a fairly hot oven, 200°C (400°F) mark 6, for 40–50 minutes for a large loaf or 30–35 minutes for small loaves, until well browned and the base sounds hollow when tapped. Turn out on to a wire rack and brush the crust of the loaf immediately with a wet pastry brush dipped in honey or syrup or with melted butter. Leave to cool.

Variations

Fruited Orange Bread

Add 175g (6oz) mixed dried fruit to the dry ingredients before adding the liquid and then proceed as for basic orange bread.

Orange Treacle Bread

450g (1lb) risen orange bread dough (ie half the basic recipe)
60ml (4tbsp) black treacle

Before shaping, put the risen dough into a bowl and add the treacle. Squeeze and knead the dough until the treacle is evenly mixed and is no longer sticky. Pour into a greased 450g (1lb) loaf tin, cover with oiled polythene and put to rise. Proceed as for basic orange bread.

Orange Nut Bread

450g (1lb) risen orange bread dough (ie half basic recipe)
100g (4oz) shelled walnuts, chopped
30ml (2tbsp) thick honey

Put the risen dough before shaping into a bowl and add the walnuts and honey. Squeeze and knead the dough until evenly mixed, then transfer to a greased 450g (1lb) loaf tin. Cover with oiled polythene and put to rise. Proceed as for basic orange bread.

Currant Bread and Malt Loaf

Currant Bread

Ingredients

450g (1 lb) strong plain white flour
5ml (1 level tsp) salt
25g (1oz) caster sugar
25g (1oz) butter or margarine
100g (4oz) currants
25g (1oz) fresh yeast or 15ml (1 level tbsp) dried yeast and 5ml (1 level tsp) caster sugar
300ml ($\frac{1}{2}$pt) warm milk and water mixed, 43°C (110°F)
Honey or syrup to glaze

Sieve the flour and salt into a bowl. Mix in the sugar and then rub in the fat until the mixture resembles fine breadcrumbs. Mix in the currants.

Dissolve the yeast in the liquid or, if you are using dried yeast, dissolve the 5ml (1tsp) caster sugar in the liquid, sprinkle the dried yeast over the top and leave in a warm place until frothy—about 10 minutes. Add the yeast liquid to the dry ingredients all at once and mix to form a firm dough, adding a little extra flour, if needed, until the dough leaves the sides of the bowl clean.

Turn on to a lightly floured surface and knead until smooth, firm and elastic. This should take about 10 minutes by hand or 3–4 minutes if you are using an electric mixer. Shape into a ball and place in a lightly oiled polythene bag with the end secured. Put to rise in a warm place until the dough has doubled in size and springs back when pressed lightly with a floured finger.

Turn out on to a floured surface, knock back and knead for about 2 minutes until smooth. Divide the dough into two equal pieces, and shape to fit 2 greased 450g (1 lb) loaf tins (see p 15 for method of shaping). Place the tins in oiled polythene bags and put to rise in a warm place until the dough reaches the top of the tins. Remove the polythene and bake in a hot oven, 220°C (425°F) mark 7, for 40–45 minutes until the bases of the loaves sound hollow when tapped. Turn on to a wire rack and brush the tops of the loaves immediately with a wet pastry brush dipped in honey or syrup. Leave to cool.

The mixture can also be made into rolls (see p 20 for shaping) but only into round bun shapes. They should be baked in a hot oven, 220°C (425°F) mark 7, for 15–20 minutes. Glaze with honey or syrup as for the loaves.

Variations

Spicy Currant Bread

To the dry ingredients together with the currants add 5ml (1 level tsp) mixed spice, 5ml (1 level tsp) ground cinnamon and the finely grated rind of 1 small lemon. Proceed as for basic currant bread.

Fruited Bread

In place of the 100g (4oz) currants, to the dry ingredients add 100g (4oz) sultanas, raisins or mixed fruit and 50g (2oz) chopped mixed peel. Also, 15–30ml (1–2 tbsp) clear honey can be used to replace the same amount of the liquid. Proceed as for basic currant bread.

Note This bread freezes well.

Malt Bread

A delicious loaf with a sticky top full of sultanas, favoured by many at tea-time.

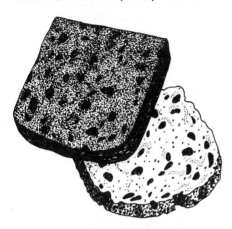

This loaf is made with household flour *not* the strong bread flour.

Ingredients

100g (4oz) malt extract
15ml (1tbsp) black treacle
25g (1oz) margarine
450g (1lb) plain white flour (*not* strong bread flour)
5ml (1 level tsp) salt
175g (6oz) sultanas
25g (1 oz) fresh yeast or 15ml (1 level tbsp) dried yeast and 5ml (1 level tsp) caster sugar
Good 150ml ($\frac{1}{4}$pt) warm water, 43°C (110°F)
Honey to glaze

Put the malt extract, black treacle and margarine in a saucepan and heat gently until thoroughly blended. Remove from the heat and allow to cool without getting completely cold. Sieve the flour and salt into a large bowl and mix in the sultanas. Dissolve the fresh yeast in the warm water or, for dried yeast, dissolve 5ml (1tsp) sugar in the water. Sprinkle the dried yeast over the top and leave in a warm place until frothy—about 10 minutes. Add the cooled malt mixture and yeast liquid to the dry ingredients and mix to form a soft and sticky dough. It may be necessary to add a little extra flour in order to make the dough leave the sides of the bowl clean. However, use as little extra flour as possible for this has to be a very soft dough to get the required result.

Turn out on to a lightly floured surface and knead the dough for about 5 minutes until it is smooth and elastic. Divide the dough into two pieces and flatten each piece to an oblong. Roll up like a Swiss roll and shape to fit two greased 450g (1lb) loaf tins, keeping the seam underneath. Place the tins in an oiled polythene bag and put to rise in a warm place until the dough reaches the top of the tins and springs back when lightly pressed with a floured finger. This should take about 1$\frac{1}{2}$ hours in a warm place, but longer in a cool one. Malt bread is a slow riser so don't worry if it takes longer than usual. Remove the polythene and bake in a fairly hot oven, 200°C (400°F) mark 6, for 35–45 minutes, until well risen and brown and the base sounds hollow when tapped. After turning out on to a wire rack, brush the tops of the hot loaves liberally with a wet pastry-brush dipped in honey. Leave to cool.

Note For a darker malt loaf replace 15ml (1tbsp) malt extract with black treacle and, if liked, add a little gravy browning. This loaf will freeze well.

Chelsea Buns

Chelsea buns are, traditionally, rolled up buns with a dried fruit filling. They are cooked to touch each other in a square cake tin and they should be pulled apart when cold to give square-shaped buns. These buns are made by the batter method.

Ingredients

225g (8oz) strong plain white flour
15g ($\frac{1}{2}$oz) fresh yeast or 7.5ml ($1\frac{1}{2}$ level tsp) dried yeast and 2.5ml ($\frac{1}{2}$ level tsp) caster sugar
100ml (4fl oz) warm milk, 43°C (110°F)
2.5ml ($\frac{1}{2}$ level tsp) salt
15g ($\frac{1}{2}$oz) butter or lard
1 egg, beaten
Approx 50g (approx 2oz) melted butter or margarine
100g (4oz) mixed dried fruit
25g (1oz) chopped mixed peel
50g (2oz) soft brown sugar
Clear honey to glaze

Put 50g (2oz) flour into a large bowl, add the fresh yeast or dried yeast, caster sugar and warm milk, and mix to a smooth batter. Put aside in a warm place until the batter froths—this should take 10–20 minutes in a warm place.

Sieve the remaining flour with the salt and rub in the fat. Add this mixture to the yeast batter, together with the beaten egg, and mix to form a soft dough which will leave the sides of the bowl clean after beating the dough. Turn out on to a lightly floured surface and knead the dough until it is smooth and elastic—about 5 minutes. Shape into a ball and place in an oiled polythene bag. Put to rise in a warm place until doubled in size—1–$1\frac{1}{2}$ hours. Grease a 17.5cm (7in) square cake tin. Remove dough from the bag, turn on to a lightly floured surface and knead thoroughly until smooth. Roll out the dough to an oblong about 30cm × 25.5cm (12in × 9in). Brush the whole surface with melted butter or margarine. Mix together the dried fruit and peel and sprinkle evenly over the dough. Sprinkle with brown sugar. Starting from the longest side, roll up the dough like a Swiss roll, sealing the end edge with a little water. Cut the roll into nine even-sized slices and place these evenly, cut-side downwards, in the prepared tin. Cover with oiled polythene and put to rise in a warm place for about 30 minutes or until the dough has risen and feels springy. Remove the polythene and bake in a moderately hot oven, 190°C (375°F) mark 5, for 30–35 minutes, until golden brown. Turn all the buns in one piece out on to a wire rack and, whilst still warm, brush the tops with a wet pastry-brush dipped in honey. Leave to get cold. This recipe makes nine buns.

Variations
Chopped glacé cherries, chopped angelica or chopped nuts may be used in place of some of the fruit. Mixed spice or cinnamon may be mixed with the brown sugar, or grated lemon, orange or grapefruit rind added.

Note These buns can be cooked on a greased baking sheet placed well apart. This will give a bun with firm crusty edges all round, unlike the soft pull-apart sides of the traditional Chelsea bun.

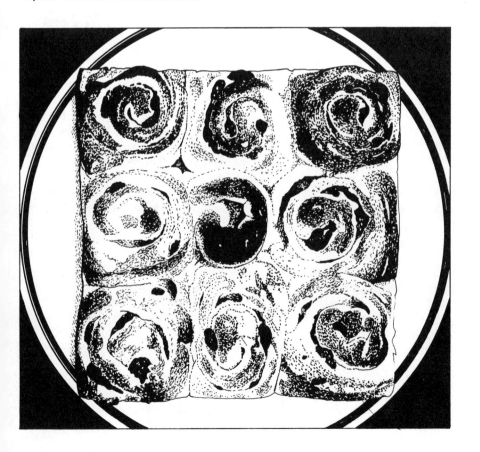

Yorkshire Tea-cakes and Fruity Bannock

Yorkshire Tea-cakes

These large flat tea-cakes can be split open and served with lots of butter. They are at their very best when served slightly warmed and they also toast well.

Ingredients

15g (½oz) fresh yeast or 7.5ml (1½ level tsp) dried yeast and 5ml (1 level tsp) caster sugar
300ml (½pt) warm milk, 43°C (110°F)
450g (1lb) strong plain white flour
5ml (1 level tsp) salt
40g (1½oz) butter or lard
25g (1oz) caster sugar
75g (3oz) currants
25g (1oz) mixed peel (optional)

Blend the fresh yeast in the warm milk. For dried yeast, dissolve 5ml (1 tsp) sugar in the milk, then sprinkle the dried yeast over the top and leave in a warm place until frothy—about 10 minutes. Sieve the flour and salt into a bowl, add the butter and rub in until the mixture resembles breadcrumbs. Stir in the sugar, currants and peel until well mixed. Add the yeast liquid to the dry ingredients and mix to form a fairly soft dough, adding a little more flour if necessary to leave the sides of the bowl clean.

Turn out on to a floured surface and knead until smooth and elastic—about 10 minutes by hand or 3–4 minutes if you are using an electric mixer. Shape into a ball and put in a lightly oiled polythene bag. Put to rise in a warm place for about 1 hour or until doubled in size. Turn on to a floured surface, knock back and knead for about 2 minutes until smooth. Divide into five or six equal-sized pieces and knead each into a round, then roll out to a circle 15–17.5cm (6–7in) in diameter. Place the tea-cakes on greased baking sheets and brush the tops with milk. Cover lightly with a sheet of greased polythene and put to rise in a warm place for about 45 minutes or until almost doubled in size. Remove the polythene and bake in a fairly hot oven, 200°C (400°F) mark 6, for about 20 minutes. Remove to a wire rack and leave to cool. The tea-cakes can be brushed with honey or syrup, if liked. To serve, split open the tea-cakes and spread thickly with butter, or toast lightly and then spread with butter. This recipe makes five or six large tea-cakes.

Note These tea-cakes can be made smaller, if preferred. Divide the dough into ten or twelve equal-sized pieces and roll out to about 7.5cm (3in). Place on a baking sheet and bake for about 15 minutes.

Fruity Bannock

As a change from the usual scone round, this type of yeasted fruit scone will tempt everyone. It is very easy to make and the fruit and spices can be varied to suit yourself.

Ingredients

225g (8oz) strong plain white flour
25g (1oz) softened butter or margarine
150ml ($\frac{1}{4}$pt) warm milk, 43°C (110°F)
15g ($\frac{1}{2}$oz) fresh yeast or 7.5ml (1$\frac{1}{2}$ level tsp) dried yeast and 5ml (1 level tsp) caster sugar
Pinch of salt
25g (1oz) caster sugar
25g (1oz) sultanas
50g (2oz) currants
25g (1oz) chopped mixed peel
Milk to glaze

Put 50g (2oz) flour into a large bowl with the softened butter, warm milk, either fresh yeast or dried yeast and 5ml (1tsp) sugar. Mix well to form a batter and leave in a warm place until frothy—about 20–30 minutes.

Sieve the remaining flour and salt into a bowl and mix in the sugar, sultanas, currants and mixed peel. Add these dry ingredients to the yeast batter and mix well to form a firm dough. Turn on to a lightly floured surface and knead well until smooth, elastic and no longer sticky—about 10 minutes by hand or 3–4 minutes if you are using an electric mixer. Shape into a ball and place in an oiled polythene bag. Put to rise in a warm place until doubled in size. The dough should spring back when pressed gently with a floured finger. This usually takes about 1 hour (see p 13 for alternate rising times). Turn out on to a floured surface, knock back and knead until smooth. Shape into a ball and flatten carefully with your hands to about a 22.5cm (9in) circle, about 1.5cm ($\frac{1}{2}$in) thick. Place on a greased baking sheet and cut into eight wedges with a sharp knife. Brush the top with milk and cover lightly with oiled polythene. Put to rise in a warm place until the dough has doubled in size and feels springy—about 45 minutes. Remove the polythene, brush with milk again, and bake in a fairly hot oven, 200°C (400°F) mark 6, for about 20 minutes. Remove to a wire rack and leave to cool. Serve split and buttered, with or without jam, honey, etc.

Note This recipe freezes well, so if you have a freezer it is worth making several of these bannocks in one batch to freeze some for later on.

Bath Buns and SallyLunn

Bath Buns

These are traditionally sweet, uneven and flattish buns with a topping of crushed sugar. The mixture is very soft and is spooned on to the baking sheets. They are often served split and buttered but can also be eaten as they are.

Ingredients

450g (1lb) strong plain white flour
25g (1oz) fresh yeast or 15ml (1 level tbsp) dried yeast
5ml (1 level tsp) caster sugar
60ml (4tbsp) water
150ml ($\frac{1}{4}$pt) milk
5ml (1 level tsp) salt
175g (6oz) sultanas
50g (2oz) chopped mixed peel
50g (2oz) caster sugar
50g (2oz) butter or margarine, melted and cooled but still running
2 eggs, beaten
Little beaten egg
Lightly crushed sugar lumps for topping

Put 100g (4oz) flour into a bowl and add the yeast and 5ml (1tsp) sugar. Warm the water and milk together to about 43°C (110°F), then add to the mixture in the bowl and mix well to form a batter. Set aside in a warm place until frothy—about 10–15 minutes. Sieve together the remaining flour and salt and then mix in the sultanas, mixed peel and sugar. Stir the melted fat and beaten egg into the yeast batter, then add the dry ingredients and mix well to form a soft dough. Turn out on to a floured surface and knead for about 5 minutes until smooth. Place in a lightly floured bowl, cover with oiled polythene and put to rise in a warm place until doubled in size. The length of time required depends on the warmth of the room but it should take 45–60 minutes.

Remove the polythene and beat the mixture with a wooden spoon or your hand to knock out all the air bubbles. Place tablespoonfuls of the mixture well apart on greased baking sheets and cover lightly with oiled polythene. Put to rise in a warm place until the buns double in size. Remove the polythene, brush each bun lightly with beaten egg and sprinkle with lightly crushed sugar lumps. Bake in a moderately hot oven, 190°C (375°F) mark 5, for about 15 minutes, until well risen and golden brown. Cool on a wire rack. This recipe makes about eighteen buns.

Sally Lunn

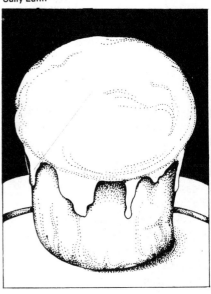

Variations

Sultanas may be replaced by raisins and/or nuts and spices; or finely grated orange or lemon rind may be added to the dry ingredients, but the buns would not then be the true Bath variety.

Sally Lunn

This is a traditional tall, round tea-bread supposed to come from Bath. It is often sliced horizontally and served with butter and jam or honey.

Ingredients

50g (2oz) butter
225ml (¼pt + 4tbsp) milk
5ml (1 level tsp) caster sugar
15g (½oz) fresh yeast or 10ml (2 level tsp) dried yeast
450g (1lb) strong plain white flour
5ml (1 level tsp) salt
2 eggs, beaten

Sugar Glaze

15ml (1tbsp) water
15ml (1tbsp) sugar

Melt the butter slowly in a pan, then remove from the heat. Stir in the milk and sugar and blend in the fresh or dried yeast. Sieve the flour and salt into a bowl and add the eggs and yeast mixture. Mix to form a soft dough, turn out on to a floured surface and knead well for about 5 minutes until smooth. Divide the dough in half and shape to fit two well greased 12.5cm (5in) round cake tins. Cover loosely with oiled polythene and put to rise in a warm place for about 1 hour, or until the dough fills the tins. Remove the polythene and bake in a very hot oven, 230°C (450°F) mark 8, for 15-20 minutes. Turn out on to a wire rack.

Boil the water and sugar together for 2 minutes, then brush the glaze quickly over the tops of the loaves while they are still warm. Leave to cool.

Pizzas

Pizza is one of the most popular dishes from Italy. It is an open savoury type of tart with a yeasted dough base. It can have a variety of toppings. Tomatoes, onions, herbs, and cheese usually feature and other ingredients such as bacon, salami, sausages, sardines, anchovies, etc give the variety. It can be served either hot or cold. The pizza can be made using left-over white bread dough or brown dough which then is brushed with oil and rolled, as in this recipe. About 450g (1 lb) made-up dough is required for a pizza.

Ingredients

15g ($\frac{1}{2}$oz) fresh yeast or 7.5ml (1$\frac{1}{2}$ level tsp) dried yeast
2.5ml ($\frac{1}{2}$ level tsp) caster sugar
Approx 150ml (approx $\frac{1}{4}$pt) warm water, 43 °C (110 °F)
225g ($\frac{1}{2}$lb) plain white flour (preferably strong)
5ml (1 level tsp) salt
15g ($\frac{1}{2}$oz) lard or margarine
Oil

Topping

450g (1 lb) onions, peeled and thinly sliced
822g (1 lb 13oz) canned tomatoes or 450g (1 lb) fresh tomatoes, skinned and sliced
10ml (2 level tsp) oregano or basil
Salt and pepper
175g (6oz) Bel Paese or processed cheese, sliced
1 can anchovies, drained
Black or stuffed green olives

Blend the fresh yeast and sugar in the warm water. For dried yeast, dissolve the sugar in the water, then sprinkle the dried yeast over the top and put in a warm place until frothy—about 10 minutes. Sieve the flour and salt into a bowl and rub in the fat. Add the yeast liquid to the dry ingredients and mix to form a fairly firm dough. Turn out on to a lightly floured surface and knead until smooth and elastic—about 10 minutes by hand or 3–4 minutes if you are using an electric mixer. Shape into a ball, place in a lightly oiled polythene bag, secure the end, and put to rise in a warm place until doubled in size. This should take $\frac{3}{4}$–1 hour in a warm place or about 2 hours at room temperature.

Turn the dough out on to a lightly floured surface, knock back and roll out to a long narrow strip. Brush all over with oil, then roll up like a Swiss roll. Carefully roll out again to a long strip and brush again with oil and roll up. Repeat this process twice more. To make one large pizza, grease a 30cm (12in) plain flan ring and place on a greased baking sheet. For two smaller pizzas, use two 20cm (8in) rings (the pizzas can be made without a ring, but some of the topping will probably slide off). Roll out the dough to one 30cm (12in) circle or two 20cm (8in) circles. Place on the greased baking sheets inside the rings and brush all over the dough with oil.

For the topping, sauté the onions in 15–30ml (1–2 tbsp) oil until soft and just beginning to colour. Spoon over the dough leaving a 2cm ($\frac{3}{4}$in) margin all round. If using canned tomatoes, partly drain and then lay them over the onions, or arrange the skinned, sliced fresh tomatoes evenly over the onions.

Sprinkle with herbs and then season
well. Put to rise for 15 minutes in a
warm place. Bake in a very hot oven
230°C (450°F) mark 8, for 20 minutes.
Remove from the oven and quickly
cover the pizza with the sliced cheese
and arrange a lattice or cartwheel
pattern with the anchovies. Decorate
with black or stuffed olives and return
to the oven for a further 20 minutes.
Cover lightly with foil if getting too
brown (smaller pizzas will take a little
less time). Remove the rings and serve
hot or leave to cool and serve cold with
salads. This recipe serves four to six
portions.

Bacon and Mushroom Pizza

Topping

25g (1oz) butter
1 clove garlic, crushed (optional)
100–175g (4–6oz) mushrooms, sliced
830g (1lb 13oz) can skinned
   tomatoes or 450g (1lb) fresh
   tomatoes, skinned and sliced
10ml (2 level tsp) mixed herbs
Salt and pepper
100g (4oz) Cheddar cheese, coarsely
   grated
225g (½lb) streaky bacon rashers,
   derinded
Few pickled walnuts or stuffed green
   olives

Melt the butter in a pan and fry the
garlic and mushrooms until soft.
Arrange over the prepared pizza dough
base. Cover with sliced tomatoes or
partly drained canned tomatoes, then
sprinkle first with herbs and then with
salt and pepper. Sprinkle the cheese
over the herbs and arrange the bacon
rashers in a lattice or cartwheel
pattern. Fill in the gaps with pieces of
pickled walnut or olives. Put to rise in
a warm place for 15 minutes. Bake in a
very hot oven, 230°C (450°F) mark 8,
for 30–40 minutes (smaller pizzas will
take a little less time).

Doughnuts

Large, sticky, sugar-covered buns with a jam filling, doughnuts are deep-fried until golden brown and then coated in caster sugar or a cinnamon and sugar mixture. They can also be fried without a filling, and when cold, be split open and filled with whipped cream and/or jam. Round American-style doughnuts are made using two pastry cutters to make the circles and are then fried in the same way.

Ingredients

225g (8oz) strong plain white flour
2.5ml ($\frac{1}{2}$ level tsp) salt
15g ($\frac{1}{2}$oz) fresh yeast or 10ml (2 level tsp) dried yeast and 2.5ml (1 level tsp) caster sugar
Approx 60ml (4 tbsp) warm milk, 43°C (110°F)
15g ($\frac{1}{2}$oz) softened butter or margarine
1 egg, beaten
Deep fat or oil for frying
Caster sugar and ground cinnamon for coating

Sieve the flour and salt into a bowl. Blend the fresh yeast in the warm milk or, for dried yeast, dissolve 5ml (1 tsp) sugar in the milk, then sprinkle the dried yeast over the top and leave in a warm place until frothy—about 10 minutes. Add the yeast liquid to the dry ingredients with the softened butter and beaten egg and mix to form a fairly soft dough which leaves the sides of the bowl clean, adding a little more milk, if necessary.

Turn out on to a floured surface and knead thoroughly until smooth—about 10 minutes by hand or 3–4 minutes if you are using an electric mixer. Place the dough in a lightly floured bowl, cover with oiled polythene and put to rise until doubled in size. This should take 45–60 minutes in a warm place; 2 hours at room temperature; up to 12 hours in a cold larder, or up to 24 hours in a refrigerator. Remember to allow refrigerated dough to return to room temperature before proceeding.

Turn out again on to a floured surface and knock back and knead for about 2 minutes until smooth. Divide into eight pieces and roll each piece into a round. Put 5ml (1 level tsp) stiff raspberry jam in the centre and draw up the edges to form a ball, making sure the dough is well joined together to enclose the jam. Put the buns on to greased and floured baking sheets, cover with oiled polythene and put to rise for 10–15 minutes until a little puffy. Heat a pan of fat or oil to 182°C (360°F) or until a 2.5cm (1in) cube of bread will brown in 1 minute.

Fry the doughnuts, a few at a time, for 5–10 minutes until golden brown. Drain thoroughly on crumpled kitchen paper and, whilst still hot, coat either in plain caster sugar or a mixture of caster sugar mixed with ground cinnamon to taste. The easist way to do this is to put the coating in a polythene bag, add the doughnuts one at a time and shake until well coated. Remove and leave to cool. Reheat the fat and cook the remaining doughnuts in the same way.

Cream Doughnuts

Shape the pieces of dough either into balls or oval shapes and put to rise as before. Fry in hot fat for 5–10 minutes until golden brown and drain and coat in sugar as before. When cold, make a

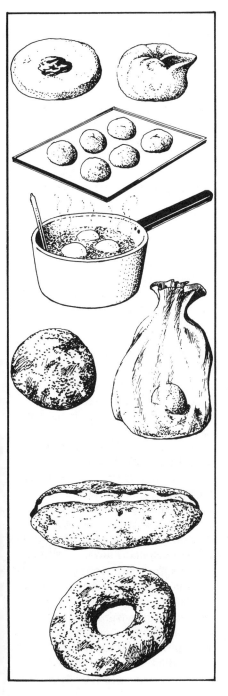

slit along the top of each doughnut and either fill with slightly sweetened whipped cream, or first add a little jam of your choice and then cover with the whipped cream.

Ring Doughnuts

Roll out the whole piece of dough to about 1cm ($\frac{1}{2}$in) thickness. Using a 7.5cm (3in) plain round cutter, cut into rounds. Then cut out the centres of each doughnut using a smaller cutter, 2.5–4cm (1–1$\frac{1}{2}$in). Transfer the rings to a greased and floured baking sheet, cover with oiled polythene and put to rise until almost doubled in size. Use the remaining dough trimmings to make more doughnuts. Fry the doughnuts a few at a time in hot deep fat until golden brown—about 5 minutes. Drain on absorbent kitchen paper and coat in sugar as for jam doughnuts. Leave to cool. These doughnuts are usually eaten as they are, but can also have either a little whipped cream piped around the top of each one, or be split open and filled with jam and/or cream.

Note Doughnuts must be eaten whilst fresh. The jam can be put into the doughnuts after proving the buns just prior to baking. To do this, make a small hole in the side and fill with jam using a long piping nozzle fitted into a bag. Make sure the hole is completely closed before cooking.

Iced Plait

An attractive, rich yeasted bread in the shape of a plait which can either be served decorated with nuts and glacé cherries or with glacé icing and the nuts and cherries.

Ingredients

225g (8oz) strong plain white flour
Pinch of salt
25g (1oz) butter or margarine
50g (2oz) caster sugar
75g (3oz) mixed dried fruit
15g (½oz) fresh yeast or 7.5ml (1½ level tsp) dried yeast and 5ml (1 level tsp) caster sugar

75ml (5 tbsp) warm milk, 43°C (110°F)
1 egg, beaten
Beaten egg to glaze
Chopped nuts and glacé cherries for decoration

Sieve the flour and salt into a bowl and rub in the butter or margarine. Mix in the sugar and dried fruit. Dissolve the fresh yeast in the milk. For dried yeast, dissolve 5ml (1 tsp) sugar in the milk, sprinkle the dried yeast over the top and leave in a warm place until frothy—about 10 minutes. Add the yeast liquid to the dry ingredients together with the egg and mix to form a fairly soft dough.

Turn out on to a lightly floured surface and knead until smooth and elastic—about 10 minutes by hand or 3–4 minutes if you are using an electric mixer. Shape into a ball and place in an oiled polythene bag. Put to rise in a warm place for about 1 hour until doubled in size and the dough springs back when lightly pressed with a floured finger (see p 13 for alternate rising times).

Turn out on to a floured surface, knock back and knead for about 2 minutes until smooth and firm. Divide into three equal pieces and roll each piece to a long, thin sausage. Place these pieces side-by-side and, beginning in the middle, plait the three pieces together towards you ; secure the ends. Turn the dough right over and plait the remaining pieces to complete the loaf, securing the end. Place on a greased baking sheet. Cover with a sheet of oiled polythene and put to rise in a warm place for about 25 minutes or until doubled in size. Remove the polythene, brush all over with beaten

Glacé Icing

225g (8oz) icing sugar
20–30ml (1½–2 tbsp) warm water, or
    orange or lemon juice
Colouring (optional)

Blend the sieved icing sugar and water
or fruit juice in a basin until smooth,
adding colouring sparingly, if liked.
This mixture gives a soft, flowing icing ;
for a firmer consistency, use only
10–15ml (¾–1tbsp) water.

egg and bake in a hot oven, 220°C
(425°F) mark 7, for about 15 minutes,
until golden brown. Cool on a wire rack.
Either brush with a wet brush dipped
in honey and sprinkle thickly with
chopped nuts and pieces of glacé
cherry, or leave until cold and then coat
with glacé icing (see below) and
sprinkle with the nuts and cherries.
Leave to set.

Variations
The plait can also be shaped into a
crescent after plaiting or have the two
ends of the plait joined together to
make a circle. Place on greased baking
sheets and put to rise and bake as
above.

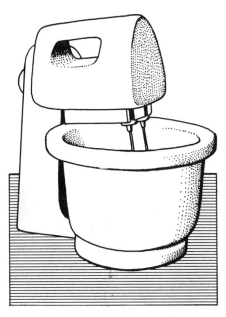

Iced Fruit Buns

Divide the dough into 50g (2oz) pieces
and either shape into buns by rolling
each piece on a lightly floured surface
with the palm of your hand or divide
each piece into two and roll to thin
sausage shapes and then twist together
securing each end. Place on greased
baking sheets, cover with oiled
polythene and put to rise until doubled
in size. Bake for 10–15 minutes.
Decorate as for the plait.

Devonshire Splits

These buns are popular for they are served split and filled with Devonshire or clotted cream and jam. They are often enjoyed on holidays in the West Country as part of a cream tea.

Ingredients

15g (½oz) fresh yeast or 7.5ml (1½ level tsp) dried yeast and 5ml (1 level tsp) caster sugar
Approx 300ml (½pt) warm milk, 43°C (110°F)
450g (1lb) strong plain white flour ·
5ml (1 level tsp) salt
50g (2oz) butter or margarine
25g (1oz) caster sugar
Devonshire or whipped cream
Raspberry jam
Icing sugar

Blend the fresh yeast in half the warm milk. For dried yeast, dissolve 5ml (1tsp) sugar in the milk, then sprinkle the dried yeast over the top and leave in a warm place until frothy—about 10 minutes. Sieve the flour and salt into a bowl. Dissolve the butter or margarine and the sugar in the remaining milk, then cool to 43°C (110°F) before adding to the dry ingredients together with the yeast liquid. Beat to form a soft, elastic dough, then turn on to a floured surface and knead until smooth —about 10 minutes by hand or 3–4 minutes if you are using an electric mixer.

Shape into a ball, put into an oiled polythene bag and put to rise until doubled in size—about 1 hour in a warm place; 2 hours at room temperature; up to 12 hours in a cold larder or up to 24 hours in a refrigerator. Remember to allow the

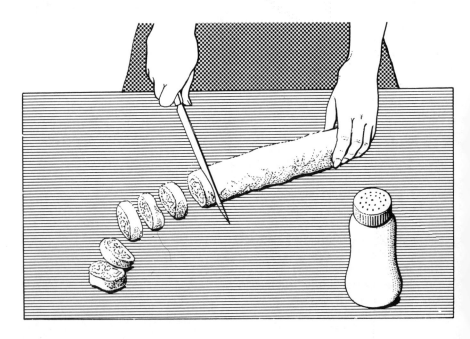

dough to return to room temperature before shaping—about 1 hour.

Turn the dough on to a floured surface, and divide into fifteen even-sized pieces. Knead each piece lightly and shape into a ball. Place on greased baking sheets and slightly flatten each bun with the palm of your hand. Cover with sheets of oiled polythene and put to rise in a warm place for about 25 minutes or until doubled in size. Bake in a hot oven, 220°C (425°F) mark 7, for 15–20 minutes. Remove to a wire rack and leave to cool. Before serving, split the buns open and spread with jam and cream. Reassemble the buns and dredge the top of each one with icing sugar. This recipe makes fifteen buns.

Note These buns freeze well but do not fill until properly thawed and ready to serve. Stale buns can be toasted first.

Swiss Buns

Divide the knocked-back dough into 50–75g (2–3oz) pieces and then shape each piece into a sausage shape using the palms of your hands. Place on well greased baking sheets. Cover with a sheet of oiled polythene and put to rise in a warm place until doubled in size. Remove polythene and bake in a hot oven, 220°C (425°F) mark 7, for about 15 minutes, until well risen and pale golden brown. Remove to a wire rack and leave to cool.

Make up a glacé icing by sieving 225g (8oz) icing sugar into a bowl and adding sufficient warm water and a little cochineal (if liked) to give a thick coating consistency. Spoon over the buns and leave to set.

Hot Cross Buns

The traditional spicy fruit bun for Easter. It is suitable to eat at any meal but often favoured for breakfast served warm with lots of butter or at tea-time either warmed or toasted. The crosses can be made in several ways. The easiest and quickest way is simply to cut a cross into the top of the bun after shaping, and then mark it again after proving, immediately before putting into the oven. Narrow strips of pastry are definitely more visible but do require the extra time to make a small amount of short crust pastry. Both methods are given here.

Ingredients

450g (1lb) strong plain white flour
25g (1oz) fresh yeast or 15ml (1 level tbsp) dried yeast
5ml (1 level tsp) caster sugar
150ml ($\frac{1}{4}$pt) warm milk, 43°C (110°F)
60ml (4tbsp) warm water, 43°C (110°F)
5ml (1 level tsp) salt
2.5ml ($\frac{1}{2}$ level tsp) ground nutmeg
2.5ml ($\frac{1}{2}$ level tsp) mixed spice
2.5ml ($\frac{1}{2}$ level tsp) ground cinnamon
50g (2oz) caster sugar
50g (2oz) chopped mixed peel
100g (4oz) currants
50g (2oz) melted butter or margarine, cooled
1 egg beaten

Pastry for Crosses (optional)

60g (2oz) plain four
Pinch of salt
15g ($\frac{1}{2}$oz) margarine
15g ($\frac{1}{2}$oz) lard or white fat
Water to mix

Sugar Glaze

45ml (3 level tbsp) caster sugar
45–60ml (3–4 tbsp) milk and water mixed

Place 100g (4oz) flour in a large bowl with fresh or dried yeast and 5ml (1tsp) sugar. Add the warm milk and water and mix well. Put in a warm place until the batter becomes frothy—this should take 10–15 minutes for fresh yeast or 20–25 minutes for dried yeast.

Sieve the remaining flour into a bowl with the salt and spices, and then mix in the sugar followed by the mixed peel and currants. Add the cooled melted butter and beaten egg to the yeast batter, followed by all the dry ingredients, and mix together to form a softish dough. Turn out on to a lightly floured surface and knead until smooth and no longer sticky—about 10 minutes by hand or 3–4 minutes if you are using an electric mixer. Shape into a ball and place in a lightly oiled polythene bag. Put to rise in a warm place for about 1$\frac{1}{2}$–2 hours until doubled in size and the dough springs

back when lightly pressed with a floured finger. This is a richly fruited dough, so it takes longer to rise than ordinary plain bread.

Turn out again on to a lightly floured surface. Knock back and knead for about 2 minutes until smooth. Divide the dough into twelve or fourteen even-sized pieces. Shape each piece into a bun by rolling on a hard surface with the palm of your hand, first of all pressing down hard, and then easing the pressure as the bun takes shape. Place the buns fairly well apart on a lightly greased baking sheet. Either cut a cross into each bun using a very sharp knife or, if using pastry crosses, leave as they are. Cover with a sheet of oiled polythene and put to rise in a warm place until doubled in size— about 30 minutes. For simple crosses, mark again using a very sharp knife and bake in a moderately hot oven, 190°C (375°F) mark 5, for 20–25 minutes

until golden brown. For pastry cross buns, while the buns are rising, make up the shortcrust pastry by rubbing the fats into the flour with a pinch of salt added, until the mixture resembles fine breadcrumbs, then mix to a pliable dough with a little cold water. Roll out very thinly on a floured surface and cut into very narrow strips about 8.5cm ($3\frac{1}{2}$in) long. Brush the strips with milk and lay two across each bun to make a cross. Bake in a moderately hot oven as for the other buns.

While the buns are cooking, make the sugar glaze by mixing the sugar, milk and water together in a small pan and bring to the boil for 2 minutes. Leave to cool. Remove the buns to a wire rack and, while still hot, brush the tops two or three times with the sugar glaze and then leave to cool.

Note These buns freeze well.

Lardy Cake and Dough Cake

Both these cakes are made from basic white bread dough with the extra ingredients added after the first rising. When baking a batch of white bread, remove a little of the dough and use to make a different sort of cake for the family. Lardy cake can be served at tea-time or warmed and served as a pudding with cream or custard.

Lardy Cake

Ingredients

675g (1½lb) risen white bread dough, using 450g (1 lb) flour (see p 14)
100g (4oz) lard or half lard and half margarine
100g (4oz) caster sugar
5ml (1 level tsp) mixed spice or cinnamon
75–100g (3–4oz) sultanas, or currants, or mixed dried druit

Remove the dough from the polythene bag and knock back. Knead well until smooth. Roll out on a floured surface to 5mm (¼in) thickness. Cover the dough with small flakes made from 50g (2oz) fat and then sprinkle with 50g (2oz) sugar, followed by 2.5ml (½tsp) spice and 40–50g (1½–2oz) dried fruit. Roll up loosely like a Swiss roll and then roll out again to an oblong. Repeat, covering the dough with the remaining fat, most of the sugar, and all the spice and fruit. Roll up loosely again. Roll out to an oblong and roll up for a third time and place in a greased baking tin about 25cm × 20cm (10in × 8in) pressing the dough down firmly to fit into the corners. Cover with

a sheet of oiled polythene and put to rise in a warm place until doubled in size. Remove polythene, brush the top of the cake with oil and sprinkle with the remaining sugar. Using a sharp knife, score the top into a criss-cross pattern. Bake in a hot oven, 220°C 425°F) mark 7, for about 30 minutes. Turn out and cool on a wire rack and serve in slices either plain or buttered.

Dough Cake

A tea-bread which can be varied by adding orange or lemon rind, other spices or a tablespoon of black treacle.

Making lardy cake

Spread fruit and spices over dough

Roll up loosely

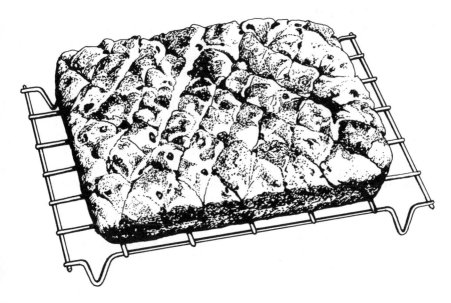

Lardy cake

Ingredients

450g (1 lb) risen white bread dough
  (see p 14)
50g (2oz) butter or margarine,
  softened
50g (2oz) caster sugar
100g (4oz) mixed dried druit
50g (2oz) chopped nuts
5ml (1 level tsp) mixed spice
Honey or syrup to glaze

Remove the dough from the polythene bag and place in a bowl. Add all the other ingredients, and knead and squeeze the mixture until evenly blended. Shape the dough to fit a greased 450g (1 lb) loaf tin and put into a large oiled polythene bag. Put to rise in a warm place until the dough reaches the top of the tin. Remove the polythene and bake in a very hot oven, 230°C (450°F) mark 8, for about 30 minutes, until the base sounds hollow when tapped. Remove from the tin to a wire rack and brush the top of the hot loaf with a wet pastry-brush dipped in honey or syrup to glaze. Leave to cool.

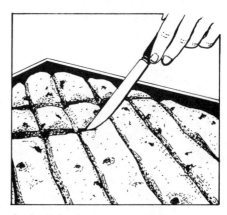

Scoring lardy cake

Scandinavian Tea Ring

A most attractive but simple to make tea-ring with a spicy sugar filling which will delight your guests. A variety of toppings can be added either on top of glacé icing or straight on to the ring after brushing with honey or syrup.

Ingredients

225g (8oz) strong plain white flour
2.5ml ($\frac{1}{2}$ level tsp) caster sugar
15g ($\frac{1}{2}$oz) fresh yeast or 7.5ml
   ($1\frac{1}{2}$ level tsp) dried yeast
100ml (4fl oz) warm milk, 43°C
   (110°F)
2.5ml ($\frac{1}{2}$ level tsp) salt
25g (1oz) margarine
$\frac{1}{2}$ egg, beaten
20g ($\frac{3}{4}$oz) melted butter or margarine
50–75g (2–3oz) soft brown sugar
10–15ml (2–3 level tsp) ground
   cinnamon or mixed spice
Glacé cherries, chopped angelica
   and/or flaked almonds or chopped
   walnuts for topping

Lemon Glacé Icing

100g (4oz) icing sugar, sieved
5ml ($\frac{1}{2}$ level tsp) finely grated
   lemon rind
Lemon juice

Put 65g ($2\frac{1}{2}$oz) flour with the sugar, fresh or dried yeast and milk into a bowl. Put aside in a warm place for about 20 minutes until frothy and the yeast dissolved. Sieve the remaining flour with the salt into a bowl and rub in the margarine until the mixture resembles fine breadcrumbs. Add the beaten egg and the flour mixture to the yeast batter and mix well to give a fairly soft dough which will leave the sides of the bowl clean.

Turn the dough on to a lightly floured surface and knead until it is smooth and no longer sticky—about 10 minutes by hand or 3–4 minutes if you are using an electric mixer (no extra flour should be necessary). Form the dough into a ball and place in a lightly oiled polythene bag, tie loosely and put to rise in a warm place until doubled in size—about 1 hour (see p 13 for alternate rising times).

Remove the risen dough from the polythene bag on to a lightly floured surface. Knock back and knead for about 2 minutes until smooth. Roll out the dough to an oblong on a floured surface to approx 30cm × 22.5cm (12in × 9in). Brush all over with the melted butter or margarine and then sprinkle with a mixture of brown sugar and spice. Starting from the long edge, roll up the dough tightly like a Swiss roll, sealing the ends together to form a ring. Place on a well greased baking sheet. Using scissors which have been brushed with oil, cut slashes at an

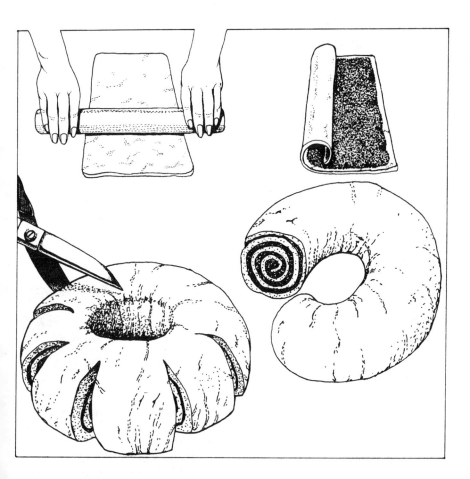

angle into the ring about two-thirds
of the way through the dough at 2.5cm
(1in) intervals. Keeping a neat shape,
carefully turn the cut sections to one
side to open up the ring a little.

Cover with oiled polythene and put
to rise in a warm place for about 30
minutes until well risen. Remove the
polythene and bake in a moderately
hot oven, 190°C (375°F) mark 5, for
30–35 minutes, until well risen and
golden brown. Remove the ring
carefully to a wire rack.

While the ring is still warm, make the
glacé icing by mixing the icing sugar
and lemon rind with sufficient lemon
juice to give a thick coating
consistency. Spoon over the tea-ring,
allowing the icing to drip down over the
cut pieces. Decorate the top with
cherries, angelica and nuts, as you
wish. Leave to cool and set before
cutting.

Danish Pastries

To achieve the required soft dough for these delicious pastries, use household plain flour—not the strong bread flour. This softer flour, together with the softened butter and folding and rolling involved, gives a very tender, flaky pastry. The fillings and toppings can be varied according to taste, and your own special filling can be added to give a wider choice. These pastries are a Danish speciality but are easy and fairly quick to make.

Ingredients

25g (1oz) fresh yeast or 15ml (1 level
    tbsp) dried yeast and 5ml (1 level
    tsp) caster sugar
Approx 150ml (approx ¼pt) water
450g (1lb) plain, not strong, flour
5ml (1 level tsp) salt
50g (2oz) lard
25g (1oz) caster sugar
2 eggs, beaten
300g (10oz) butter
Beaten egg to glaze

Blend the fresh yeast with the water. For dried yeast, dissolve the sugar in warm water 43°C (110°F), then sprinkle the dried yeast over the top and leave in a warm place until frothy—about 10 minutes.

Sieve the flour and salt into a bowl, rub in the lard; then mix in the sugar. Add the yeast liquid and beaten eggs to the dry ingredients and mix to form a soft, elastic dough, adding a little more water if necessary. Turn out on to a lightly floured surface and knead lightly by hand for about 2–3 minutes, until smooth. Put the dough into a

lightly oiled polythene bag and chill in a refrigerator for 10 minutes. Soften the butter with a knife and shape into an oblong about 10cm × 25cm (4in × 10in). Roll out the dough on a lightly floured surface to a 27.5cm (11in) square and spread the rectangle of butter down the centre third of the dough. Enclose the butter by folding the two flaps of pastry over to just overlap in the middle, and seal the top and bottom with the rolling-pin.

Turn the dough so that the folds are to the sides and roll into a strip three times as long as it is wide. Fold the bottom third of the dough upwards and the top third down and seal the edges. Put in the polythene bag and put to rest in a refrigerator for 10 minutes. Repeat the rolling, folding and resting of the dough twice more, leaving it to chill for 30 minutes after the last folding. The dough is then ready for use.

Make up the required fillings and prepare the toppings.

Fillings

Almond Paste

15g (½oz) butter
75g (3oz) caster sugar
75g (3oz) ground almonds
1 egg, beaten
Almond essence

Cream the butter and sugar together until soft, then stir in the almonds and add sufficient egg to mix to a pliable consistency. Add a few drops of almond essence to taste.

Cinnamon Butter

50g (2oz) butter
50g (2oz) caster sugar
10ml (2 level tsp) ground cinnamon

Cream the butter and sugar together until fluffy and then beat in the ground cinnamon until well mixed.

Confectioner's Custard

1 whole egg, separated
1 egg yolk
50g (2oz) caster sugar
30ml (2 level tbsp) plain flour
30ml (2 level tbsp) cornflour
300ml (½pt) milk
Vanilla essence

Cream the egg yolks and sugar together in a bowl until really thick and pale in colour. Beat in the flour and cornflour and a little cold milk to make a smooth paste. Heat the rest of the milk gently (preferably in a non-stick pan) until almost boiling and, stirring continuously, pour on to the egg mixture. Return the mixture to the saucepan and, continuing to stir, cook slowly over a gentle heat, until the mixture just comes to the boil. Remove the saucepan from the heat. Whisk the egg whites until stiff and fold into the custard. Add vanilla essence to taste and return the pan to cook over a very gentle heat for 2–3 minutes. Cool before using. Cover the pan with a lid or cling-film, to prevent a skin forming whilst cooling.

Dried Fruit Filling

25g (1oz) butter
25g (1oz) brown sugar
Pinch of ground nutmeg
25g (1oz) currants
25g (1oz) sultanas

Cream the butter and sugar together. Beat in nutmeg to taste and the dried fruits.

Toppings
Apricot jam or redcurrant jelly
Flaked and chopped almonds, plain and toasted
Glacé cherries and angelica

White Glacé Icing

100–175g (4–6oz) icing sugar, sieved
Little flavouring essence (optional)
15–30ml (1–2 tbsp) warm water

Put the icing sugar into a bowl and add flavouring essence. Gradually beat in sufficient warm water to give a thick coating consistency. Add more water or sugar to adjust the consistency.

Shaping and Baking Danish Pastries

Crescents

Roll out thinly one quarter of the dough into a 22.5cm (9in) circle. Cut this circle into eight even-sized wedges. Put 1 tsp almond paste, confectioner's custard, dried fruit filling (see p 65) or even a little stewed apple at the wide base of each piece of dough. Roll carefully and fairly loosely to the point. Curve into a crescent shape and place on a lightly greased baking sheet. Cover lightly with oiled polythene and put to rise in a warm place for 20–30 minutes until puffy. Brush with beaten egg and bake in a hot oven, 220°C (425°F) mark 7, for 10–15 minutes. Remove to a wire rack and, while still hot, brush with a little white glacé icing (see p 65) and sprinkle with nuts. Leave until cold and set. This recipe makes eight pastries.

Windmills and Imperial Stars

Roll out thinly one quarter of the dough and cut into 7.5cm (3in) squares. Make diagonal cuts from each corner to within 1cm ($\frac{1}{2}$in) of the centre. Put a piece of almond paste in the middle and fold one corner of each cut section to the centre of the square securing each tip with a little beaten egg. Place on a greased baking sheet. Cover with lightly oiled polythene and put to rise in a warm place for 20–30 minutes until puffy, then brush with beaten egg and bake in a hot oven, 220°C (425°F) mark 7, for about 20 minutes. Remove to a wire rack and, while still hot, brush with white glacé icing (see p 65) and sprinkle with toasted flaked almonds

and pieces of glacé cherry and/or angelica to make windmills. For imperial stars, finish the centres with a spoonful of confectioner's custard (see p 65) and possibly a piece of glacé cherry, and brush the star projections with glacé icing. Leave to cool and set.

Fruit Pinwheels

Roll out thinly one quarter of the dough and cut into an oblong 30cm × 20cm (12in × 8in). Spread all over with the dried fruit filling (see p 65), adding a little chopped mixed peel and chopped glacé cherries, if liked. Roll up like a Swiss roll from the short end, securing the end with beaten egg. Cut into 2.5cm (1in) thick slices and place, cut-side downward, on a greased baking sheet. Flatten slightly. Cover with oiled polythene and put to rise in a warm place until puffy—about 20 minutes. Brush with beaten egg and bake in a hot oven, 220°C (425°F) mark 7, for 15–20 minutes, until golden brown. Remove to a wire rack and either brush with glacé icing or with a

wet pastry-brush dipped in honey and sprinkle with toasted flaked almonds. Leave to cool and set. This recipe makes eight pastries.

Cocks Combs

Roll out one quarter of the dough and cut into strips 11 cm × 12.5cm (4½in × 5in). Spread half the width of each strip with almond paste, confectioner's custard (see p 65) or stewed apple sprinkled with cinnamon and currants. Fold over the other half, sealing the edges with beaten egg. Make four or five cuts into the folded edge of the pastry and place on a greased baking sheet, curving it to open out the comb. Cover with oiled polythene, put to rise in a warm place until puffy—about 20 minutes. Brush with beaten egg and bake in a hot oven, 220°C (425°F) mark 7, for about 20 minutes. Remove to a wire rack and, while still hot, brush with glacé icing and sprinkle with toasted almonds. This recipe makes six to eight pastries.

Cushions

Roll out thinly one quarter of the dough and cut into 7.5cm (3in) squares. Put a little almond paste, confectioner's custard or other filling to taste (see p 65) in the centre and either fold two alternate corners to overlap slightly in the centre and secure with beaten egg, or fold all four corners into the centre to overlap a little and secure with beaten egg. Place on greased baking sheets and cover with oiled polythene. Put to rise in a warm place for 20–30 minutes until puffy, then brush with beaten egg and bake in a hot oven, 220°C (425°F) mark 7, for about 15 minutes. Remove to a wire rack and, while still hot, brush lightly with glacé icing (see p 65). Sprinkle with nuts and cherries and put a spoonful of confectioner's custard (see p 65) or redcurrant jelly in the centre of each one. This recipe makes eight pastries.

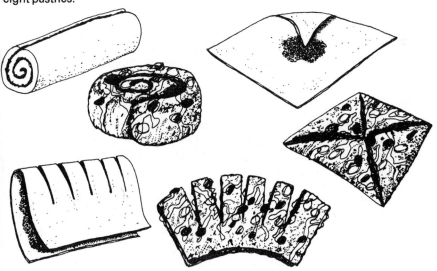

Croissants

These are the classic crisp and flaky rolls of a continental breakfast, the taste of which often lingers long after a holiday. They are best served warm. The secret of making a good croissant is to have both the dough and the fat firm so that they make two definite layers. The pastry is light because it is made by a combination of two methods of aeration : the yeast fermentation of a rich yeast dough, and the trapping of air with the fat as in flaky pastry. The pastry must be kept cold throughout the preparation with only the final rising at a warm temperature after shaping. To get the layering even, roll the dough thinly and use a margarine that is hard and waxy—not a soft type at room temperature. The dough must be wrapped in polythene each time when chilled to prevent cracking and a skin forming. Whilst rolling, keep the dough in shape with straight sides and square corners to make the folding up and layering even, and work quickly when handling the dough to prevent it from becoming soft and warm.

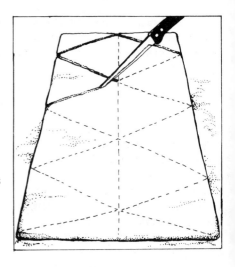

Ingredients

25g (1oz) fresh yeast or 15ml (1 level tbsp) dried yeast and 5ml (1 level tsp) caster sugar
300ml less 60ml ($\frac{1}{2}$pt less 4tbsp) warm water 43°C (110°F)
450g (1lb) strong plain white flour
10ml (2 level tsp) salt
25g (1oz) lard
1 egg, beaten
100–175g (4–6oz) hard margarine

Egg Glaze

1 egg, beaten
2.5ml ($\frac{1}{2}$ level tsp) caster sugar
15–30ml (1–2 tbsp) water

Blend the fresh yeast into the water. For dried yeast, dissolve the sugar in the water, then sprinkle the dried yeast over the top and leave in a warm place until frothy—about 10 minutes. Sieve the flour and salt together into a bowl, add the lard and rub in. Add the yeast liquid and beaten egg, and mix well to form a dough. Turn out on to a lightly floured surface and knead thoroughly until smooth and even—10–15 minutes by hand or about 5 minutes if you are using an electric mixer.

Roll out the dough to a rectangle about 50cm × 20cm × 5mm (20in × 8in × $\frac{1}{4}$in) thick, taking care to keep the edges straight and the corners square. Divide the margarine into three. Soften each piece of margarine with a knife, then use one part to dot evenly over the top two-thirds of the dough, leaving a small

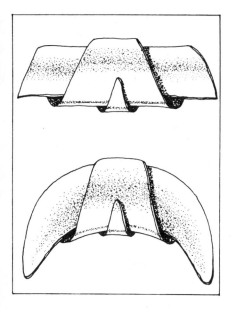

Shaping Croissants

Roll the dough out on a lightly floured surface to a rectangle about 57.5cm × 35cm (23in × 14in). Cover with lightly oiled polythene and leave to rest for 10 minutes. Trim the dough to 52.5cm × 30cm (21in × 12in) and then cut in half lengthwise. Cut each strip into six triangles 15cm (6in) high with a 15cm (6in) base (see diagram). Make the egg glaze by mixing together the egg, sugar and water and use to brush all over the dough. Roll up each triangle loosely, starting from the wide base to the point and finishing with the tip underneath. Bend into a crescent shape and place on ungreased baking sheets. Brush the top of each croissant with egg glaze and put each baking sheet into a lightly oiled polythene bag. Close bags and put to rise at room temperature for about 30 minutes, until light and puffy. Remove the polythene and brush again with egg glaze. Bake in a hot oven, 220°C (425°F) mark 7, for about 20 minutes. This recipe makes twelve croissants.

border clear all round. Fold into three by bringing up the bottom plain third first, then folding the top third over the other two. Turn the dough so that the fold is on the right-hand side and then seal the edges with a rolling-pin. Roll out the dough gently again to a long strip by gently pressing the dough at intervals with the rolling-pin. Repeat with the other two portions of margarine, taking care all the time to keep the dough in a neat rectangle. Place the dough in a lightly oiled polythene bag and put to rest in a refrigerator for 30 minutes.

Remove from the bag and roll out and fold as before (without adding any fat, of course) three times more. Replace in the polythene bag and return to the refrigerator for at least 1 hour. The dough can be left in the refrigerator overnight or for two or three days at this stage, ready to make into croissants at any time.

Note Croissants are best served warm. To reheat, wrap lightly in foil before putting into a hot oven for a few minutes.

69

Soda Bread and Scone Rounds

Soda Bread (*without yeast*)

Ingredients

450g (1lb) plain white flour
10ml (2 level tsp) bicarbonate of soda
10ml (2 level tsp) cream of tartar
5ml (1 level tsp) salt
50g (2oz) lard or margarine
15ml (1 tbsp) lemon juice
300ml ($\frac{1}{2}$pt) milk

Sieve together into a bowl the flour, bicarbonate of soda, cream of tartar and salt. Rub in the lard or margarine until the mixture resembles fine breadcrumbs. Add the lemon juice to the milk to make it turn sour (or use sour milk or buttermilk, if available), and add this to the dry ingredients and mix to a soft manageable dough, using a palette knife. Turn on to a floured surface and, using your hands, shape into a round about 17.5cm (7in) across.

Transfer the dough to a greased baking sheet and mark into quarters with a sharp knife. Dredge the top with flour or sprinkle with coarse sea salt.

Bake in a hot oven, 220°C (425°F) mark 7, for about 30 minutes, until well risen and golden brown. Cool on a wire rack and eat whilst fresh—stale soda bread is very unpalatable.

Brown Soda Bread

Use 225g (8oz) plain, white flour and 225g (8oz) plain, wholemeal flour, and follow the recipe for white soda bread.

Scone Rounds (*without yeast*)

These are light textured scones which are quick and easy to prepare and bake. The variations make them suitable to serve with any meal to replace traditional bread. They also freeze well.

Ingredients

450g (1lb) self-raising flour
Pinch of salt
100g (4oz) butter or margarine
40–50g (1$\frac{1}{2}$–2oz) caster sugar
2 eggs, beaten
Approx 175ml (6fl oz) milk
   (preferably sour)

Sieve the flour and salt into a bowl. Add the butter or margarine and rub in until the mixture resembles fine breadcrumbs. Mix in the sugar. Make a well in the centre of the mixture and add the eggs. Add sufficient milk to mix to a soft dough. Turn out on to a floured surface, divide into two equal pieces and flatten out each one with your hand to a round about 2cm ($\frac{3}{4}$in) thick.

Transfer to greased or floured baking sheets and mark each round deeply into eight wedges. Either leave plain or dredge with flour. Bake in a very hot oven, 230°C (450°F) mark 8, for 15–20

minutes, until well risen and browned. Turn on to a clean cloth on a wire rack, wrap up and leave to cool. Break into wedges as required.

Alternative Sweet Toppings

The rounds can be brushed with beaten egg or milk and, if liked, be sprinkled with one of the following before baking : demerara sugar, chopped shelled walnuts, cinnamon or mixed spice, crushed sugar lumps, etc.

Fruited Scone Rounds

Add to the rubbed in dry ingredients 100g (4oz) currants, raisins or sultanas ; or 100g (4oz) mixed dried fruit ; or the grated rind of 1 large orange or lemon ; or a mixture of fruit and 50g (2oz) mixed peel or chopped nuts.

Wholemeal Scone Rounds

Replace half the self-raising flour with brown self-raising flour or brown plain flour mixed with 7.5ml ($1\frac{1}{2}$ level tsp) baking powder, and follow the recipe for basic scone rounds.

Savoury Scone Rounds

Prepare the basic scone round mixture, omitting the sugar and adding any of the following to the dry ingredients : 75–100g (3–4oz) finely grated cheese ; or 30–45ml (2–3tbsp) freshly chopped herbs ; or 3–4 cloves crushed garlic or the equivalent of powdered garlic. Sprinkle the tops with flour, or grated cheese or rock salt, or brush with egg or milk.

Note Using cutters, or by cutting the dough into triangles or squares, the mixture can also be made into scone rounds of various sizes, ie 2.5cm (1in), 4cm ($1\frac{1}{2}$in), 5cm (2in), etc. Place on a greased or floured baking sheet with the scones almost touching each other. Bake as for the basic scone rounds for 12–15 minutes. Cool on a wire rack wrapped in a clean cloth.

PRESERVING AND PICKLING

Rosemary Wadey

Introduction

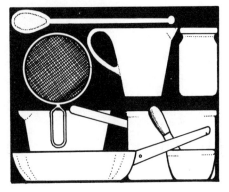

In these days of highly priced vegetables and fruits it is only common sense either to grow your own and then preserve them in various ways for future use or to buy in when there is an abundant supply or glut of the particular items you want and preserve them. Picking your own from large growers is also becoming more popular and brings the price down really low for of course, it cuts out all the overheads otherwise incurred.

Freezing is one excellent way of preserving fruit and vegetables but not everyone owns a deep freeze ; so this book concentrates on preserving the produce in other ways. Pickles, chutneys, jams, jellies, and bottling can use up an enormous amount of produce and will keep it in excellent condition if the few simple rules for each particular method of preserving are followed. Commercial chutneys and pickles as well as jams are now very expensive, whilst home processing is neither difficult nor very costly and the results are often so much better than the commercial equivalent. Also there is such enormous scope for mixing and altering ingredients and flavours in favourite preserves to create exciting new and even better ones.

Only use fresh crisp vegetables for pickling. Damaged or blemished produce will not keep well or give good results when finished so is better used in chutneys when the marked part can be cut out and discarded. Windfall apples can, however, be used if the correct weight is made up after cutting out the damaged part of the fruit.

Vegetables need to be brined before pickling to remove the surplus water. If this is omitted the water in the vegetables will dilute the vinegar so that it will not be strong enough to preserve the vegetables and they will go off. Use table salt to make the brine allowing 50g (2oz) per 600ml (1pt) water ; and rinse the vegetables in cold running water after removing from the brine or the resulting pickle will be too salty.

Equipment for Pickles and Chutneys

To prevent an unpleasant metallic taste forming in the finished pickle or chutney, all pans made of brass, copper and iron must be avoided. Instead use enamel-lined pans or those made of aluminium or stainless steel. This includes basins and bowls used for brining so always use glass or china for this stage. For the same reason do not use metal sieves but always have a nylon or hair one at hand. Keep one or two large wooden spoons especially for pickle- and chutney-making for the flavour does become attached and might be passed on to something else the spoon is used for.

Jars used for pickling, as for all

preserves, must be sound and clean. They can be ordinary jam jars or special pickling (or bottling) jars but they must be properly covered with a special vinegar-proof top to prevent the evaporation of vinegar during storage which causes the preserve to shrink badly and the surface to dry out into a tough leathery skin, which ruins the pickle or chutney. So use one of the following covers :

1   Special preserving skin sold in rolls to be cut off to the required size, or a vinegar-proof paper.

2   Metal or Bakelite caps which have a special vinegar-proof lining (without the lining the acid in the preserve will eat through the metal).

3   Large corks which are first boiled for 10 minutes in water before use and then covered with greaseproof paper and tied down firmly with string.

4   Greaseproof paper covers which are then covered with a circle of muslin which has been dipped in melted paraffin wax or fat, tied down with string, which then sets firm when it dries out.

All jars should be well filled and covered with a waxed disc (except with pickles with pieces of vegetable or fruit in vinegar or a syrup), keeping the waxed side touching the preserve. Chutneys, jams and jellies are usually covered with a vinegar-proof top or dampened cellophane cover whilst still hot, but marmalades are more usually covered when cold. Jars must be wiped down and clearly labelled with name of preserve and the date. All pickles and chutneys need a little time to mature before use but the times recommended vary and are stated in the individual recipes.

Vinegar

The vinegar used in pickles and preserves is the preserving agent and is obviously very important. Because of this it is advisable to use the best quality vinegar whether it be malt or distilled (white). The colour is no indication of strength but the malt vinegar often gives a better flavour to chutneys. However, the white vinegar (turned colourless only by further distilling) gives a much better appearance to light coloured pickles such as onions, cucumber, cauliflower, etc, but has the same preserving qualities as malt vinegar. To give the spicy flavour to the pickles, the vinegar is usually infused with spices and herbs which flavour the vegetables, etc. Commercial spiced vinegar is now available in small bottles and bulk containers but recipes for spicing vinegar are given in the book.

Note Remember chutneys are cooked in an uncovered pan to allow the necessary evaporation. If something is cooked in a covered pan the recipe will say so, otherwise in this book leave the lid off the pan. One metric teaspoon : 5ml ; one metric tablespoon : 15ml.

Pickles

Pickled Cucumber

Ingredients

3 cucumbers
450g (1lb) onions
45ml (3 level tbsp) salt
600ml (1pt) white vinegar
175g (6oz) caster sugar
7.5ml (1½ level tsp) celery seed
5ml (1 level tsp) mustard seed

Wipe the cucumbers and slice thinly.
Put into a large bowl. Peel the onions
and slice thinly and then mix with the
cucumbers. Sprinkle with the salt, mix
well and leave to stand for about an
hour. Pour off the brine, rinse the
cucumber and onion thoroughly in
cold water and then drain very well.
Put the vinegar into a saucepan with
the sugar, celery seed and mustard

seed and heat gently until the sugar
has dissolved. Bring to the boil and boil
for 3 minutes. Pack the cucumber and
onion slices tightly into jars and cover
completely with the hot vinegar. Cover
at once whilst hot with a vinegar-proof
top and store in a cool dry place for
2–3 weeks before use.

Pickled Mushrooms

Ingredients

900g (2lb) small young mushrooms
White vinegar
3–4 blades of mace
5ml (1 level tsp) white pepper
10ml (2 level tsp) salt
7.5ml (1½ level tsp) ground ginger
1 onion, peeled and finely chopped
  (optional)
1 bayleaf (optional)

If using cultivated mushrooms just trim off the stalks. With field mushrooms, unless they are the tight button ones, trim off the stalks and peel carefully. Wash all mushrooms thoroughly in salted water and drain well. Discard any damaged or blemished ones. Either put mushrooms into a saucepan or an ovenproof casserole adding just sufficient vinegar to cover and then mix in all the other ingredients. Bring slowly up to the boil on the top of the cooker and simmer very gently until just tender and the mushrooms have shrunk ; or cover casserole and cook in a cool oven 170°C (325°F) mark 3 for about 20 minutes or until tender. Remove the mushrooms and pack into clean jars. Strain the vinegar and bring back to the boil. Pour the hot liquid over the mushrooms to cover completely. Cover at once whilst hot with a vinegar-proof top.

Note 350g (¾lb) raw mushrooms will usually fill a 450g (1lb) jar but it will vary with the larger and smaller mushrooms.

Apple and Onion Pickle

Ingredients

900g (2lb) cooking apples (or windfalls)
900g (2lb) onions
100g (4oz) sultanas
2.5ml (½ level tsp) whole peppercorns
20 cloves
50g (2oz) chillies
2 pieces root ginger, bruised
30ml (2 level tbsp) salt
1.1l (2pt) white or malt vinegar
50g (2oz) demerara sugar (optional)

Peel, core and chop the apples and plunge them immediately into boiling water for 3 minutes. Drain very thoroughly. This will prevent apples from discolouring and tenderize them sufficiently for the pickle. Peel the onions and chop finely ; then mix with the apples and sultanas. Pack into hot dry jars. Tie the peppercorns, cloves, chillies and ginger in a piece of muslin and place in a saucepan with the salt, vinegar and sugar, if used. Leave to infuse for 1 hour then bring up to the boil and simmer for 10 minutes. Remove the muslin bag and pour the boiling vinegar into the jars to completely cover the contents. Cover with vinegar-proof tops whilst still hot and store in a cool, dry place for 1–2 weeks before using.

Preparing Spiced Vinegar

There is a quick and a slow method of making a spiced vinegar and although the quick method is more often used, the longer soaking of the slow method gives better results. With both ordinary spiced and sweet spiced vinegar use one of these methods :
Either put the vinegar with all the spices into a saucepan and bring slowly to the boil. Pour into a bowl, cover with a plate and leave to stand for at least 2 hours or until cold. Strain and use as required. Or put the cold vinegar into a large container with all the spices and cover tightly with a vinegar-proof top. Leave to stand for about 2 months before straining off to use. Both vinegars will keep for some time after spicing.
Recipes for spiced vinegar are given in the book.

Pickles

Pickled Onions

Ingredients

2.7–4.5kg (6–10lb) pickling onions
900g (2lb) salt
Water

Spiced Vinegar

2l (3½pt) vinegar, white or malt
15g (½oz) blade mace
15g (½oz) whole allspice
15g (½oz) whole cloves
Piece of cinnamon stick
12 whole peppercorns

Choose small even-sized pickling onions which should be firm and without any sign of sprouting at the top. Wash, then place in a large container. Make a brine of 4.5l (1gal) water to 450g (1lb) salt, pour over the onions and leave to soak for 12 hours. Drain onions, peel and replace in a fresh brine made in the same way and leave to soak for 24–36 hours. Make the spiced vinegar by putting all the ingredients into a pan and bringing slowly up to the boil. Pour into a bowl, cover and leave until cold—at least 3 hours. Strain and use. (If individual spices are unavailable use 50–75g [2–3oz] pickling spice but this will probably give a little different flavour each time, for commercially packed pickling spice differs from make to make and availability of spices. There is also a commercial spiced vinegar available on the market packed in 1.1l [2pt] and 4.5l [1 gal] containers.)

Remove the onions from the brine, and drain very well. Pack into jars or bottles as tightly as possible and cover with cold spiced vinegar. Cover with a vinegar-proof top and label the jars. Store in a cool dry place for 3 months before using.

Pickled Cauliflower

Ingredients

2–3 medium sized cauliflowers
100g (4oz) salt
1.1l (2pt) vinegar—white or malt
4 blades of mace
15ml (1tbsp) whole allspice
15ml (1tbsp) whole cloves
Piece cinnamon stick
6 whole peppercorns

Use firm tight headed cauliflowers and break into small florets, discarding the tough stalks and leaves. Make a brine with the salt and 1.1l (2pt) water and put in the cauliflower. Cover and leave to soak overnight. The next day rinse off surplus salt from the cauliflower and drain thoroughly. Pack tightly into jars. Put the vinegar into a saucepan with the spices and bring slowly up to

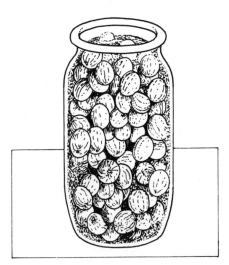

the boil. Pour into a bowl, cover and leave to stand for at least 2 hours. Strain the cold vinegar and pour into the jars to cover the cauliflower. Cover with a vinegar-proof top and store in a cool, dry place for 6–8 weeks before use.

Pickled Red Cabbage

Ingredients

1 large firm red cabbage (about
  2kg [5lb])
Salt

Spiced Vinegar

1.1l (2pt) vinegar
6–8 blades of mace
15ml (1tbsp) whole allspice
15ml (1tbsp) whole cloves
Piece of cinnamon stick
6 whole peppercorns

Remove any limp, marked and tatty outside leaves from the cabbage then cut it into quarters. Remove the hard white core from the centre of the cabbage and then slice each quarter

into fine shreds. This can be done either by using a sharp knife or by using a hand shredding machine or an electric shredder. Place the shredded cabbage in a large bowl layering it up with salt. Cover bowl and leave to stand overnight. To make the spiced vinegar put all the ingredients into a pan and bring slowly up to the boil. Pour into a bowl, cover and leave until cold —at least 3 hours. Strain and use. (If individual spices are unavailable use 40g [1½oz] pickling spice from a packet.) The next day drain the cabbage, rinse off the salt and drain again very thoroughly. Pack fairly tightly into jars and cover completely with cold spiced vinegar. Cover with a vinegar-proof top. Store for about a week before using in a cool dry place.

Note Pickled cabbage should be used fairly quickly for it tends to go limp after 2–3 months.

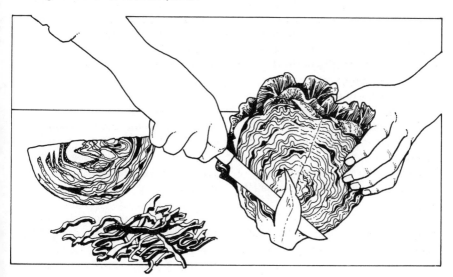

Pickles

Pickled Gherkins

Ingredients

450g (1 lb) gherkins
Salt
600ml (1 pt) vinegar—white or malt
5ml (1 level tsp) black peppercorns
5ml (1 level tsp) whole allspice
3–4 cloves
1 blade of mace

Wash the gherkins, do not peel; trim
and place in a bowl. Make up a brine
using 100g (4oz) salt to 1.1l (2pt)
water and pour over the gherkins.
Cover and leave to soak for 3 days.
Drain gherkins, rinse off the salt and
drain again and then pack into large
jars. Put the vinegar into a saucepan
with the spices, bring to the boil and
simmer for 10 minutes. Pour the hot
vinegar over the gherkins, cover
tightly and leave in a warm place for
about 24 hours. Strain off the vinegar,
boil it up and pour back over the
gherkins. Cover and leave for another
24 hours. Repeat this process several
times until the gherkins become a good
green colour. Strain off the vinegar
again. Pack the gherkins evenly and
tightly into fairly small jars and cover
with the boiling vinegar. Seal at once
with a vinegar-proof top and leave for
several weeks before use. (Extra spiced
vinegar may be required for the final
topping up in which case make half the
above quantity.)

Note Gherkins are the fruit of a small
variety of cucumber, but are not always
easy to get hold of. The best varieties

to use are small and dark green with a
rough skin, but small ridge or
immature cucumbers can also be used
if they are not longer than 6–7.5cm
(2½–3in). For sweet pickled gherkins
add 50–75g (2–3oz) demerara sugar
for malt vinegar or white sugar for
white vinegar per 600ml (1pt).

Pickled Beetroot

Ingredients

1.4–1.8kg (3–4lb) young beetroots
Salt
About 1.3l (2¼pt) spiced vinegar (see
   pickled cabbage)

Wash the beetroots thoroughly taking
care not to damage the skins. Put into
a saucepan and cover with water
adding 25g (1oz) salt per 600ml (1pt).
Bring to the boil, cover and simmer
gently until tender, about 1½–2 hours
depending on size. (Beetroots can also
be wrapped in foil and baked in a
moderate oven 180°C (350°F) mark 4
for 1¼–2 hours or until tender.) Cool
beetroots then carefully rub off the
skins and remove any blemishes from
the flesh. Cut into thin slices or dice the
beetroots. Pack into jars and cover with
cold spiced vinegar adding 15g (½oz)
salt per 600ml (1pt) if the beetroots
were baked in foil. Cover with a
vinegar-proof top. Store in a cool dry
place for at least two weeks before
using and use up within 3–4 months
for the beetroot to stay in prime
condition.

Note For longer storage pack diced
beetroot fairly loosely into 450g (1lb)
jars and cover with boiling spiced
vinegar. Cover as above and keep for

at least a month before using.

The delicious tiny beetroots about the size of a walnut can be pickled whole.

Red Tomato Pickle

Ingredients

1.4kg (3lb) red tomatoes
75g (3oz) salt
450g (1lb) brown sugar
600ml (1pt) vinegar—brown or white
1–2 cloves garlic, crushed
1 blade of mace
Piece of cinnamon stick
5ml (1 level tsp) whole allspice

Peel tomatoes, if liked, by plunging first into boiling water for about 20 seconds and then into cold water, or wipe over carefully. Cut into thick slices. Make up a strong brine using 75g (3oz) salt to 600ml (1pt) water and add the tomatoes ; leave to soak for 4–5 hours. Rinse off excess salt and drain well. Put the sugar, vinegar, garlic, mace and allspice in a saucepan and heat gently until the sugar dissolves then bring to the boil. Add the tomatoes, bring back to the boil and simmer for 2 minutes. Carefully remove the tomatoes and pack straight away in layers into hot clean jars. Boil the vinegar until it begins to thicken, then strain and pour over the tomatoes to fill the jars. Cover at once with a vinegar-proof top, and label. Store in a cool dry place for 1–2 weeks before using.

Note When available yellow tomatoes can also be pickled in this way. Tiny tomatoes (red or yellow) can be peeled and left whole to pickle.

Pickles

Mixed Pickle

Ingredients

1kg (2½lb) prepared mixed vegetables
  (eg cauliflower, small cucumbers,
  shallots, French beans, etc.)
Salt

Spiced Vinegar

1.1l (2pt) vinegar
3–4 blades of mace
15ml (1tbsp) whole allspice
15ml (1tbsp) whole cloves
Piece of cinnamon stick
6 whole peppercorns

Cut the cauliflower into small florets
discarding tough stalks and leaves;
peel and dice the cucumber (or wipe
and leave the skin on if preferred);
peel the shallots; top and tail and cut
beans into 1–2cm (½–¾in) slices. Put
all the vegetables into a bowl sprinkling
liberally with salt, cover and leave for
48 hours in a cool place; or if
preferred make a brine using 100g
(4oz) salt to 2 pints water, add the
vegetables and leave to soak for
24 hours. Make the spiced vinegar by
putting all the ingredients into a
saucepan and bring slowly up to the
boil. Pour into a bowl, cover and leave
until cold—at least 3 hours. Strain and
use. (If individual spices are
unavailable use 40–50g [1½–2oz]
pickling spice.) Wash off all the salt
from the vegetables and drain very
thoroughly. Pack the vegetables neatly
into jars but not too tightly or the
vinegar will not have room to circulate
freely. Fill up with cold spiced vinegar,
cover with vinegar-proof tops and
label. Store in a cool dry place for at
least 2 weeks before using.

Piccalilli

This is a special type of pickle which is
a great favourite with many people
because of its spicy mustard sauce.
It is delicious with all cold meats and
is useful for sandwiches and to serve
with snacks.

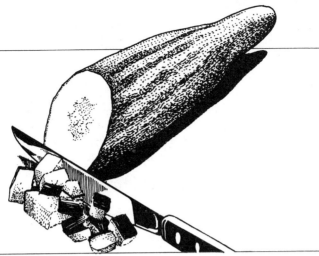

Ingredients

2.7kg (6lb) prepared vegetables
   (eg cucumber, beans, small onions,
   marrow, cauliflower, green tomatoes,
   etc)
450g (1lb) salt
250g (9oz) caster sugar
20g ($\frac{3}{4}$oz) dry mustard
10ml (2 level tsp) ground ginger
1.7l (3pt) white vinegar
60ml (4 level tbsp) flour or cornflour
25–30ml (1$\frac{1}{2}$–2 level tbsp) turmeric

Either peel or wipe the cucumber then
cut into dice; top, tail and slice the
beans; peel onions and cut in half or
quarters if large; peel, remove seeds
and dice the marrow; cut cauliflower
into small florets discarding tough
stalks and leaves; cut green tomatoes
into small pieces, if used. Either layer up
the prepared vegetables with the salt
in a large bowl or make a brine by
adding it to 4.5l (1 gal) water, and add
the vegetables; leave for 24 hours
keeping the vegetables under the brine
with a weighted plate. Drain the
vegetables and rinse off all the salt and
then drain again very thoroughly. Mix
the sugar, mustard and ginger with
1.5l (2$\frac{1}{2}$pt) of the vinegar in a large
saucepan then add all the drained
vegetables. Bring slowly up to the boil
and simmer gently for 10–20 minutes
until the vegetables are tender-crisp
(or tender, if preferred) but not soft and
mushy. Blend the flour and turmeric
into the remaining vinegar until
smooth and stir into the cooked
vegetables. Bring back to the boil for
2–3 minutes. Pack the vegetables into
hot clean jars as tightly as possible,
filling up with more sauce. Cover
whilst still hot with vinegar-proof tops,
and label. Store in a cool dry place for
at least 2 weeks before using.

Note For a hot sharp piccalilli (instead
of the sweeter milder recipe given
above) use the same vegetables and
salt as above but use the following
ingredients for the sauce, making it in
the same way: 15g ($\frac{1}{2}$oz) turmeric;
40g (1$\frac{1}{2}$oz) dry mustard; 25–40g
(1–1$\frac{1}{2}$oz) ground ginger; 20g ($\frac{3}{4}$oz)
flour or cornflour; 175g (6oz) white
sugar and 1.1l (2pt) white vinegar.

Sweet Pickles

This sweet type of pickle is often preferred to the more vinegary types and it is a particularly good accompaniment to cold meats. As well as having a higher proportion of sugar added to the vinegar, they are usually made with all fruit or at least more fruit than vegetable. Whole fruits to be pickled need pricking with a darning needle, cocktail stick or thin skewer before heating otherwise they will shrivel up during pickling. A brine is not usually necessary for this type of pickle for the excess moisture evaporates during cooking, unlike the vegetables which have little or no cooking.

Pickled Pears

Ingredients

900g (2lb) hard pears
900g (2lb) white sugar
900ml (1½pt) white vinegar
Few whole cloves

Peel the pears, quarter and remove the cores, then cut the flesh into dice. Cook the pears in a little boiling water until just soft then drain very well. Meanwhile put the sugar, water and cloves into a saucepan, heat gently until the sugar dissolves, then bring to the boil and simmer for about 20 minutes. Add the well drained fruit to the syrup and continue to boil for a further 15 minutes. Pour into hot jars, filling well with the pears and cover at once with vinegar-proof tops. Store in a cool dry place for 6 months before using.

Spiced Pears

Ingredients

2.7kg (6lb) hard pears (small or medium sized)
400g (14oz) white sugar
15–20ml (3–4 level tsp) salt
1.1l (2pt) water
1.1l (2pt) distilled or white wine vinegar
2 cinnamon sticks
Strip of thinly pared lemon rind
5ml (1 level tsp) whole cloves

Peel the pears, cut into quarters and remove the cores. Dissolve 50g (2oz) sugar and the salt in the water and bring slowly to the boil making sure the sugar is dissolved. Add the pears to the boiling water, remove from the heat and cover tightly. Leave to stand until cool. Put the remaining sugar into a pan with the vinegar, cinnamon sticks, lemon rind and cloves and heat gently until the sugar dissolves; then bring to the boil. Drain the pears very well and add to the vinegar syrup in the pan. Bring back to the boil then remove from the heat and leave to get cold. Boil up again slowly and repeat the cooling and boiling process twice more. Leave to get cold once more then pack the pears into small jars and cover with the syrup. Do not seal jars but fill up for the next four days with the surplus syrup until no more syrup is absorbed by the fruit; then cover as usual with a vinegar-proof top. Keep for several weeks before using.

Note Spiced pears are excellent with pork.

Pickled Peaches

Ingredients

900g (2lb) white sugar
600ml (1pt) white vinegar
15g ($\frac{1}{2}$oz) whole cloves
15ml ($\frac{1}{2}$oz) whole allspice
Small piece of cinnamon stick
Small piece of root ginger, bruised
Thinly pared rind of 1 lemon or orange
1.8kg (4lb) freestone peaches

Dissolve the sugar slowly in the vinegar. Crush the spices and tie in a piece of muslin with the cinnamon stick, ginger and lemon or orange rind

and add to the saucepan. Cut the peaches into quarters then remove the stones and carefully remove the peel. (If peaches are difficult to peel, dip the whole fruit quickly first into boiling water and then into cold water and then the skins should easily rub off. Cut into quarters and remove the stones after peeling.) Add the quartered peaches to the syrup and simmer gently until the peaches are just soft. Drain the fruit and pack neatly and fairly tightly into small warm jars. Boil the syrup hard until it begins to thicken. Pour sufficient syrup over the fruit to cover and fill up the jars. Cover with a vinegar-proof top whilst still hot. Store for 2–3 months before using.

Note In freestone fruit the skin and stone separate easily whereas with cling-stone varieties the flesh is firmer and is firmly attached to the stone thus making it difficult to cut the fruit into neat quarters or slices.

Sweet Pickles

Pickled Plums

Ingredients

1.4kg (3lb) Victoria plums
300ml ($\frac{1}{2}$pt) white vinegar
450g (1lb) white sugar
25g (1oz) ground cinnamon
5ml (1 level tsp) mixed spice

Remove stalks from the plums, wipe them over well and discard any which are bruised or have bad blemishes. Prick each plum two or three times with a wooden cocktail stick or small skewer to prevent them from shrivelling up during the pickling process. Place the fruit in a deep bowl. Put the vinegar into a saucepan with the sugar and spices and heat gently until the sugar dissolves, then bring up to the boil and boil until slightly reduced. Strain through a double layer of muslin and then bring back to the boil in a clean saucepan. Pour over the plums, cover bowl and leave for 2 days. Strain off the syrup and bring back to the boil. Pour over the plums again and leave for 2–3 days. Strain off the syrup again and boil up in a pan. Pack the plums into small jars and cover with warm syrup. Cover at once with a vinegar-proof top. Store for 6–8 weeks before using.

Note Other varieties of plums may be used.

Pickled Damsons

Ingredients

1.8kg (4lb) firm ripe damsons
900g (2lb) white sugar
600ml (1pt) white vinegar
1 blade mace
Small piece root ginger
5ml (1 level tsp) ground allspice
10ml (2 level tsp) ground cloves
Piece of thinly pared lemon rind

Remove the stems from the fruit, wash well and dry; then prick each damson twice with a cocktail stick or fine skewer. Put the sugar, vinegar and spices into a saucepan and heat gently until the fruit is almost tender—but take care not to let the skins break. Drain well and pack the fruit into small clean jars. Boil the syrup until slightly reduced —about 10 minutes—then strain through a double layer of muslin and pour into the jars to cover the fruit. The next day strain off the syrup and boil up then pour back over the damsons. Repeat this process for the next 2–3 days. Cover with a vinegar-proof top whilst still hot and label. Store in a cool, dry place for a few weeks before use.

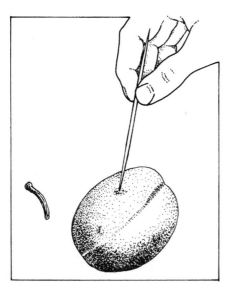

Pickled Rhubarb

Ingredients

1.4kg (3lb) prepared young tender
  rhubarb
900g (2lb) white sugar
600ml (1pt) white vinegar
15g ($\frac{1}{2}$oz) whole cloves
7.5ml (1$\frac{1}{2}$ level tsp) whole allspice
15–25g ($\frac{1}{2}$–1oz) whole root ginger,
  bruised
Small piece of cinnamon stick
Thinly pared rind of $\frac{1}{2}$ lemon

Wash the rhubarb and dry well then
cut into 2cm ($\frac{3}{4}$in) lengths. Put the
sugar into a saucepan with the vinegar
and spices and heat gently until the
sugar dissolves. Add the rhubarb and
simmer very gently until the fruit is
almost tender—but take great care not
to let it break up and become mushy.
Leave to get cold then strain off all the
syrup, and the spices (optional). Pack
the rhubarb into small warmed jars ;
reboil the syrup until syrupy—about
10 minutes—and then pour into the
jars to cover the fruit. Cover at once
with vinegar-proof tops whilst still hot
and label. Store in a dark, cool and dry
place for 6–8 weeks before use.

Spiced Orange Rings

Ingredients

8–10 firm medium-sized oranges
900ml (1$\frac{1}{2}$pt) white vinegar
675g (1$\frac{1}{2}$lb) white sugar
15ml (1 level tbsp) ground cloves
2 pieces cinnamon stick
5ml (1 level tsp) whole cloves

Wipe the oranges thoroughly,
scrubbing off any stubborn marks, but
do not peel. Cut into thin even slices

0.5cm ($\frac{1}{4}$in) thick. Put the oranges into
a saucepan in layers and barely cover
with water. Bring to the boil, cover and
simmer gently for about $\frac{3}{4}$ hour or until
the orange rind is really tender. Drain
well and put the cooking liquid back
into a saucepan with the vinegar, sugar
and spices. Heat gently until the sugar
dissolves then bring up to the boil and
simmer for 10 minutes. Replace the
orange rings a few at a time in the
syrup and simmer gently until the rind
becomes clear. Remove the rings
straight to warm jars and pack neatly.
Continue with all the orange rings.
Boil the syrup again until it begins to
thicken and then leave to cool but not
get cold. Strain and pour over the
orange rings to cover and fill the jars.
Add a few of the cloves to each jar and
cover with a vinegar-proof top. Store
in a cool, dark place for several weeks
before using.

Note These orange rings are particularly
good served with cold ham, turkey,
chicken and duck and make very
attractive gifts.

Vinegars

Fruit Vinegars

These are usually made with soft fruits and are used like a cordial. Fruit which is in good condition but which is a little bruised or too wet for freezing or jam is excellent for this purpose. Fruit vinegars used to be an old-fashioned remedy for curing sore throats and colds, and can also be used to replace wine vinegar in salad dressings to give unusual flavours and colours to the salads.

The prepared and washed fruits are put into a large glass or china bowl and roughly broken up with a wooden spoon. Add 600ml (1pt) white wine vinegar or best malt vinegar per 450g (1lb) fruit to the bowl and mix lightly. Cover the bowl with a cloth and leave to stand for 3–4 days giving an occasional stir. Then strain off the liquid through a double layer of muslin into a large saucepan. Add 450g (1lb) white sugar to each pint of juice and heat gently until the sugar dissolves. Bring up to the boil and boil for 10 minutes then cool and pour into warmed clean dry bottles. Cork tightly and label. Blackberries, raspberries and blackcurrants are the most usual fruits to use.

Flavoured Vinegars

Home-made herb flavoured vinegars are very useful in the kitchen—it is a simple process but takes time, usually from two to six weeks, for the vinegar to absorb the flavour of the herbs. A wide mouthed jar should be thoroughly cleaned and then half filled with freshly gathered herbs (just before they flower for the best results) eg tarragon, mint, thyme, marjoram or basil. Then fill up the jar with the best vinegar—either malt or white wine. Cover and store in a cool, dry and dark place until sufficiently flavoured. Strain the vinegar through a double layer of muslin, taste and add more vinegar if the herb flavour is too strong (or label the bottle stating that it is double strength). Pour into bottles and cork tightly. Use in salad dressings, mayonnaise, etc.

Preserved Mint in Vinegar

Ingredients

225g ($\frac{1}{2}$lb) freshly picked mint leaves
600ml (1pt) malt vinegar
450g (1lb) white sugar

Wash and dry the mint leaves removing all the stems. Chop the mint finely and put into small wide-necked jars. Put the vinegar into a saucepan with the sugar and heat gently until the sugar dissolves then bring it just up to the boil. Leave to get cold. Pour the vinegar over the mint mixing it lightly until evenly coated then seal the jar to make it airtight. Store in a dark cool place. To use the mint for mint sauce, spoon out a little of the concentrated mint and liquid into a small jug and add sufficient fresh vinegar to give the desired consistency. If it is too strong add a little water in place of the vinegar.

Preserved Horse-radish in Vinegar

Ingredients

Plump horse-radish roots
5ml (1 level tsp) salt
White vinegar

Wash and clean the horse-radish then either scrape, mince or grate it. Plunge immediately into a boiling solution of brine—5ml (1 level tsp) salt to 600ml (1pt) water—for 1 minute. This helps to keep the colour of the horse-radish. Drain thoroughly and pack into small warmed jars. Cover at once with boiling white vinegar and seal to make the jars airtight.

To make the preserved horse-radish into horse-radish cream sauce to serve with roast beef, smoked trout or to use in sandwiches put 15ml (1 level tbsp) into a small bowl and mix in 2.5–5ml ($\frac{1}{2}$–1 level tsp) made mustard, 5ml (1 level tsp) caster sugar, 60ml (4tbsp) double cream, lightly whipped, and salt and pepper to taste.

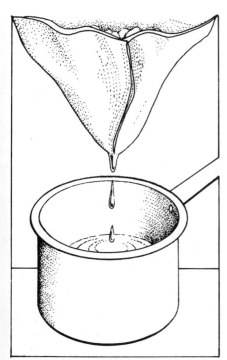
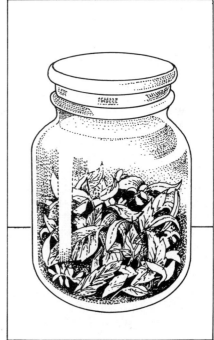

Sauces and Ketchups

Home-made sauces and ketchups usually have one predominating flavour, ie tomato, mushroom, plum, etc with spices added to bring out rather than disguise the main flavour. Remember that sauces and ketchups will thicken more as they cool so take this into consideration during cooking and also remember to use the same types of sieves and pans as for chutneys. In other words use hair, nylon or stainless steel sieves and enamel-lined, stainless steel or aluminium pans, for many metals give an unpleasant metallic taste to chutneys and for this reason avoid using copper, brass or iron pans.

Sauces and ketchups can ferment after bottling so they need to be sterilized immediately after filling as described below:

Use bottles with screw tops or corks. Heat the bottles in a cool oven, 150°C (300°F) mark 2 and boil the caps or corks for 10 minutes. Use a deep pan and either put an upturned plate or thick wad of newspaper in the bottom and then stand the filled and sealed jars on this. Fill the pan with cold water to reach the necks of the bottles and then heat gently to reach simmering point 76°C (170°F). Simmer at this heat for 30 minutes. Remove the bottles and stand on a board or pad of cloth and tighten screw-topped bottles or push the corks in further with cork-topped bottles. If using corks, when the bottles are partly cooled they should be coated in melted paraffin wax and secured with wire. Store the cold, labelled bottles in a cool dry place.

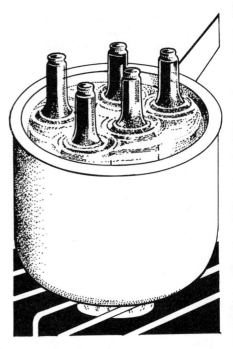

Ripe Tomato Sauce

Ingredients

10g ($\frac{1}{4}$oz) whole allspice
4–5 blades of mace
Piece of cinnamon stick
600ml (1pt) white vinegar
5.4kg (12lb) ripe tomatoes
40g (1$\frac{1}{2}$oz) salt
Good pinch of cayenne pepper
7.5ml (1$\frac{1}{2}$ level tsp) paprika pepper
30ml (2 tbsp) chilli vinegar
450g (1lb) white sugar

Put the spices into a piece of muslin and tie loosely. Put with the vinegar into a pan and bring to the boil. Remove from the heat, cover pan and leave to infuse for 2 hours. Remove spices. Wipe tomatoes and slice. Place in a pan and cook gently without any added liquid until they are pulpy. Rub through a sieve, return to the pan and add the salt, cayenne and paprika and continue to cook gently until the mixture begins to thicken. Then add the spiced vinegar, sugar and chilli vinegar and continue to boil until the mixture thickens to the consistency of thick cream, stirring from time to time. Pour into hot bottles leaving a 2.5cm (1 in) headspace and put on screw tops (not too tightly) or corks. Sterilize for 30 minutes, seal tightly, cool and label and store in a cool dry place.

Note If chilli vinegar is unavailable, tarragon or garlic vinegar can be substituted or a little powdered garlic may be added to the sauce and extra vinegar omitted.

Inexpensive Tomato Sauce

Ingredients

900g (2lb) ripe tomatoes, roughly chopped
450g (1lb) cooking apples, peeled, cored and chopped
225g ($\frac{1}{2}$lb) shallots or onions, peeled and chopped
300ml ($\frac{1}{2}$pt) white vinegar
225g ($\frac{1}{2}$lb) white sugar
10ml (2 level tsp) salt
10 whole cloves
3 pieces root ginger, bruised or 10ml (2 level tsp) ground ginger
2–3 chillies

Put the tomatoes, apples and onions in a pan without any extra liquid and cook very gently until soft, in a covered pan. Stir occasionally, and take care not to let the vegetables burn. Add the vinegar, sugar, salt and spices and bring back to the boil. Cover pan and

simmer for about $\frac{1}{2}$ hour. Rub the sauce through a sieve and return to a clean pan. Bring back to the boil, and simmer uncovered, for about 15 minutes or until thickened. Pour into hot bottles leaving a 2.5cm (1 in) headspace, seal and sterilize for 30 minutes. Complete sealing bottles, cool and label and store in a cool dry place.

Green Tomato Sauce

Ingredients

1.4kg (3lb) green tomatoes, thinly sliced
450g (1lb) cooking apples, peeled, cored and chopped
1 onion or 6–8 shallots, peeled and chopped
225g ($\frac{1}{2}$lb) sugar, brown or white
5ml (1 level tsp) ground pickling spice
2.5ml ($\frac{1}{2}$ level tsp) ground pepper
2.5ml ($\frac{1}{2}$ level tsp) dry mustard
10ml (2 level tsp) salt
2 cloves garlic, crushed (optional)
300ml ($\frac{1}{2}$pt) vinegar—malt or white
Gravy browning to colour (optional)

Put all the ingredients except the gravy browning into a large pan and bring slowly up to the boil, stirring frequently until the sugar has dissolved and everything is well mixed. Cover pan and simmer gently for about an hour, stirring occasionally until very soft. Rub the sauce through a sieve and return to a clean pan. Add gravy browning to give the desired colour and bring the sauce back to the boil. Pour into hot bottles leaving a 2.5cm (1 in) headspace and seal and sterilize for 30 minutes. Complete sealing bottles, cool, label and store in a cool, dry place.

Sauces and Ketchups

Plum Sauce

Ingredients

3.6kg (8lb) plums, washed, stoned and
 quartered
450g (1lb) onions, peeled and
 chopped
225g ($\frac{1}{2}$lb) currants, sultanas or
 raisins
1.1l (2pt) vinegar, malt or white
15g ($\frac{1}{2}$oz) root ginger, bruised
15g ($\frac{1}{2}$oz) whole allspice
3–4 chillies
10ml (2tsp) whole peppercorns
5ml (1 level tsp) dry mustard (optional)
Piece of cinnamon stick
450g (1lb) sugar, brown or white
50g (2oz) salt

Put the plums into a saucepan with the
onions, currants, 600ml (1pt) vinegar
and all the spices. Bring to the boil,
cover and simmer gently for about
$\frac{1}{2}$ hour or until tender, stirring
occasionally. Rub the sauce through a
sieve and return to a clean pan with
the remaining vinegar, sugar and salt.
Return slowly to the boil, making sure
the sugar has dissolved then simmer
for about 1 hour or until the sauce is
the consistency of thick cream. Pour
into hot bottles leaving a 2.5cm (1in)
headspace and seal and sterilize for
30 minutes. Complete sealing bottles,
cool, label and store in a cool and dry
place.

Note The different coloured plums
which are available will vary the
colour of the finished sauce and malt
vinegar and brown sugar, if used, will
darken the sauce considerably.

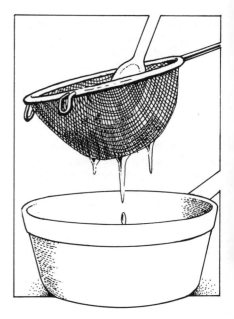

Mushroom Ketchup

Ingredients

1.4kg (3lb) mushrooms, washed
75g (3oz) salt
600ml (1pt) vinegar, malt or white
5ml (1 level tsp) whole peppercorns
5ml (1 level tsp) whole allspice
2.5ml ($\frac{1}{2}$ level tsp) ground mace
2.5ml ($\frac{1}{2}$ level tsp) ground ginger
8 whole cloves
Small piece of cinnamon stick

Break the mushrooms up roughly and
place in a bowl. Sprinkle with the salt,
cover and leave to stand for about 12
hours. Rinse off the excess salt and
drain mushrooms well. Place in a
saucepan and mash well with a
wooden spoon. Add the vinegar and
spices and bring to the boil. Cover and
simmer gently for about $\frac{1}{2}$ hour or until
the excess vinegar is absorbed. Press
the liquid out through a fine sieve and

pour quickly into hot bottles leaving a 2.5cm (1in) headspace. Seal and sterilize for 30 minutes then complete the sealing of bottles, cool, label and store in a cool, dry place.

Note Either cultivated or field mushrooms can be used for this recipe but with large field ones it is necessary to remove the stalks and peel them first.

Walnut Ketchup

Ingredients

35–40 green walnuts
75g (3oz) onion or shallots, finely chopped
75g (3oz) salt
900ml (1½pt) spiced vinegar (see pickled onion recipe on p 78)

Use green immature walnuts, before the shells have formed. Test each

walnut by pricking with a needle, and if any shell can be felt, discard the nut. Cut the walnuts in halves and crush them and then place in a bowl with the onions and salt. Bring the vinegar to the boil, pour over the walnuts, stir well to dissolve the salt and leave to stand, in a covered bowl in a cool place, for 5 days. Each day give the mixture a good stir. Pour the liquid through a fine sieve into a saucepan and bring to the boil. Simmer very gently for about 50 minutes then pour into hot bottles. Seal and sterilize for 30 minutes then complete sealing bottles, cool, label and store in a cool, dry place.

Note Commercially prepared spiced vinegar can be used, if preferred.

Chutneys

A chutney is a mixture of fruits and/or vegetables, either fresh and/or dried which are cooked with sugar, spices and vinegar until thick and pulpy. The basic ingredients such as apples, plums, red and green tomatoes, pears, gooseberries etc are preserved by the vinegar, spices and salt used in cooking. The additional ingredients such as onions, garlic, dates, sultanas, raisins and spices will add the flavours. Tough vegetables are improved by partly cooking in some of the vinegar before adding the rest of the ingredients. Use brown sugar and brown malt vinegar for richer flavour but white sugar and white distilled vinegar for light coloured produce and to keep its bright colour.

Most chutneys will improve in flavour with keeping and should store for 2–3 years. The finished chutney should be fairly smooth and have a mellow flavour although, once you have achieved a good chutney, the spiciness and sweetness can be altered to your own taste. By mincing part or all of the main ingredients, the texture will be smoother, but chopped ingredients can still give a smooth texture with long slow cooking.

Sieves used for chutneys, as for pickles, must be of hair, nylon or stainless steel, and pans be enamel-lined, stainless steel or aluminium to prevent the unpleasant metallic taste caused by iron, copper and brass. The chutney should be bottled while hot in clean, warmed jars and a vinegar-proof cover used, otherwise, if paper covers are used, the contents will have shrunk badly after a short storage with a very hard and dry top surface. Metal caps can be used if they are well lacquered, fitting plastic covers are suitable and a special vinegar-proof paper is available which

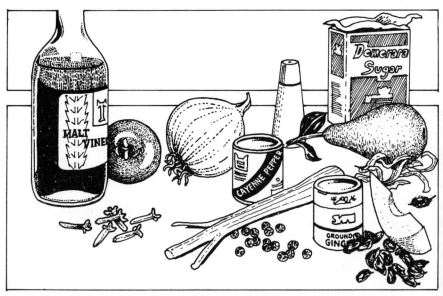

can be cut to size and used several times.

The muslin bag of spices added to chutneys when cooking should be removed before bottling.

Red Tomato Chutney

Ingredients

450g (1lb) onions
900ml (1½pt) malt vinegar
1.1kg (2½lb) ripe tomatoes
675g (1½lb) cooking apples
10ml (2 level tsp) salt
Good pinch of cayenne pepper
350g (¾lb) brown sugar
10ml (2 level tsp) ground ginger
50g (2oz) pickling spice
350g (¾lb) sultanas or chopped raisins

Peel and chop the onions finely and put into a preserving pan or large saucepan with half the vinegar and bring to the boil. Simmer gently until the onion is almost tender. Meanwhile peel the tomatoes (by first plunging into boiling water for 30 seconds then into cold water when the skins will split and peel off easily) and then chop. Peel, core and chop the apples finely. Add the tomatoes and apples to the pan with the remaining vinegar, salt, cayenne, sugar, ginger and sultanas. Tie the spices in a muslin bag and add to the chutney. Bring back to the boil slowly making sure the sugar has dissolved and then continue to cook slowly until thick and no liquid remains on the top, stirring occasionally to prevent burning. Remove bag of spices and pour chutney into hot jars. Seal whilst hot with a vinegar-proof cover and label. Cool and store in a cool dry place.

Tomato and Marrow Chutney

Ingredients

1.8kg (4lb) ripe tomatoes
450g (1lb) prepared marrow (ie peeled and seeds removed)
350g (¾lb) onions, peeled
15g (½oz) salt
5ml (1 level tsp) mixed spice
2.5ml (½ level tsp) paprika
25g (1oz) pickling spice
350g (¾lb) sugar
300ml (½pt) vinegar

Peel the tomatoes as for red tomato chutney and then slice thinly. Finely chop the marrow and onions and put into a preserving pan or large saucepan with the tomatoes. Stir in the salt, mixed spice and paprika and add the pickling spices tied in a muslin bag. Cook gently without any added liquid for about 1½ hours until very tender, stirring from time to time to prevent sticking. Dissolve the sugar in the vinegar and add to the chutney, mixing well. Continue to cook until the chutney becomes thick and there is no excess liquid on the top—about 20–30 minutes—again stirring occasionally to prevent sticking. Pour into hot jars and seal whilst hot with vinegar-proof covers. Label, cool and store in a cool dry place.

Note Either malt vinegar and brown sugar or white vinegar and white sugar can be used in this recipe.

Chutneys

Tomato and Date Chutney

Ingredients

900g (2lb) green tomatoes
450g (1lb) cooking apples
225–350g ($\frac{1}{2}$–$\frac{3}{4}$lb) stoned dates
450g (1lb) onions
225g ($\frac{1}{2}$lb) sultanas
600ml (1pt) vinegar
50g (2oz) salt
5ml (1 level tsp) ground ginger
3 cloves garlic, crushed
2.5ml ($\frac{1}{2}$ level tsp) whole cloves
2.5ml ($\frac{1}{2}$ level tsp) crushed allspice
5ml (1 level tsp) mustard seed
2–3 chillies
Piece of cinnamon stick
450g (1lb) brown sugar

Wipe the tomatoes and slice or chop; peel, core and chop the apples; chop the dates; and peel and finely chop the onions. Put all these vegetables into a preserving pan or large saucepan with the sultanas, vinegar (malt or white), salt, ginger and garlic. Tie the cloves, allspice, mustard seed, chillies and cinnamon stick in a muslin bag and add to the pan. Bring to the boil and simmer for about $\frac{3}{4}$ hour until tender, stirring occasionally. Add the sugar and heat gently until dissolved, then simmer until the chutney becomes thick and there is no extra liquid on the surface. Remove the bag of spices and pour the chutney into hot jars. Seal with a vinegar-proof cover, then label and store in a cool, dry place.

Note Red tomatoes can be used in this recipe in which case add the grated rind and juice of 1 lemon and cut the sugar to 350g ($\frac{3}{4}$lb).

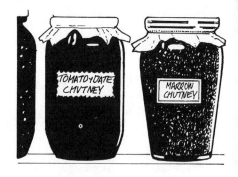

Marrow Chutney

Ingredients

1.4kg (3lb) prepared marrow (ie peeled and seeds removed)
50g (2oz) salt
225g ($\frac{1}{2}$lb) onions, peeled and chopped
350g ($\frac{3}{4}$lb) cooking apples, peeled and chopped
225g ($\frac{1}{2}$lb) sultanas or raisins
175g (6oz) demerara sugar
900ml (1$\frac{1}{2}$pt) malt vinegar
15ml (1 level tbsp) whole pickling spice
2–3 pieces root ginger, bruised

Cut the marrow into small dice and place in a bowl. Sprinkle with the salt, cover and leave to stand overnight. Rinse off the salt, drain the marrow thoroughly and put into a preserving pan or large saucepan. Add the onions, apples, sultanas, sugar and vinegar. Tie the spices and ginger in a muslin bag and add to the pan. Heat gently until the sugar has dissolved, stirring frequently, then bring to the boil and simmer gently until thick with no liquid on top. Stir occasionally. Remove the bag of spices and pour into hot jars. Seal whilst hot with vinegar-proof covers, label and store in a cool dry place.

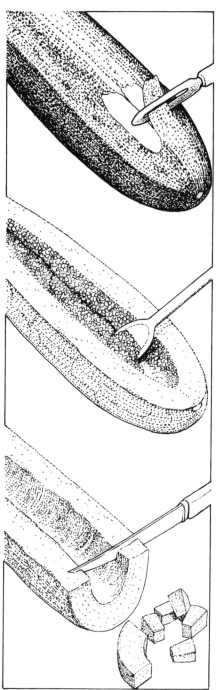

Green Tomato Chutney

Ingredients

1.8kg (4lb) green tomatoes
450g (1lb) cooking apples
350g ($\frac{3}{4}$lb) onions, peeled
225g ($\frac{1}{2}$lb) sultanas
15g ($\frac{1}{2}$oz) salt
450g (1lb) brown sugar
750ml (1$\frac{1}{4}$pt) vinegar
1 clove garlic, crushed
15ml (1 level tbsp) mustard seed
6 whole cloves
3 pieces root ginger, bruised
Good pinch of cayenne pepper
10ml (2 level tsp) curry powder
   (optional)

Wipe the tomatoes and remove stalks.
Peel, quarter and core the apples.
Coarsely mince the tomatoes, apples
onions and sultanas and put into a
preserving pan or large saucepan with
the salt, sugar and vinegar. Tie the
garlic, mustard seed, cloves and ginger
in a muslin bag and add to the pan with
the cayenne and curry powder, if used.
Heat gently, stirring frequently, until
the sugar has dissolved and then cook
gently for about 2 hours or until thick
and pulpy with no extra liquid on the
top. Stir occasionally during cooking to
prevent sticking. Remove bag of spices
and pour the chutney into hot jars.
Seal whilst hot with a vinegar-proof
cover. Label and store in a cool dry
place.

Note If preferred the tomatoes, apples
and onions can be thinly sliced or
chopped and the sultanas can be left
whole.

Chutneys

Orchard Chutney

Ingredients

675g (1½lb) plums (freestone if
   possible)
900g (2lb) red tomatoes, peeled and
   sliced
900ml (1½pt) malt vinegar
15g (½oz) unpeeled garlic
450g (1lb) onions, peeled
1.1kg (2½lb) cooking apples, peeled
   and cored
225g (½lb) raisins
450g (1lb) demerara sugar
50g (2oz) salt
30ml (2 level tbsp) whole pickling
   spice

Wash the plums, cut in halves and
remove the stone if a freestone variety.
If not leave them whole. Put the plums,
tomatoes and vinegar into a preserving
pan or large saucepan and bring to the
boil. Simmer gently until the contents
are soft. Remove the plum stones if
they have not been removed. Peel the
garlic and mince it finely with the
onions, apples and dried fruit. Add to
the plum mixture and mix well, then
stir in the sugar and salt and the spices
tied in a muslin bag. Heat gently until
the sugar has dissolved, stirring
frequently and then bring to the boil
and simmer until everything is tender,
well reduced and thick—about 2 hours.
When all the liquid is absorbed pour
into hot jars and cover whilst hot with
vinegar-proof covers. Label and store
in a cool dry place.

Green Tomato and Pear Chutney

Ingredients

900g (2lb) green tomatoes
900g (2lb) pears
450g (1lb) onions
225g (½lb) celery
225g (½lb) raisins
2.5ml (½ level tsp) cayenne pepper
2.5ml (½ level tsp) ground ginger
10ml (2 level tsp) salt
1.1l (2pt) malt vinegar
12 whole peppercorns
4–5 whole cloves
675g (1½lb) demerara sugar

Wipe the tomatoes and slice thinly ;
peel, core and chop the pears ; peel and
finely chop the onion ; and finely chop
the celery. Put these ingredients into a
preserving pan or large saucepan with
all the other ingredients except the
sugar and with the peppercorns and
cloves tied in a muslin bag. Simmer
gently until soft—about ½ hour. Add the
sugar and stir until dissolved then
simmer until the chutney thickens and
excess liquid is absorbed. Pour into hot
jars, seal with a vinegar-proof cover,
label and store in a cool, dry place.

Beetroot Chutney

Ingredients

1.1kg (2½lb) cooked beetroot
225g (½lb) onions
450g (1lb) cooking apples
225g (½lb) raisins
15g (½oz) salt
225g (½lb) brown sugar
600ml (1pt) malt vinegar
15ml (1 level tbsp) whole pickling
   spice
4 whole cloves

Peel the beetroot and chop finely. Peel and chop or mince the onions, apples and raisins and put into a preserving pan or large saucepan with the salt, sugar, vinegar and spices tied in a muslin bag. Heat gently until the sugar has dissolved and then bring to the boil and simmer until the onion is tender and the mixture thickened. Add the beetroot and continue until thick and well blended and there is no excess liquid on the surface. This should take about $\frac{1}{2}$ hour. Remove the bag of spices and pour the chutney into hot jars. Seal whilst hot with vinegar-proof covers and then label and store in a cool dry place.

Pepper Chutney

Ingredients

6 red peppers
6 green peppers
900g (2lb) green tomatoes
450g (1lb) onions, peeled
450g (1lb) cooking apples, peeled and cored
450g (1lb) sugar
25g (1oz) salt
2.5ml ($\frac{1}{2}$ level tsp) ground pepper
900ml (1$\frac{1}{2}$pt) vinegar
50g (2oz) whole pickling spice
2-3 pieces root ginger, bruised
6 cloves

Deseed the peppers and discard with the stems and then mince the flesh coarsely with the tomatoes, onions and apples. Put into a preserving pan or large saucepan with the sugar, salt, pepper and vinegar. Tie the spices, ginger and cloves in a muslin bag and add to the pan. Heat gently until the sugar has dissolved, stirring frequently. Bring to the boil and simmer for 2-3

hours or until the chutney is thick with no extra liquid on the surface. Remove the bag of spices and pour the chutney into hot jars. Seal with a vinegar-proof cover while still hot. Label jars and store in a cool dry place.

Pumpkin Chutney

Ingredients

675g (2$\frac{1}{2}$lb) prepared pumpkin (ie peeled and seeds removed)
350g ($\frac{3}{4}$lb) onions
225g ($\frac{1}{2}$lb) ripe tomatoes
350g ($\frac{3}{4}$lb) cooking apples
175g (6oz) sultanas
30ml (2 level tbsp) salt
10ml (2 level tsp) ground ginger
2.5ml ($\frac{1}{2}$ level tsp) ground black pepper
10ml (2 level tsp) ground allspice
4 cloves garlic, crushed
600ml (1pt) malt vinegar
450g (1lb) brown sugar

Finely chop the pumpkin; peel and finely chop the onions and tomatoes; and peel, core and chop the apples. Place these ingredients in a preserving pan or large saucepan with all the other ingredients except the sugar and bring to the boil. Simmer gently for about $\frac{3}{4}$ hour or until soft, stirring occasionally. Stir in the sugar until dissolved and then continue to simmer for 1-1$\frac{1}{2}$ hours, until the chutney is very thick and with no extra liquid on the surface. Stir fairly frequently as it thickens to prevent sticking or burning. Pour the chutney into hot jars and seal whilst hot with vinegar-proof covers and then label and store in a cool dry place.

Chutneys

Rhubarb Chutney

Ingredients

2.3kg (5lb) rhubarb, trimmed
450g (1lb) onions
900ml (1½pt) vinegar
Grated rind of 1 large lemon
15g (½oz) salt
15g (½oz) ground ginger
25g (1oz) ground mixed spice
10ml (2 level tsp) ground cinnamon
1–2 cloves garlic, crushed
900g (2lb) sugar

Wash the rhubarb and cut into 1.5cm (½in) lengths. Peel and mince the onions, or chop finely if preferred. Put the rhubarb and onions into a preserving pan or large saucepan with 300ml (½pt) vinegar, the lemon rind, salt and spices. Bring to the boil and simmer gently until the rhubarb is mushy. Add the remaining vinegar and sugar, heat gently until the sugar has dissolved, stirring frequently; and then boil the chutney until it is thick with no liquid on top. Stir occasionally to prevent sticking. Pour into hot jars, seal with vinegar-proof covers whilst hot and label. Store in a cool dry place.

Rhubarb and Ginger Chutney

Follow the above recipe but increase the ground ginger to 25g (1oz) or more to taste and, if available, add 50–100g (2–3oz) very finely chopped stem or crystallized ginger with the remaining vinegar and sugar.

Pear Chutney

Ingredients

1.4kg (3lb) pears
450g (1lb) onions
450g (1lb) ripe tomatoes
1 small pepper, red or green
225g ($\frac{1}{2}$lb) sultanas
450g (1lb) demerara sugar
15g ($\frac{1}{2}$oz) salt
1.25ml ($\frac{1}{4}$ level tsp) cayenne pepper
2.5ml ($\frac{1}{2}$ level tsp) ground ginger
1.1l (2 pt) malt vinegar
8 peppercorns
4 whole cloves

Peel, core and finely chop the pears ; peel and finely chop or mince the onions ; peel and slice the tomatoes and deseed and chop the pepper. Place these ingredients in a preserving pan or large saucepan, cover and cook gently without any extra added liquid until soft, stirring from time to time. Put the sugar, salt, cayenne, ginger and vinegar into a pan and heat gently until the sugar dissolves then add to the softened mixture. Tie the peppercorns and cloves in a muslin bag, add to the pan and bring up to the boil. Simmer, uncovered, until the chutney becomes thick without any liquid on the top. Remove the muslin bag, pour into hot jars and seal with vinegar-proof covers as usual. Label and store in a cool dry place.

Peach Chutney

Ingredients

900g (2lb) peaches
450g (1lb) onions, peeled and chopped
175g (6oz) raisins
225g ($\frac{1}{2}$lb) soft brown sugar
300ml ($\frac{1}{2}$pt) vinegar
Grated rind and juice of 1 lemon
Grated rind and juice of 1 small orange
5ml (1 level tsp) salt
5ml (1 level tsp) dry mustard
5ml (1 level tsp) ground ginger
Good pinch of chilli powder
Piece of cinnamon stick

Wash the peaches, remove skins if liked by plunging first into boiling water for $\frac{1}{2}$ minute and then into cold water when they should rub off easily. Remove stones and slice the fruit and then place it in a preserving pan or large saucepan with the onions, raisins, sugar, vinegar and all the remaining ingredients. Heat gently until the sugar has dissolved, stirring frequently ; then bring to the boil. Simmer uncovered, until the chutney becomes thick and there is no liquid on the top, stirring occasionally to prevent sticking and burning. Remove the cinnamon stick and pour chutney into hot jars. Seal whilst hot with a vinegar-proof cover and label. Store in a cool dry place.

Note Unripe peaches can be used for this recipe in which case increase the sugar content to 450g (1lb). Also cheap damaged peaches can be used if weighed after cutting out all the bad and blemished parts of the fruit.

Chutneys

Plum Chutney

Ingredients

1.4kg (3lb) plums
450g (1lb) cooking apples
225g ($\frac{1}{2}$lb) carrots
225g ($\frac{1}{2}$lb) onions
1.1l (2pt) vinegar
225g ($\frac{1}{2}$lb) raisins
40g (1$\frac{1}{2}$oz) salt
5ml (1 level tsp) ground cloves
10ml (2 level tsp) ground cinnamon
10 ml (2 level tsp) ground ginger
10ml (2 level tsp) ground allspice
450g (1lb) sugar

Wash the plums and remove the stalks
and any blemished parts of the fruit.
Cut into quarters and remove the
stones. Peel and core the apples, peel
the carrots and the onions and either
chop finely, mince or grate these three
ingredients. Put the plums into a
preserving pan or large saucepan with
the apples, carrots and onions and half
the vinegar. Bring to the boil and
simmer gently until everything is very
tender. Add the remaining ingredients
and heat gently until the sugar has
dissolved. Bring to the boil and simmer
until the chutney is thick and with no
extra liquid on the surface. Pour into
hot jars and seal whilst hot with
vinegar-proof covers. Label and store
in a cool dry place.

Note Malt vinegar and brown sugar
will give a richer darker chutney than
white sugar and white vinegar and the
colour of the plums used will also vary
the colour.

Variations Cider vinegar can be used in
place of half or all the vinegar; the
carrots can be omitted; and sultanas
can be used in place of raisins. For a
hotter chutney tie 4–5 chillies in a
muslin bag and add 5–10ml (1–2 level
tsp) curry powder.

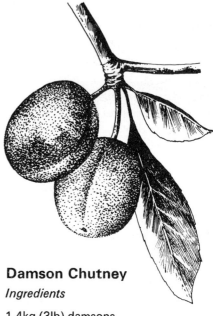

Damson Chutney

Ingredients

1.4kg (3lb) damsons
450g (1lb) cooking apples
350g ($\frac{3}{4}$lb) onions
225g ($\frac{1}{2}$lb) raisins
450g (1lb) brown sugar
900ml (1$\frac{1}{2}$pt) vinegar
7.5ml (1$\frac{1}{2}$ level tsp) salt
2.5ml ($\frac{1}{2}$ level tsp) ground allspice
20g ($\frac{3}{4}$oz) ground ginger
2 cloves garlic, crushed (optional)

Wash the damsons; peel, core and
chop the apples; peel and chop the
onions and chop the raisins. Put in a
preserving pan or large saucepan with
all the other ingredients. Heat gently
until the sugar has dissolved, stirring

frequently, then bring to the boil. Simmer for about 1½ hours, removing the damson stones as they rise to the surface, until the chutney is thick and without any extra liquid on the surface. Remove any more visible damson stones and then pour the hot chutney into hot jars. Seal at once with vinegar-proof covers then label jars and store in a cool dry place.

Note Purple plums can be used in place of the damsons and 2.5–5ml (½–1 level tsp) dry mustard and 1.25–2.5ml (¼–½ level tsp) cayenne can be added to give a hotter chutney. White vinegar and sugar give a brighter chutney whilst brown sugar and malt vinegar give a richer, darker chutney.

Blackberry Chutney

Ingredients

450g (1lb) cooking apples
1.4kg (3lb) blackberries
450g (1lb) onions
20g (¾oz) salt
25g (1oz) dry mustard
25g (1oz) ground ginger
5ml (1 level tsp) ground mace
5ml (1 level tsp) cayenne pepper
600ml (1pt) vinegar
450g (1lb) brown sugar

Peel, core and chop the apples and put into a preserving pan or large saucepan with the blackberries and peeled and finely chopped onions. Add all the remaining ingredients except the sugar and bring to the boil. Simmer for about 1 hour or until everything is soft and mushy. Rub the chutney through a nylon sieve to remove all the pips and put in a clean pan. Add the sugar and

heat gently until it has dissolved. Bring back to the boil and simmer until thick with no extra liquid on the surface. Pour the chutney into hot jars and seal with vinegar-proof covers. Label jars and store in a cool dry place.

Blackberry chutney

Chutneys

Gooseberry Chutney

Ingredients

1.4kg (3lb) gooseberries
225g ($\frac{1}{2}$lb) onions, peeled
225g ($\frac{1}{2}$lb) raisins or sultanas
450g (1lb) sugar, brown or white
300ml ($\frac{1}{2}$pt) water
15g ($\frac{1}{2}$oz) salt
15ml (1 level tbsp) ground ginger
2.5ml ($\frac{1}{2}$ level tsp) cayenne pepper
600ml (1pt) vinegar, malt or white

Wash the gooseberries and top and tail. Either roughly cut up the gooseberries and chop the onions finely or, for a smoother chutney, mince the gooseberries, onions and raisins. Put into a preserving pan or large saucepan with the water and simmer gently until soft and mushy. Add all the other ingredients and heat gently until the sugar has dissolved, then bring to the boil and simmer until the chutney becomes thick and there is no extra liquid on the surface. Pour the chutney into hot jars and seal whilst still hot with vinegar-proof covers. Label and store in a cool dry place.

Note For a variation use half tarragon vinegar and half malt or white vinegar. Brown sugar and malt vinegar will give a richer darker coloured chutney than white vinegar and white sugar.

Apple and Onion Chutney

Ingredients

1.4kg (3lb) cooking apples
1.4kg (3lb) onions
1–2 green peppers
225g ($\frac{1}{2}$lb) sultanas
Grated rind and juice of 2 lemons
600ml (1pt) malt vinegar
25g (1oz) whole pickling spice
675g (1$\frac{1}{2}$lb) demerara sugar

Peel, core and chop the apples ; peel and finely chop or mince the onions and deseed and finely chop or mince the peppers. Place in a preserving pan or large saucepan with the sultanas, grated rind and juice of the lemons, vinegar and pickling spices tied in a muslin bag. Bring to the boil and simmer for $\frac{1}{2}$ hour. Stir in the sugar heating gently until dissolved and then bring back to the boil and simmer until the chutney is thick and with no extra liquid on the surface. Remove the bag of spices and pour into hot jars. Seal whilst hot with vinegar-proof covers, label the jars and store in a cool dry place.

Apple Chutney

Ingredients

1.4kg (3lb) cooking apples
450g (1lb) onions
150ml ($\frac{1}{4}$pt) water
350g ($\frac{3}{4}$lb) white sugar
225g ($\frac{1}{2}$lb) golden syrup
100g (4oz) dates or raisins, chopped
20g ($\frac{3}{4}$oz) ground ginger
10ml (2 level tsp) ground cinnamon
3 chillies (tied in muslin)
5ml (1 level tsp) ground allspice
20g ($\frac{3}{4}$oz) salt
600ml (1pt) white vinegar

Peel and core the apples and either chop or coarsely mince. Peel the onions and finely chop or mince. Put apples, onions and water in a pan, cover and simmer for about 20 minutes or until soft. Add the remaining ingredients and heat gently until the sugar and syrup have dissolved. Mix well and bring to the boil. Simmer until the chutney becomes thick with no extra liquid on the surface. Remove the

chillies and pour into hot jars. Seal whilst still hot with vinegar-proof covers and label. Store in a cool dry place.

Indian Style Chutney

Ingredients

900g (2lb) cooking apples
225g ($\frac{1}{2}$lb) onions
2–3 large cloves garlic, crushed
900ml (1$\frac{1}{2}$pt) malt vinegar
450g (1lb) dark soft brown sugar
225g ($\frac{1}{2}$lb) raisins, chopped
75–100g (3–4oz) stem or crystallized
     ginger, chopped
10ml (2 level tsp) salt
15ml (1 level tbsp) dry mustard
2.5ml ($\frac{1}{2}$ level tsp) cayenne pepper
2.5ml ($\frac{1}{2}$ level tsp) ground allspice

Peel, core and slice the apples and put into a preserving pan or large saucepan with the peeled and finely chopped or minced onions. Add the garlic and vinegar and bring to the boil. Simmer gently until the mixture is soft and reduced to a pulp. The mixture can be liquidized or sieved at this stage to give a really smooth texture if liked. Add the remaining ingredients, heating gently until the sugar has dissolved then simmer for about $\frac{1}{2}$–$\frac{3}{4}$ hour or until the chutney becomes thick and without any excess liquid on the surface. Pour into hot jars and seal with vinegar-proof covers. Label jars and store in a cool dry place for 2–3 months before using.

Jams

Jams are a most rewarding preserve to make for they will use up any glut of fruit you may have in your garden or get hold of cheaply. A good jam should be clear and bright, with a good colour, be well set but not too stiff, with a good flavour and must keep well. To help achieve this result, first use a heavy preserving pan, where possible made from heavy aluminium, stainless steel or enamel-lined. Old-fashioned unlined copper or brass pans can be used for jams, jellies and marmalades (but not chutneys because of the vinegar) but they must be properly cleaned and any tarnishes or discolourations removed with a special cleaner before use ; and they will destroy some of the vitamin C content of the jam ; also do not leave the preserve to stand around in this type of pan for long. A thick base is necessary for jams tend to burn after the sugar is added ; a wide top is necessary to help with the evaporation of water during cooking and it must be deep enough to prevent boiling over. A large saucepan can be used if a preserving pan is not available but the cooking time may be a little longer for the narrower top will cut down the speed of evaporation.

It is an idea to keep a large wooden spoon especially for jam making (and another for chutneys) for they become discoloured easily but are better than metal spoons. A slotted spoon is also good for removing scum from the surface and also for removing stones from jams such as damson when it is not possible to remove them before cooking. Any sieves used should be made of nylon.

A good supply of clean and sound jam jars is necessary. The sizes can vary to suit your own needs but 450g (1 lb) and 900g (2lb) are the most useful. Wash well in warm soapy water, rinse and dry before use. Then before potting the jam put the jars into a warm oven to heat up. Pouring hot jam into cold jars will break them and waste the jam. Commercial covers are sold in packets containing waxed discs (remember wax side touching the jam), cellophane covers, rubber bands and labels.

Fruit used for jam should be sound and ripe or just underripe—if overripe fruit is used the pectin content may be rather low. Pectin is the absolute necessity in fruit to set the jam with the addition of sugar and acid. Some fruits are rich in pectin and acid ie cooking apples, red and blackcurrants, gooseberries, damsons, Seville oranges, lemons and limes which easily give a good setting jam ; apricots, loganberries, raspberries, most plums and gages have a reasonable content but strawberries, cherries, pears, marrows and rhubarb have only a low content and need a helping hand with the addition of lemon juice or a high pectin fruit juice ie redcurrant juice. Lemon juice is the most often used for it not only aids the setting but often brings out the flavour of the fruit. Allow 30ml (2tbsp) lemon juice to 1.8kg (4lb) fruit with poor setting qualities. A commercial pectin is available from chemists and can also be used following the manufacturer's directions or you can make your own pectin extract (see below). In some cases only extra acid (tartaric or citric acid) is required to help extract the pectin from the fruit tissues and bring out the flavour. Use 2.5ml ($\frac{1}{2}$ level tsp) per 1.8kg (4lb) fruit.

Home-made Pectin Extract

Take 900g (2lb) fruit (sour cooking apples, crab apples, redcurrants, gooseberries, apple peelings or windfalls) and cut it up without peeling or coring. Put into a pan with 600–900ml (1–1$\frac{1}{2}$pt) water. Stew gently for about $\frac{3}{4}$ hour or until well broken down and mushy. Strain through a jelly bag and use 150–300ml ($\frac{1}{4}$–$\frac{1}{2}$pt) of this juice to 1.8kg (4lb) fruit that is low in pectin.

Sugar is essential for jam making and the type used can be granulated, lump or preserving crystals. Granulated will cause more scum on top of the jams but is the cheapest. Add the sugar after the fruit has been cooked and is quite tender with the contents of the pan well reduced in volume. Remove from the heat and stir in until dissolved before reheating or the sugar will burn and spoil the jam. Too little sugar added will cause the jam to ferment whilst too much will cause crystallization during storage. A knob of butter added after the sugar has dissolved will help to prevent foaming and the resulting scum forming on the surface.

To test the jam for a set is very important for whilst under-boiled jam will not set, over boiling will make it too stiff and lose volume. There are three main ways of testing. The easiest and most accurate method is with a sugar thermometer. The warmed thermometer is placed in the jam when the sugar has dissolved and when it reaches 105°C (221°F), a set should be obtained. There are some fruits which are ready 1° lower or need 1° more but this can be double checked by using one of the other methods as well. For the flake test remove some jam on a wooden spoon and then let the jam drop off. If it has been boiled long enough, the drops will run together to form flakes which will then break off sharply. The saucer test is very simple—put a little jam on a cold saucer and leave it to cool. Push your finger across the jam when it should wrinkle. Remember to remove jam from the heat whilst doing this or it may overcook. Return jam to the pan and continue a little longer if it does not wrinkle.

Once setting point is reached pour the hot jam straight away into warmed jars filling them right up to the neck. However, with whole fruit jams such as strawberry, and marmalades, the jam must be left to stand for up to 15 minutes before potting to prevent the fruit rising in the jars. Cover with a waxed disc whilst hot—wax side downwards—making sure it lies flat to come in contact with the jam. Either cover at once with a dampened cellophane round secured with a rubber band or leave until cold before doing so. Hot or cold covering is a matter of preference. Label jars and store in a cool, dark and dry place.

Jams

Strawberry Jam (1)

Ingredients

1.6kg (3½lb) strawberries
45ml (3tbsp) lemon juice
1.4kg (3lb) sugar

Hull the strawberries and wipe over any which are dirty. It is better not to wash unless absolutely necessary. Put the fruit into a preserving pan with the lemon juice and heat very gently in their own juice until really soft—about 30 minutes, stirring frequently. Add the sugar and stir until dissolved and bring up to the boil. Boil hard without further stirring until setting point is reached, 105°C (221°F). Remove any scum from the surface then leave the jam to stand for about 15 minutes to prevent the fruit rising in the jars. Pour into clean warmed jars and cover whilst hot with wax discs and then with a dampened cellophane circle. Leave to cool, label and store in a cool, dark place. Approx yield : 2.3kg (5lb).

Strawberry Jam (2)

Ingredients

1.8kg (4lb) strawberries
900g (2lb) redcurrants or 15ml (1 level tbsp) citric or tartaric acid
1.8kg (4lb) sugar

If using redcurrants, wash them carefully and put into a saucepan with about 150ml (¼pt) water. Simmer gently till very tender, mash well and either pass through a very fine sieve or strain through a jelly bag to obtain the juice. Hull the strawberries and wipe any that are dirty. Wash only if absolutely necessary. Put into a preserving pan with the redcurrant juice and bring to the boil. Simmer gently until very tender then stir in the sugar until dissolved. Boil rapidly, without stirring for about 15 minutes or until setting point is reached, 105°C (221°F). Cool for about 15 minutes to prevent the fruit rising and cover whilst hot with waxed discs and then with a dampened cellophane circle. Leave to cool, label and store in a cool, dark place. Approx yield : 3.2kg (7lb).

Note Strawberries are low in pectin content and need either lemon juice or an acid to aid the setting. If using acid, make the jam as for Strawberry Jam (1), adding the acid to the pan with the strawberries.

Raspberry Jam (1)

Ingredients

1.8kg (4lb) fresh raspberries
1.8kg (4lb) sugar

Hull the fruit, look over carefully and wash only if necessary. Put into a preserving pan with no extra water and heat gently until the juice begins to run, and then simmer in its own juice for about 15–20 minutes or until really soft. Stir in the sugar until dissolved and then bring back to the boil and boil rapidly until setting point is reached, 105°C (221°F). Pour into warmed jars, cover with a wax disc and then with a dampened cellophane circle. Cool, label and store in a cool, dark place. Approx yield : 2.3kg (5lb).

Raspberry Jam (2)

Ingredients

2.3kg (5lb) fresh raspberries
2.7kg (6lb) sugar

Look over the fruit carefully and wash only if necessary. Place in a preserving pan with no added water. Simmer very gently until the juice begins to flow and then bring to the boil and boil for 10 minutes. Warm the sugar in a low oven and stir into the raspberries until dissolved. Bring back to the boil quickly and boil rapidly for 2 minutes. Pour into warmed jars, cover whilst hot with a waxed disc and then with a dampened cellophane circle. Cool, label and store in a cool, dark place. Approx yield : 4.5kg (10lb).

Note This jam does not set very firmly but has a good colour and a really fresh-fruit flavour.

Blackcurrant Jam

Ingredients

1.8kg (4lb) blackcurrants
1.7l (3pt) water
2.7kg (6lb) sugar

Remove the stalks from the fruit and then wash carefully. Drain fruit well and put into a preserving pan with the water. Bring to the boil and simmer gently until the fruit is soft and the contents of the pan well reduced. If the fruit is still tough at this stage the finished jam will still remain tough, so take care to cook sufficiently. Add the sugar and stir until it has dissolved. Bring back to the boil and boil rapidly until setting point is reached 105°C (221°F). Remove any scum from the surface then pour into warmed jars. Cover with waxed discs and a dampened cellophane circle. Cool, label and store in a cool, dark place. Approx yield : 4.5kg (10lb).

Jams

Gooseberry and Strawberry Jam

Ingredients

900g (2lb) ripe gooseberries
450ml (¾pt) water
900g (2lb) strawberries
1.8kg (4lb) sugar

Top and tail the gooseberries and wash well. Put into a preserving pan with the water, bring to the boil and simmer until soft. Add the hulled and wiped strawberries and cook for a further 20–30 minutes until tender but not overcooked. Stir in the sugar until dissolved then boil rapidly until setting point is reached—about 20 minutes, 105°C (221°F). Cool for about 15 minutes then pour into hot jars. Cover with waxed discs and then a dampened cellophane circle. Cool, label and store in a cool, dark place. Approx yield : 2.3–2.7kg (5–6lb).

Note This jam has an excellent flavour and the acidity of the gooseberries gives the strawberries the pectin needed for a good set.

Gooseberry Jam

Ingredients

1.8kg (4lb) gooseberries
750ml (1¼pt) water
2.3kg (5lb) sugar

The colour of the finished jam will depend on the type of fruit used and its maturity as well as the length of boiling after adding the sugar. Longer boiling gives a deeper red colour but to get the greenest jam use a copper or brass pan for the cooking.

Top and tail the gooseberries and wash. Drain well and put into a preserving pan with the water and bring to the boil. Simmer gently until the fruit is quite tender (if the skins are tough at this point they will still be so in the finished jam) and the contents of the pan well reduced. Add the sugar and stir until dissolved. Bring back to the boil and boil rapidly until setting point is reached, 105°C (221°F). Remove scum from the surface and then pour into warmed jars. Cover with a waxed disc and then a dampened cellophane circle. Cool, label and store in a cool, dark place. Approx yield : 4.5kg (10lb).

Note For a pleasant variation add 14–16 well washed heads of elderflowers (tied in a muslin bag) to the pan with the gooseberres and water. Before adding the sugar, remove the bag, squeezing out all the juice and continue as above.

Pumpkin Jam

Ingredients

1.4kg (3lb) prepared pumpkin (ie
    peeled and seeds removed)
900ml–1.1l (1½–2pt) water
50g (2oz) root ginger, bruised or
    7.5ml (1½ level tsp) ground ginger
Grated rind of 2 lemons (optional)
Juice of 2 lemons
1.4kg (3lb) sugar
50–75g (2–3oz) preserved ginger,
    finely chopped (optional)

Cut the pumpkin into small dice and
put into a preserving pan with the water
and ginger (tie root ginger in a muslin
bag). Bring to the boil, cover and
simmer very gently until the pumpkin
is mushy and very tender. Remove
from the heat and mash thoroughly.
Stir in the lemon rind (if used) and
juice and the sugar until dissolved.
Bring back to the boil and boil rapidly
until setting point is reached, 105°C
(221°F), stirring occasionally as the
jam will be very thick and tends to
stick. Remove the bag of ginger, then
stir in the chopped ginger, if used, and
pour the jam into warmed jars. Cover
with a waxed disc and then a
dampened cellophane circle. Cool,
label and store in a cool, dark place.
Approx yield : 2kg (4½lb).

Marrow Jam

Ingredients

2.3kg (5lb) prepared marrow (ie
    peeled and seeds removed)
Finely grated rind and juice of 3 large
    lemons
50g (2oz) root ginger, bruised or
    7.5ml (1½ level tsp) ground ginger
2.3kg (5lb) sugar

There are two methods of making this
jam :

Method 1   Cut the marrow into cubes
about 1cm (½in) square. Place in a
steamer and steam gently until just
tender, then put into a bowl with the
grated rinds and juice of the lemons and
the bruised ginger tied in a muslin bag.
Add the sugar and leave to stand in a
covered bowl for 24 hours. Transfer to a
preserving pan and heat gently until all
the sugar has dissolved, stirring
frequently. Bring to the boil and cook
until the marrow is transparent and the
syrup thick and continue until setting
point is reached, 105°C (221°F).
Remove the bag of ginger and any
scum on the surface and leave to stand
for 5–10 minutes. Pour into warmed
jars, cover with waxed discs and a
dampened cellophane circle. Cool,
label and store in a cool, dark, place.
Approx yield : 3.4kg (7½lb).

Method 2   Place the cubed marrow
(as above) in a bowl with about 450g
(1lb) sugar and leave to stand
overnight in a covered bowl. The next
day put the lemon juice and rinds,
bruised ginger tied in a muslin bag and
the marrow into a preserving pan and
bring slowly to the boil. Simmer gently
for about ½ hour, then stir in the
remaining sugar and return to the boil.
Continue to boil fairly gently until the
marrow becomes transparent, the
syrup is thick and setting point is
reached. Remove the muslin bag and
pot and cover as above.

Jams

Rhubarb and Ginger Jam

Ingredients

1.4kg (3lb) prepared rhubarb
1.4kg (3lb) sugar
Juice of 2 lemons
Grated rind of 1 lemon (optional)
25g (1oz) root ginger, bruised
50–75g (2–3oz) preserved or
   crystallized ginger, finely chopped
   (optional)

Wash the rhubarb, drain well and cut into small chunks. Put into a bowl layered up with the sugar and lemon juice and cover bowl. Leave to stand overnight. The next day transfer this mixture to a preserving pan adding the lemon rind, if used, and root ginger tied in a muslin bag. Bring slowly to the boil, stirring frequently until the sugar has dissolved. Boil rapidly for 15 minutes then remove the muslin bag, and add the chopped ginger, if used. Continue to boil until the rhubarb is transparent and setting point is reached, 105°C (221°F). Remove any scum from the surface and pour into warmed jars. Cover with waxed discs and then with a dampened cellophane circle. Cool, label and store in a cool, dark place. Approx yield : 2.3kg (5lb).

Rhubarb and Lemon Jam

Make as above but omit both the root and preserved ginger and use the finely grated rind of 3 lemons and 2.5–5ml ($\frac{1}{2}$–1 level tsp) ground mixed spice.

Rhubarb and Raspberry Jam

Ingredients

1.8kg (4lb) prepared rhubarb
300ml ($\frac{1}{2}$pt) water
900g (2lb) raspberries
2.7kg (6lb) sugar

Wash the rhubarb and drain well and cut into small chunks. Put into a pan with the water and bring to the boil, cover and simmer until tender and mushy. Remove the lid, add the raspberries and continue to simmer until the fruit is tender and the contents of the pan reduced. Add the sugar, stirring continuously until dissolved and then bring back to the boil. Boil rapidly until setting point is reached, 105°C (221°F). Remove any scum from the surface and pour into warmed jars. Cover with waxed discs and a

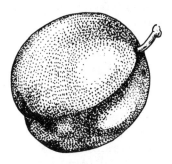

dampened cellophane circle. Cool, label and store in a cool, dark place. Approx yield : 4.5kg (10lb).

Note Loganberries, if available, can be used in place of raspberries. The softer and slightly damaged raspberries unsuitable for freezing can be used for this recipe.

Plum Jam

Ingredients

2.7kg (6lb) plums
300–900ml ($\frac{1}{2}$–1$\frac{1}{2}$pt) water
2.7kg (6lb) sugar

Remove stalks from the fruit then wash and drain well. Cut the plums in halves and remove the stones. Crack some stones and remove the kernels, if liked. If the plums are not the freestone variety leave them whole. Put the plums and kernels into a preserving pan with the water and bring to the boil. Simmer gently until the fruit is very soft and the contents of the pan well reduced. (If using whole fruit remove the stones as they rise to the surface with a slotted spoon.) Add the sugar and stir until well dissolved then bring to the boil. Boil rapidly until setting point is reached, 105°C (221 °F), remove any scum from the surface and pour into warm jars. Cover with waxed discs and a dampened cellophane circle. Cool, label and store in a cool, dark place. Approx yield : 4.5kg (10lb).

Note: Dark coloured plums will obviously give a richer darker finished jam than the lighter varieties. Green and yellow gages when available can be used in this way to make jams.

The amount of water used depends on the juiciness of the fruit and also on the fruit content required in the finished jam. Use less water with very juicy plums and gages and more with the drier varieties.

Cherry Jam

Ingredients

1.8kg (4lb) cherries (Morello or May
    Duke are best)
Juice of 3 lemons or 7.5ml (1$\frac{1}{2}$ level
    tsp) tartaric or citric acid
1.6kg (3$\frac{1}{2}$lb) sugar

Wash and stone the cherries and put the fruit into a preserving pan. Crack a few of the stones and remove the kernels to add to the pan with the lemon juice or acid. Bring to the boil slowly and simmer very gently until the fruit is really tender, stirring occasionally to prevent sticking. Add the sugar and stir until dissolved, then bring back to the boil and boil rapidly until setting point is reached, 105°C (221 °F). Remove any scum from the surface, pour into warmed jars, cover with waxed discs and then with dampened cellophane circles. Cool, label and store in a cool, dark place. Approx yield : 2.3kg (5lb).

Note Cherries are low in pectin and consequently this jam has only a light set, but the flavour is very good. A firmer setting jam needs a fruit such as redcurrants or gooseberries added to supply the lacking pectin. Use 900g (2lb) cherries, 450g (1lb) redcurrants or other fruit, 150ml ($\frac{1}{4}$pt) water and 1.4kg (3lb) sugar and make as for blackcurrant jam (see p 109) cooking the cherries and other fruit together.

Jams

Fig Jam

Ingredients

675g (1½lb) fresh green figs
350–450g (¾–1lb) tart cooking apples
Finely grated rind of 2 lemons
Juice of 4 lemons
675g (1½lb) sugar

Wash the figs and remove stalks, then slice. Peel, core and slice the apples and put into a pan with the prepared figs, lemon rind and juice. Bring to the boil, cover pan and cook very gently, stirring from time to time, until the figs are very tender. (If the figs are tough at this stage they will remain tough in the finished jam.) Add the sugar and stir until dissolved then bring back to the boil and boil rapidly for 15 minutes. Continue to boil until setting point is reached, 105°C (221°F). Remove any scum from the surface, pour into warmed jars and cover first with waxed discs and then a dampened cellophane circle. Cool, label and store in a cool, dark place. Approx yield : 900g (2lb).

Rose Petal Jam (1)

This is an unusual, novelty jam with a strong, distinctive flavour. Use thin-petalled roses where possible when they are full blown for the best results—and use it sparingly.

Ingredients

450g (1lb) rose petals
675g (1½lb) sugar
300ml (½pt) water
Juice of half lemon

Pick the petals when they are dry from full blown roses and then cut off the white base of each petal. Cut petals into uneven pieces and place in a bowl with half the sugar. Mix well, cover bowl and leave to stand in a cool place for 48 hours. Dissolve the remaining sugar slowly in the water in a pan without boiling and then add the lemon juice and rose petal mixture (which will have darkened in colour and have a very strong scent). Bring up to the boil and simmer gently for about 15–20 minutes until the jam thickens then continue until setting point is reached, 105°C (221°F). Remove any scum from the surface and cool for a few minutes before pouring into warmed jars. Cover with waxed discs and a dampened cellophane circle. Cool, label and store in a cool dark place. Approx yield : 900g (2lb).

Rose Petal Jam (2)

Ingredients

100g (4oz) rose petals
675g (1½lb) sugar
15ml (1tbsp) lemon juice
150ml (¼pt) rose water
150ml (¼pt) water

Prepare the rose petals as for recipe above then put into a bowl. Dissolve the sugar with the lemon juice, rose water and water in a pan over a gentle heat, stirring continuously, then bring to the boil and simmer for 5 minutes. Pour over the petals, mix well, cover bowl and leave to stand overnight. The next day turn the rose petal mixture into a saucepan and bring up to the boil. Simmer gently, stirring continuously, for about 30 minutes until the syrup thickens and setting point is reached, 105°C (221°F). Continue as above.

Rosehip and Apple Jam

Another unusual preserve making use of the hedgerow rosehips and apples which can be windfalls if they are weighed after cutting out bad and bruised parts of the fruit.

Ingredients

900g (2lb) ripe rosehips
1.7l (3pt) water
900g (2lb) tart cooking apples
725–900g (1¾–2lb) sugar

Wash the rosehips thoroughly and drain. Put into a pan with the water, bring to the boil, cover and simmer until very soft and pulpy. Strain through a jelly bag overnight. Peel, core and chop the apples and put into a pan with the very minimum of water and cook gently in a covered pan until a soft pulp. Stir occasionally to prevent sticking. Add the rosehip juice and the

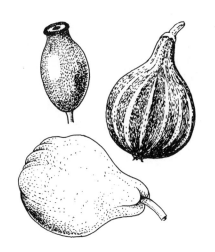

sugar and stir until the sugar has dissolved. Bring up to the boil and boil rapidly until setting point is reached, 105°C (221°F). Remove any scum from the surface and pour at once into warmed jars. Cover with waxed discs and a dampened cellophane circle and cool, label and store in a cool, dark place. Approx yield : 1.6kg (3½lb).

Quince Jam

When available, quinces make a most delicious jam.

Ingredients

900g (2lb) quinces
225g (½lb) apples
900ml (1½pt) water
1.4kg (3lb) sugar

Wash the fruit well then peel, core and finely chop the flesh. Put all the peelings and cores into a pan with the roughly chopped up apples (including peel and cores) and the water. Bring to the boil, cover and simmer gently until pulpy. Strain the juice through a jelly bag then replace in a clean saucepan. Add the chopped quince flesh and simmer gently until quite tender but still in cubes, and the contents of the pan are reduced by about one-third. Add the sugar and stir until dissolved, then bring to the boil and boil rapidly until setting point is reached, 105°C (221°F). Remove any scum from the surface and leave to stand for 15 minutes before potting to prevent the fruit rising. Pour into warmed jars, cover with waxed discs and then a dampened cellophane circle. Cool, label and store in a cool, dark place. Approx yield : 2.3kg (5lb).

Jellies

The same principles apply to jelly making as to jam making with a few extra considerations, and as with jam, to get the correct set of the jelly there must be pectin, acid and sugar present. The finished jelly should be clear in colour with a good set (but not too stiff) and a good fruity flavour. To achieve this only fruits which give a really good set should be used (see jams p 106) unless the good setters are mixed with a lesser setting fruit.

Jellies take longer to make than jams because of the time involved in allowing the cooked pulpy fruit to drip through a jelly bag. However, the smooth results overcome the problems of those who do not like or cannot digest tough skins or pips found in some jams.

The fruit to be used needs little preparation, but thorough washing is essential. Use ripe fruit for preference but slightly underripe is acceptable. Take care with overripe fruit for the pectin content is much lower. Cut out any bad or damaged parts from the fruit and cut up larger varieties roughly—but do not remove peel, cores or pips. Put into a pan with sufficient water to just cover (hard fruits such as currants and quinces need more water and the softer ones less water) and cook slowly until the fruits are really tender so that all the juices can be extracted and all the acid and pectin present are dissolved in the water. The pulp has to be strained through a jelly bag or double thickness of clean tea-towel, sheet or piece of muslin which has previously been scalded. The bag can be tied to a cupboard door, upturned chair, etc, but must be left to drip until no more juice appears—this takes several hours or overnight. Do not prod or squeeze the bag whilst straining or the jelly will become cloudy. The strained juice is often called the extract.

The extract is then put into a clean pan with sugar and boiled until setting point is reached, 105°C (221°F) as for jam. On average allow 450g (1lb) sugar to each 500ml (approx 1pt) juice, and heat gently stirring frequently, until the sugar has dissolved, before boiling hard. Setting point is usually reached after about 10 minutes boiling without further stirring. Scum must be removed from the surface before potting with a slotted spoon or by straining through a piece of scalded cloth. Pour into warmed jars, tilted to prevent trapping air bubbles, and cover at once whilst very hot with waxed discs. Dampened cellophane covers can be put on when the jelly is hot or cold. Small jars usually 225–450g ($\frac{1}{2}$–1lb) in size are used for jellies. Take care not to tilt jars until completely cold and set.

It is not practical to quote the yields for jellies because of the varying losses incurred on straining the juice due to the ripeness of the fruit, length of time allowed for dripping, etc.

Note In the jelly recipes, the metric equivalent of 1pt has been rounded down to 500ml, to give the correct consistency.

Apple and Blackberry Jelly

Ingredients

1.8kg (4lb) blackberries
900g (2lb) cooking apples
1.1l (2pt) water
Sugar

Wash the blackberries thoroughly and pick them over and then drain well. Put into a pan. Wash the apples, cut into rough slices removing any bad pieces (but not the cores or skins) and add to the blackberries with the water. Bring to the boil and simmer gently for about an hour or until very tender. Mash the fruit well and then strain through a jelly bag or cloth. Measure the strained juice and return it to a clean pan with 450g (1lb) sugar to each 500ml (approx 1pt) juice. Heat gently until the sugar has dissolved, stirring frequently, then bring up the the boil and boil rapidly until setting point is reached, 105°C (221 °F). Remove any scum from the surface and pour into warmed jars. Cover with waxed discs and then a dampened cellophane circle. Cool, label and store in a cool, dark place.

Bramble Jelly

Ingredients

1.8kg (4lb) blackberries
Juice of 2 lemons or 7.5ml (1½ level
    tsp) tartaric or citric acid
450ml (¾pt) water
Sugar

Wash the blackberries thoroughly and pick them over, then drain well. Put into a pan with the lemon juice or acid and the water and bring to the boil. Simmer until really soft and pulpy—about an hour ; then mash well. Strain through a jelly bag or cloth, measure the strained juice and return it to a clean pan. Add 450g (1lb) sugar to each 500ml (approx 1pt) strained juice and heat gently until the sugar has dissolved, stirring frequently. Bring to the boil and boil rapidly until setting point is reached, 105°C (221 °F). Remove any scum from the surface and pour into warmed jars. Cover with waxed discs and a dampened cellophane circle ; then cool, label and store in a cool, dark place.

Jellies

450g (1lb) sugar to each 500ml (approx 1pt) juice and heat gently until the sugar has dissolved. Bring to the boil and boil rapidly until setting point is reached, 105°C (221°F). Remove any scum from the surface and pour into warmed jars. Cover with waxed discs and a dampened cellophane circle then cool, label and store in a cool, dark place.

Note Half quinces and half cooking apples can be used for this recipe especially when quinces are hard to get. It is not then necessary to use the lemon rind and juice or acid, but a little lemon juice does help the flavour.

Quince Jelly

Ingredients

1.8kg (4lb) quinces
Thinly pared rind and juice of 3
  lemons or 15g ($\frac{1}{2}$oz) tartaric or
  citric acid
3.4l (6pt) water
Sugar

Wash the quinces well and drain, then cut up into fairly small pieces. Put into a pan with 2.3l (4pt) water and the lemon rind and juice or the acid and bring to the boil. Simmer for about 1 hour or until the fruit is really soft and pulpy. Mash well and then strain through a jelly bag or cloth. Return the quince pulp to the pan with the remaining water and simmer for a further hour to make a second extract, and strain through the bag again. Mix the two strained juices together and measure. Put into a clean pan with

Crab Apple Jelly

Ingredients

1.8kg (4lb) crab apples
1.4l (2$\frac{1}{2}$pt) water
Few whole cloves, little bruised root
  ginger or thinly pared orange or
  lemon rind (optional)
Sugar

Wash the crab apples and cut into quarters. Put into a preserving pan with the water and add the cloves, ginger, or fruit rind, if used. Bring to the boil and simmer for about 1$\frac{1}{2}$ hours or until the crab apples are very soft and pulpy. Mash the fruit well then strain through a jelly bag or cloth. Measure the strained juice and put into a clean pan with 450g (1lb) sugar to each 500ml (approx 1pt). Heat gently until the sugar has dissolved, stirring frequently, then bring to the boil and boil rapidly until setting point is reached, 105°C (221°F). Remove any scum from the surface then pour into warmed jars. Cover with waxed discs

118

and then a dampened cellophane circle. Cool, label and store in a cool, dark place.

Note Apple jelly is made in the same way as this recipe but as apples give a rather bland jelly, one of the suggested flavourings or a few blackberries, blackcurrants or raspberries should be added to give it more flavour. Also make japonica jelly in this way.

Gooseberry and Elderflower Jelly

Ingredients

1.8kg (4lb) gooseberries
1.4–1.7l (2½–3pt) water
About 16 heads of elderflowers
Sugar

Wash the gooseberries (but don't top and tail) and place in a pan with the water to cover. Wash the elderflowers carefully and add to the pan. Bring to the boil and simmer until the fruit is really soft and pulpy. Strain through a jelly bag or cloth and measure the juice. Put into a clean pan with 450g (1lb) sugar to each 500ml (approx 1pt) juice and heat gently until dissolved. Bring to the boil and boil rapidly until setting point is reached, 105°C

(221°F). Remove any scum from the surface, pour into warmed jars and cover with waxed discs and then a dampened cellophane circle. Cool, label and store in a cool, dark place.

Note The elderflowers may be omitted. For an orange flavoured gooseberry jelly add the finely pared rinds of 2 oranges in place of the elderflowers.

Gooseberry and Redcurrant Jelly

Ingredients

1.1kg (2½lb) gooseberries
675g (1½lb) redcurrants
Approx 500ml (approx 1pt) water
Sugar

Wash the gooseberries and redcurrants carefully but do not remove stalks or top and tail. Place in a pan with the water (or more if necessary to cover the fruit), and bring to the boil. Simmer until very soft and pulpy, mash well and strain through a jelly bag or cloth. Measure the juice and put into a clean pan. Add 450g (1lb) sugar to each 500ml (approx 1pt) juice and heat gently until dissolved. Bring to the boil and boil rapidly until setting point is reached, 105°C (221°F). Remove any scum from the surface and pour into warmed jars. Cover with waxed discs and then a dampened cellophane circle. Cool, label and store in a cool, dark place.

Note The water can be increased to 900ml–1l (1½–1¾pt) to give a little less concentrated jelly.

Jellies

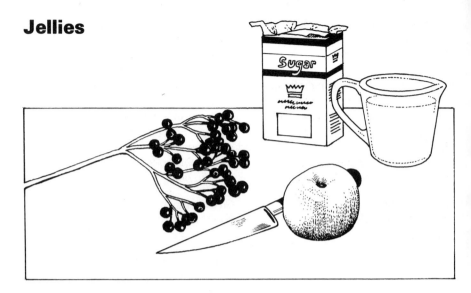

Apple and Elderberry Jelly

Ingredients

900g (2lb) elderberries
900g (2lb) cooking apples
500ml (approx 1pt) water
Sugar

Wash the elderberries and put into a pan with just sufficient water to cover. Wash the apples and chop up roughly (without removing peel or cores) and put into another pan with just sufficient water to cover. Simmer both fruits gently until very soft and pulpy. Mash the fruits well and strain the combined fruits through a jelly bag or cloth. Measure the juice and put into a clean pan with 450g (1lb) sugar to each 500ml (approx 1pt) juice. Heat gently until the sugar has dissolved, stirring frequently, and then bring to the boil and boil rapidly until setting point is reached, 105°C (221°F). Remove any scum from the surface, pour into warmed jars and cover first with a waxed disc and then a dampened cellophane circle. Cool, label and store in a cool, dark place.

Blackcurrant and Apple Jelly

Ingredients

675g (1½lb) blackcurrants
675g (1½lb) cooking apples
2.8l (5pt) water
Sugar

Wash the blackcurrants and place in a pan. Wash the apples and cut up roughly (without removing peel or cores) and add to the blackcurrants with the water. Bring to the boil and simmer gently until the contents are very soft and pulpy—about 1 hour. Mash the fruit well and strain through a jelly bag or cloth. Measure the juice into a clean pan and bring to the boil for 5 minutes. Add 450g (1lb) sugar to each 500ml (approx 1pt) juice and heat gently until dissolved. Bring back to the boil and boil rapidly until setting

120

point is reached, 105 °C (221 °F).
Remove any scum from the surface and
pour into warmed jars. Cover with
waxed discs and dampened cellophane
circles. Cool, label and store in a cool,
dark place.

Apple and Orange Jelly

Ingredients

4 sweet oranges
1.4kg (3lb) cooking apples
1.7l (3pt) water
Sugar

Wash the oranges and cut into slices
without removing peel or pith. Wash
the apples and roughly chop without
removing the peel or cores. Put both
fruits into a pan with the water and
bring to the boil. Simmer gently until all
the fruit is very tender—1$\frac{1}{4}$–1$\frac{1}{2}$ hours.
Mash well and strain through a jelly
bag or cloth. Measure the strained
juice and put into a clean pan. Add
450g (1lb) sugar to each 500ml
(approx 1 pt) juice and heat gently until
dissolved, stirring frequently. Bring to
the boil and boil rapidly until setting
point is reached, 105 °C (221 °F).
Remove any scum from the surface and
pour into warmed jars. Cover with
waxed discs and a dampened
cellophane circle. Cool, label and store
in a cool, dark place.

Note A little orange colouring can be
added to the jelly before potting if the
colour is a little pale.

Apple and Lemon Jelly

Make as apple and orange jelly but use
4 lemons in place of the oranges.

Damson Jelly

Ingredients

1.8kg (4lb) damsons
1.1l (2pt) water
Sugar

Wash the damsons well and place in a
pan with the water. Bring to the boil and
simmer gently until the fruit is very soft
—about $\frac{1}{2}$ hour. Mash well and strain
through a jelly bag or cloth. Measure
the juice and put into a clean pan. Add
450g (1lb) sugar to each 500ml
(approx 1pt) strained juice and heat
gently until the sugar has dissolved,
stirring frequently. Bring to the boil and
boil rapidly until setting point is
reached, 105 °C (221 °F). Remove any
scum from the surface, pour into
warmed jars and cover first with waxed
discs and then with dampened
cellophane circles. Cool, label and
store in a cool, dark place.

Note Damson jelly is often made in
preference to jam because of the
difficulty of removing all the stones
from the jam. For damson and apple
jelly use 900g (2lb) damsons, 1.8kg
(4lb) cooking apples and 1.4l (2$\frac{1}{2}$pt)
water; cook the damsons and roughly
chopped apples, without removing
peel or cores, together and continue
as above.

Jellies

Redcurrant Jelly

This is a popular jelly for serving with meats and for this purpose it should have a firm consistency and piquant flavour.

Ingredients

1.4kg (3lb) redcurrants
500ml (approx 1pt) water
Sugar

Wash the fruit without removing the stalks and place in a saucepan with the water. Bring to the boil and simmer gently until very soft and pulpy. Mash well and strain through a jelly bag or cloth. Measure the strained juice and put into a clean pan adding 450g (1lb) sugar to each 500ml (approx 1pt) juice. Heat gently until dissolved, stirring frequently, and bring to the boil. Boil rapidly until setting point is reached, 105°C (221°F), then remove any scum from the surface. Pour into warmed jars quickly. This must be done quickly for a concentrated redcurrant jelly tends to set fast. Cover with waxed discs and then dampened cellophane circles. Cool, label and store in a cool, dark place.

Note For a less concentrated and slightly less firm jelly, increase the water to 900ml–1l (1½–1¾pt).

Redcurrant and Apple Jelly

A more economical jelly than redcurrant jelly, still suitable to serve with meats but also good as a preserve.

Ingredients

900g (2lb) redcurrants
900g (2lb) cooking apples
1.4l (2½pt) water
Sugar

Wash the redcurrants without removing the stalks and put into a saucepan. Wash the apples and roughly chop or slice without removing the peel or cores, and add to the pan with the water. Bring to the boil and simmer until the fruits are really tender and mushy. Mash well and strain through a jelly bag or cloth. Measure the strained juice into a clean pan and add 450g (1lb) sugar to each 500ml (approx 1pt) juice. Heat gently until dissolved, stirring frequently and then bring to the boil. Boil rapidly until setting point is reached, 105°C (221°F) then remove any scum from the surface. Pour into warmed jars, cover with waxed discs, then dampened cellophane circles and cool, label and store in a cool, dark place.

Mint Jelly (1)

This is a pleasant mint-flavoured apple jelly suitable for use as a preserve or to serve as a mild accompaniment to meats.

Ingredients

1.4kg (3lb) green skinned cooking
    apples
1.3l (2¼pt) water, approx
A bunch of freshly picked mint
Juice of 2 lemons or 5ml (1 level tsp)
    tartaric or citric acid
Sugar
Green colouring (optional)
45–60ml (3–4tbsp) freshly chopped
    mint or a few sprigs of mint, bruised

distributed through the set jelly. Pour into small warmed jars, cover with waxed discs and then dampened cellophane circles. Cool, label and store in a cool, dark place.

Mint Jelly (2)

With added vinegar this jelly has a piquant flavour suitable to serve with meats.

Ingredients

1.4kg (3lb) green skinned cooking
   apples
500ml (approx 1pt) water
A bunch of freshly picked mint
750ml (1¼pt) white distilled vinegar
Sugar
45–60ml (3–4tbsp) freshly chopped
   mint
Green colouring (optional)

Wash the apples and chop roughly without removing the peel or cores. Put into a pan with the water and bunch of mint and bring to the boil. Simmer gently until the fruit is really soft and pulpy, stirring occasionally to prevent it sticking. Add the vinegar and simmer for a further 5 minutes. Strain through a jelly bag or cloth and measure the strained juice into a clean pan. Add 450g (1lb) sugar to each 500ml (approx 1pt) juice and heat gently until dissolved, stirring frequently. Bring to the boil and boil rapidly until setting point is reached. Remove any scum from the surface, stir in the mint and a few drops of green colouring, if liked. Leave to stand for a few minutes before pouring into small warm jars. Cover with waxed discs and a dampened cellophane circle. Cool, label and store in a cool, dark place.

The greener the skins of the apples the better, for red skinned ones do not give a good coloured jelly. Wash the apples, chop roughly (without removing peel or cores), and put into a pan with the water, mint and lemon juice or acid. Bring to the boil and simmer until soft and pulpy. Mash well and strain through a jelly bag or cloth. Measure the strained juice and put into a clean pan with 450g (1lb) sugar to each 500ml (approx 1pt) juice. Heat gently until the sugar has dissolved, stirring frequently, then bring to the boil and boil for 5 minutes. Either add the chopped mint (or add the bruised mint to the jelly for 3–4 minutes whilst continuing to boil). Remove the sprigs of mint and continue to boil until setting point is reached, 105°C (221°F). Remove any scum from the surface and stir in a little green colouring, if liked. Leave to stand until a thin skin forms on the surface, if using chopped mint, as this helps to keep it evenly

Marmalades

A marmalade is a jam, jelly or pulp in which slices or pieces of peel or fruit are suspended. Seville oranges, lemons, grapefruit and limes are the most usual 'marmalade fruits' but sweet oranges and tangerines can also be combined with these fruits to give other flavours.

The method of making marmalade is basically very similar to jam making but extra time is needed to prepare and cook the tough peel of the citrus fruit which would otherwise spoil the finished marmalade. The pectin required to set the finished marmalade is found in the pips and the white pith so the pips must be tied in a muslin bag and the peel with pith attached (although if very thick, some may be pared off), finely shredded.

The peel can be evenly shredded by hand, or by using a slicer to do the job— however hand shredding is always preferred. The peel can also be minced but this gives a thick jam-like finished preserve, which some people do not like. The shredded peel (fine or medium according to taste) can be soaked in the measured water overnight before cooking to help soften the peel but it is not essential. The cooking time is longer than for jams—usually at least an hour—and because of this more water is used to allow for the evaporation. The contents of the pan should be reduced by about half, and the peel really soft before adding the sugar—failure to do so is one of the most common reasons for marmalade failing to set and gives tough and chewy pieces in the finished preserve. This first softening process can be done in a pressure cooker to save time allowing 600ml (1pt) water to each 450g (1lb) fruit, but the amount cooked at one time is much smaller. 900g (2lb) is the usual amount to make in a pressure cooker but follow the manufacturer's instructions. Once tender add the sugar and proceed as usual.

Once the sugar has been added and slowly dissolved as for jams, the rapid boiling to reach setting point usually takes a little longer than with jams and the longer the boiling, the darker the colour of the finished marmalade. A little black treacle can be added with the sugar if you like really dark marmalade, ie 25g (1oz) to each 2.7kg (6lb) sugar. Allow the marmalade to stand in the pan for 5–10 minutes after removing the scum from the surface before potting to prevent the peel rising in the jar. Place the waxed discs immediately on the hot marmalade. The cellophane covers can be put on hot or cold as preferred but are more usually added when the marmalade is cold. Label and store in a cool, dark place. Allowing the marmadade to mature for a few weeks before use is advisable but it can be used at once. Marmadades should keep well for at least two years if properly made, covered and stored.

When making jelly marmalade it is essential to test for pectin content before adding the sugar, or the finished marmalade may not set. To do this take 5ml (1tsp) of the juice from the cooked fruit (ie just before adding the sugar) and put into a glass. When cool add 15ml (1tbsp) methylated spirits and shake well. Leave for 1 minute and if it forms a good jelly clot there is plenty of pectin. If it does not form a clot then it requires extra pectin which can be obtained either by boiling further to reduce the bulk and then retesting before adding the sugar or by adding lemon juice, 30ml (2tbsp) to each 1.8kg (4lb) fruit and then retesting. This test can also be used for jams, and jellies which use fruit with low pectin content to be certain of a good set.

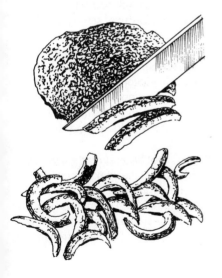

Note Marmalade fruits with a short season like Seville oranges and limes can be scrubbed, packed in suitable containers and frozen until required. The semi-thawed fruit should then be cooked by the method for lemon marmalade (see p 126).

Seville Orange Marmalade

Ingredients

1.4kg (3lb) Seville oranges
2.6–3.4l (4$\frac{1}{2}$–6pt) water
Juice of 2 lemons
2.7kg (6lb) sugar

Wash the fruit thoroughly, scrubbing off any stubborn marks. Cut the fruit in halves, squeeze out the juice and pips and remove the membrane. Tie the pips and membrane in a muslin bag. Cut the peel into thin shreds (or to taste) and put into a preserving pan with the orange juice, water, lemon juice and bag of pips. Bring to the boil and simmer gently, uncovered, until the contents of the pan are reduced by about half and the peel is really tender —about 2 hours. Remove the muslin bag and squeeze out all the juice from it. Add the sugar and stir until completely dissolved. Bring to the boil and boil rapidly until setting point is reached, 105°C (221°F). Remove any scum from the surface and leave to stand for about 5–10 minutes. Pour into warmed jars and cover with waxed discs (wax side downwards) whilst hot. Finish with cellophane tops when hot or cold and then label and store in a cool, dark place. Approx yield : 4.5kg (10lb).

Marmalades

Mixed Fruit Marmalade

Ingredients

4 lemons
2 sweet oranges } total weight
2 grapefruit } 1.4kg (3lb)
2.6–3.4l (4½–6pt) water
2.7kg (6lb) sugar

Wash the fruit thoroughly. Cut lemons and oranges in halves and squeeze out the juice and pips. Pare off the rind of the grapefruit without too much of the white pith, then peel off the remainder of the pith and any stringy parts of the fruit and put into a muslin bag with the lemon and orange pips. Either finely shred, coarsely shred or mince all the peels according to taste and put into a preserving pan with the fruit juices. Roughly chop up the grapefruit flesh discarding the pips and add to the pan with the water. Add the muslin bag and bring to the boil. Simmer for 1–1½ hours or until the peel is really soft and the contents of the pan reduced by about half. Remove the muslin bag, squeezing out all the juice and stir in the sugar until dissolved. Bring to the boil and boil rapidly until setting point is reached, 105°C (221°F). Remove any scum from the surface and leave to stand for about 10 minutes. Pour into warmed jars and cover with waxed discs at once. Finish with cellophane tops when hot or cold. Label and store in a cool, dark place. Approx yield : 4.5kg (10lb).

Note This marmalade can be made at any time of the year for it does not require Seville oranges.

Lemon or Lime Marmalade

Ingredients

1.4kg (3lb) thin skinned lemons or limes
2.6–3.4l (4½–6pt) water
2.7kg (6lb) sugar

This marmalade can be made in the same way as Seville orange marmalade, or in the following way :
Weigh the preserving pan before you start. Wash whichever fruit you use and remove the stem end. Put the fruit with the water in a pan with a tight fitting lid and simmer gently for 1½–2 hours or until the fruit is really soft. Remove from the pan and slice or chop the fruit finely, separating out the pips. (A knife and fork is the best thing to use for this.) Return the fruit and juice to the cooking liquor and weigh. It should weigh 2.3kg (5lb) (plus weight of pan) but if not, boil it further until it does. Add the sugar and stir until dissolved then boil rapidly until setting point is reached. Remove any scum from the surface and leave to stand for 5–10 minutes. Pour into warmed jars and cover immediately with waxed discs. Finish with cellophane tops when hot or cold. Label and store in a cool, dark place. Approx yield : 4.5kg (10lb).

Note It is not necessary to weigh the pan if you test the cooked fruit for pectin content (see p 106) before adding the sugar. This method can also be used for other fruit marmalades and is especially good for using frozen whole fruit.

Orange Jelly Marmalade

Ingredients

900g (2lb) Seville oranges
2.6l (4½pt) water
Juice of 2 large lemons
1.4kg (3lb) sugar

To make sure of a good set this marmalade must be tested for pectin content (see p 106) before adding the sugar.

Scrub the oranges and dry and then pare off the rind free of any of the white pith. Shred this peel very finely and put into a pan with 600ml (1pt) water. Bring to the boil, cover and simmer for about 1½ hours or until very tender. Meanwhile roughly chop up the remaining fruit including pith etc and put into a pan with 1.4l (2½pt) water and the lemon juice. Bring to the boil and simmer in a covered pan for about 2 hours until really soft and pulpy. Strain the orange shreds and add the liquid to the cooked pulp. Strain this pulp through a jelly bag for about 15 minutes into a bowl, without squeezing it. Return the pulp to the pan with the remaining water and simmer for a further 20 minutes. Strain the pulp again until it stops dripping and then mix it with the first extract. Test the extract for pectin and if it doesn't clot, boil it rapidly to reduce a little and retest. Add the sugar, stirring until dissolved, then add the orange shreds. Boil rapidly until setting point is reached, 105°C (221°F). Remove any scum from the surface and leave to stand for 15 minutes before pouring into warmed jars. Cover at once with waxed discs and finish with cellophane tops when hot or cold. Do not move or tilt the jars until set. Label and store in a cool, dark place. Approx yield: 2.3kg (5lb).

Ginger Marmalade

Ingredients

3 Seville oranges
1.4l (2½pt) water
675g (1½lb) cooking apples
1.5kg (3¼lb) sugar
100g (4oz) preserved ginger, finely chopped
10ml (2 level tsp) ground ginger

Wash the oranges thoroughly then remove the peel. Shred this peel finely and put into a pan. Chop up the flesh separating the tough membranes and pips and tie these in a muslin bag. Add the flesh, juice and muslin bag to the pan with the water and bring to the boil. Simmer for about 1½ hours or until the contents of the pan are reduced by half and the peel is very soft. Remove the muslin bag squeezing out all the juice. Meanwhile peel, core and chop the apples roughly and put into a pan with 45–60ml (3–4tbsp) water. Simmer gently until well pulped then stir into the cooked and reduced orange mixture with the sugar, chopped and ground ginger. When the sugar has dissolved, boil rapidly until setting point is reached, 105°C (221°F). Remove any scum from the surface and leave to stand for 15 minutes before pouring into warmed jars. Cover with waxed discs immediately and with cellophane covers when hot or cold. Label and store in a cool, dark place. Approx yield: 2.3kg (5lb).

Bottling

The success or failure of home bottling depends largely on efficient sterilization. The object of preserving fruits in bottles is to kill the yeasts and moulds already present in the cells on the surface of the fruits and to prevent them and others spreading into the container which would cause fermentation and eventually rotting in the jars. This is done by heating the fruit to sterilize and inactivate the enzymes present and then sealing whilst hot.

Bottling Jars and Covers

These are wide-necked glass jars with either glass caps or metal discs which are secured by screw bands or clips. A new rubber ring or metal disc fitted with a special seal should be used each time for bottling, but the jars can be used many times provided they are clean and sound. Jars are widely available in sizes ranging from 450g (1 lb) up to 1.8kg (4 lb), as are the replacement tops. A check of the soundness of bottles must be made before starting. To do this, fill the jar with water, put on the lid, then turn jar upside down and leave for 10 minutes. If there is a leak, it will then be apparent. Wash all jars thoroughly in hot soapy water, rinse out but do not dry for the fruit slips more easily into a wet jar.

What Can I Bottle?

Almost any type of fruit can be bottled provided you follow the general rules for preparing and processing. The fruit used must be fresh and sound, clean (wash if dirty or gritty) and just ripe.

Do not use overripe fruit for it tends to ferment more easily. Also grade fruits into sizes for each bottle and use a bottle of the appropriate size.

Preparation of Fruits for Bottling

Apples

(**slices**) Peel, core and slice or cut into rings. During preparation prevent discolouration by immersing in a brine solution (10ml/2 level tsp salt to 1.1l/2pt cold water). Rinse quickly in cold water before packing into jars.

Apples

(**solid pack**) Prepare as above for slices then blanch in boiling water for $1\frac{1}{2}$–3 minutes until the fruit is pliable and just tender. Drain and pack tightly into jars.

Apricots

(**whole**) Remove stalks and rinse in cold water. Or cut fruit in half carefully by twisting in half and removing the stone. Pack quickly before cut surfaces begin to discolour. Some stones can be cracked and the kernels added to the jar.

Blackberries

Discard any unsound fruit, stalks and leaves, and wash.

Blackberries with Apples

Prepare the apples as for solid pack then mix with the washed blackberries and pack into jars.

Blackcurrants and Redcurrants

Pick over carefully, remove stalks and wash.

Cherries

(**whole**) Remove stalks and wash fruit. (**stoned**) Remove stones with a cherry stoner or small knife collecting any juice to add to the fruit. To improve the colour and flavour of black or white cherries add 5ml (1 level tsp) citric acid to each 2.3l (4pt) syrup.

Damsons

Remove stalks and wash.

Figs

Remove stems, peel if liked. Add 2.5ml ($\frac{1}{2}$ level tsp) citric acid to each 600ml (1pt) syrup used to help the figs keep well. Pack with an equal weight of syrup.

Gooseberries

Use small green fruit for pies and the larger ones for stewed fruit. Top and tail, taking a small slice from each end of the fruit or prick the skins well to prevent shrivelling when preserved in syrup.

Peaches

Dip in boiling water for $\frac{1}{2}$ minute then plunge into cold water; peel off the skins. Leave whole or cut in halves and remove the stones as for apricots.

Pears

(**cooking**) Not the best fruit for bottling as they are very hard, but they can be prepared as for dessert pears and then stewed gently in syrup—100–175g (4–6oz) sugar to 600ml (1pt) water—until tender. Pack into jars.

Pears

(**dessert**) Peel, halve and core

carefully using a teaspoon. During preparation put into a brine solution using 10ml (2 level tsp) salt and 7.5ml (1$\frac{1}{2}$ level tsp) citric acid to each 1.1l (2pt) water. Rinse in cold water before packing.

Plums and Gages

(**whole**) Remove stalks and wash. (**halved**) Only possible with free-stone varieties. Make a cut round the fruit, twist in half and remove stone. Crack some stones and add the kernels to the jars. Pack quickly to prevent discolouration.

Quinces

Prepare as for cooking pears and preserve in small jars for they are usually only used in small quantities and mixed with other fruit.

Raspberries and Loganberries

Hull, pick over carefully and do not wash unless absolutely essential.

Rhubarb

Use thick stalks for made up dishes and the tender young stalks to serve as stewed fruit. Cut into 2.5–5cm (1–2in) lengths and pack carefully into jars. It is easier to pack if soaked overnight in hot syrup to soften the fruit. Use the syrup for topping up.

Strawberries

These do not really bottle well but can be done by soaking overnight in the syrup. Then pack drained fruit into jars. Boil syrup until reduced to its original amount before adding to the jars.

Tomatoes

See p 134 for method and bottling instructions.

Bottling

Packing the Fruit

Pack into jars (with inside of jar wet) in layers using a long-handled packing spoon or the handle of a wooden spoon. It must be packed tightly but without bruising or damaging the fruit. Some large fruits need to be halved, sliced or cut into rings. The tighter packed and fuller the jar, the less risk there is of the fruit rising after the sterilizing process, which can cause some shrinkage.

Syrup

Fruit may be preserved in syrup or water, but syrup usually gives a better flavour and colour to the fruit and keeps it better after long storage, but it does cause the fruit to rise in the jars. The strength of syrup used can vary but 225g (8oz) sugar to 600ml (1pt) water is the usual strength although for tightly packed fruits the syrup should be heavier, ie 275–300g (10–11oz) per 600ml (1pt). Use granulated or loaf sugar and dissolve it in half the water, then bring to the boil for 1 minute, remove from the heat, add the remaining water and leave to cool. This saves time in cooling syrup for use with the slow water bath method of sterilizing using a thermometer (see later. Use hot (not boiling) syrup for the quick water bath method and boiling syrup for oven methods and pressure cookers.

When to add the syrup depends on which method of sterilizing is used, so see separate methods, but when jars are full, in all methods give the bottles a quick jerk to free as many air bubbles as possible before sealing down.

Sterilizing

There are several ways of sterilizing the bottles but the two most often used are the water bath method and the oven method (see pp 130 and 132). A pressure cooker can also be used (see p 134).

Checking for Seal

After processing the bottles, it is important to test for an airtight seal. To do this remove the screw band or clip and try to lift the jar by the cap or disc. If it holds firm then there is a good seal but if it comes off there may be a flaw in the rim of the jar or cover. If several fail to seal it is more likely to be a fault in the sterilizing process. The fruit can be reprocessed but it will lose a lot of its quality so is probably best used up quickly.

The Water Bath Method (Slow) of Sterilizing

This method of sterilizing is the more accurate way but it does require a large pan (ie an old zinc bath or bucket or a very large saucepan) which is about 5cm (2in) deeper than the tops of the bottles, a thermometer (a sugar one will do), bottling tongs (or wooden washing tongs) to remove the bottles quickly from the water bath, and a false bottom for the water bath which can be a metal grid, wooden trellis, wad of newspapers or folded cloths.

1 Fill up the fruit filled jars with cold syrup and put the metal discs and screw bands in place (or the rubber bands and glass discs) and then turn the screw bands back a quarter turn.

2 Put the jars in the water bath on the hob and cover completely with cold water (or at least up to the necks if

complete submersion is impossible).

3 Heat the water gently until it reaches 54 °C (130 °F) in one hour, checking the temperature regularly with the thermometer then continue heating to reach the processing temperature as suggested on the chart, taking about half an hour and checking the temperature regularly.

4 Maintain this temperature for the time stated on the chart.

5 Remove the jars carefully with the tongs and stand on a wooden surface or a thick pad of newspapers.

6 Tighten the screw bands immediately.

The quick water bath method can be used if you do not have a thermometer. Fill the packed jars with hot (but not boiling) syrup. Cover as for the slow water bath method and put into a bath of warm water. Bring the water to simmering point in 25–30 minutes and keep at simmering point for the time stated on the chart.

Note Soft and stone fruits can be bottled as a pulp to make pies, sauces, ice cream, etc. Stew in the minimum of water until only just cooked. At this stage the fruit can be liquidized and/or sieved if liked. Pour the boiling pulp into hot jars and put on the covers as above. Immerse in a pan of hot water up to the necks and bring the water up to boiling point. Keep boiling for 5 minutes, then remove the jars and screw down immediately. Cool, label and store.

Sterilization Times for the Water Bath Method (as suggested by the Long Ashton Research Station)

Type of Fruit	Slow Method	Quick Method
Soft fruit (normal pack) : blackberries, currants, loganberries, mulberries, raspberries, gooseberries and rhubarb for made-up dishes, apples (sliced)	Raise from cold in 90 minutes and maintain as below 74 °C (165 °F) for 10 minutes	Raise from warm 38°C (100°F), to simmering 88°C (190°F) in 25–30 minutes and maintain as below For 2 minutes
Soft fruit (tight pack) : as above, including gooseberries and rhubarb to serve as stewed fruit Stone fruit (whole) : Apricots, cherries, damsons, gages and plums	82°C (180°F) for 15 minutes	For 10 minutes
Apples (solid pack), apricots (halved), nectarines, peaches pineapple, plums (halved)	82°C (180°F) for 15 minutes	For 20 minutes
Figs, pears	88°C (190°F) for 30 minutes	For 40 minutes

Bottling

The Oven Method of Sterilizing

The advantage of the oven method of sterilizing is that jars can be processed one at a time and no special equipment is required. It isn't quite so exact as the water bath method because the temperature throughout the oven doesn't stay constant all the time and it is easier to overcook the fruit. Use only one central shelf in the oven and stand the bottles far enough apart to allow the heat to circulate freely. Tall jars are not suitable for this method. There is a wet pack and dry pack method for sterilizing in the oven.

Wet Pack

This method avoids the difficulty of filling hot jars with boiling syrup. Heat the oven to 150 °C (300 °F) mark 2. Pack the warmed jars with fruit then fill with boiling syrup or water to within 2.5cm (1in) of the top. Put on the rubber rings and glass caps or metal discs but not the clips or screw bands. Stand the filled jars on a baking sheet padded with newspaper (to catch any liquid that boils over) leaving 5cm (2in) between each jar. Place in the centre of the oven and process for the time stated on the chart below. Remove the jars one by one to a wooden surface or wad of newspaper and put on clips or screw bands—screwing the bands as tightly as possible. Leave until quite cold then test for airtightness. Label and store.

Dry Pack

Heat the oven to 130 °C (250 °F) mark $\frac{1}{2}$. Pack the prepared fruit into bottles but do not add any liquid. Put on the caps but *not* the rubber rings, metal discs with rims, screw bands or clips. Stand the jars on a newspaper lined baking sheet with 5cm (2in) between each one. Put into the centre of the oven and process for the time stated on the chart. Remove the jars one at a time from the oven to a wooden surface and fill up each bottle with fruit from an extra bottle if the contents have shrunk at all. Fill up immediately with boiling syrup and give each bottle a good jerk to dispel the air bubbles ; then cover with the rubber bands, caps or metal discs and secure with clips or put on the screw bands tightly. Leave to get cold and test for air-tightness. The success of this method depends on filling the jars and sealing them as quickly as possible after being taken from the oven. (This dry pack method is not recommended for fruits which discolour in the air, eg apples, pears and peaches.)

Note With both oven methods, the time required varies with the different types of fruit, tightness of the pack in the bottle and the total load in the oven at one time. The load is calculated according to the total capacity of the jars.

Processing Times for Oven Methods (as recommended by the Long Ashton Research Station)

Type of Fruit	Wet Pack		Dry Pack	
	Pre-heat oven to 150°C (300° F) mark 2. Process time varies with quantity in oven, as shown below		Pre-heat oven to 130°C (250°F) mark ½. Process time varies with quantity in oven, as shown below	
	Quantity	Time in minutes	Quantity	Time in minutes
Soft fruit (normal Pack): blackberries, currants, loganberries, raspberries, gooseberries and rhubarb (for made-up dishes)	450g–1.8kg (1–4lb)	30–40	450g–1.8kg (1–4lb)	45–55
	2–4.5kg (4½–10lb)	45–60	2–4.5kg (4½–10lb)	60–75
Apples (sliced)	450g–1.8kg (1–4lb)	30–40	Not recommended	
	2–4.5kg (4½–10lb)	45–60		
Soft fruit (tight packs): as above including gooseberries and rhubarb for stewed fruit	450g–1.8kg (1–4lb)	40–50	450g–1.8kg (1–4lb)	55–70
	2–4.5kg (4½–10lb)	55–70	2–4.5kg (4½–10lb)	75–90
Stone fruit (dark whole): cherries, plums, damsons	As soft fruit (tight pack)		As soft fruit (tight pack)	
Stone fruit (light whole): apricots, cherries, gages, plums	As above		Not recommended	
Apples (solid pack), apricots (halved), nectarines, peaches, plums (halved), strawberries (soaked)	450g–1.8kg (1–4lb)	50–60	Not recommended	
	2–4.5kg (4½–10lb)	65–80		
Figs	450g–1.8kg (1–4lb)	60–70	450g–1.8kg (1–4lb)	80–100
	2–4.5kg (4½–10lb)	75–90	2–4.5kg (4½–10lb)	105–125
Pears	As figs		Not recommended	

Bottling

Bottling Tomatoes

There are three different methods of bottling tomatoes :

Whole unpeeled tomatoes (recommended for oven sterilizing). Use small and medium ripe but firm fruit, uniform in size. Remove stalks, wash or wipe and pack into jars. Fill up with a brine of 10ml (2 level tsp) salt to each 1.1l (2pt) water.

Solid pack (no water added). Use any sized firm fruit and peel after dipping first into boiling water for ½ minute then into cold water. Leave small fruit whole, but halve or quarter larger fruit. Pack really tightly with no air spaces making it impossible to add water. To improve the flavour sprinkle about 5ml (1 level tsp) salt and 2.5ml (½ level tsp) sugar over the fruit to fill a 450g (1lb) jar.

In their own juice. Peel tomatoes as for solid pack and pack tightly into jars. Stew a few tomatoes in a covered pan with 5ml (1 level tsp) salt to each 900g (2lb) fruit, strain the juice and use to fill up the jars.

With pressure cooker sterilizing for whole or halved tomatoes in brine, process the tomatoes for 5 minutes at low (2.25kg/5lb) pressure following pressure cooker method on p 135.

Pressure Cooker Method

This is a much shorter form of processing with an exact temperature control. The cooker must have a 'low'

Processing Chart for Tomatoes

	Oven Method		Water Bath Method	
	Wet Pack Pre-heat oven to 150°C (300°F) mark 2, process as below	Dry Pack Pre-heat oven to 130°C (250°F) mark ½, process as below	Slow Method Raise from cold in 90 minutes and maintain as below	Quick Method Raise from warm 38°C (100°F) to simmering 88°C (190°F) in 25–30 minutes and maintain for :
Whole tomatoes	450g–1.8kg (1–4lb) for 60–70 minutes 2–4.5kg (4½–10lb) for 75–90 minutes	450g–1.8kg (1–4lb) for 80–100 minutes 2–4.5kg (4½–10lb) for 105–125 minutes	88°C (190°F) for 30 minutes	40 minutes
Solid pack tomatoes (halved or quartered)	450g–1.8kg (1–4lb) for 70–80 minutes 2–4.5kg (4½–10lb) for 85–100 minutes	Not recommended for solid packs	88°C (190°F) for 40 minutes	50 minutes

2.25kg (5lb) pressure control and unless it has a domed lid, only the 450g (1lb) jars will fit in.

Prepare the fruit as for ordinary bottling taking note of the additional information on the chart below. Pack the fruit into clean warm jars up to the top and cover with boiling syrup or water to within 2.5cm (1in) of the top of the bottles. Position the rubber bands and caps or metal discs and add clips or put on screw bands tightly and then give a quarter turn back. Heat the jars gently by standing in a bowl or pan of boiling water. Put the rack in the bottom of the pressure cooker and add 900ml (1½pt) water (with 15ml [1tbsp] vinegar to prevent discolouration). Bring to the boil, pack the bottles into the cooker with newspaper between each to prevent them touching and put on the lid without the weight. Heat until steam comes from the vent then put on the low (2.25kg/5lb) pressure control and bring to pressure on a low heat. Reduce the heat and maintain for the time given in the chart. It is important to keep the pressure constant for any change will cause liquid to be lost from the jars and this may cause under processing. Remove the pressure cooker from the heat and leave to cool and reduce the pressure for 10 minutes at room temperature, before removing the lid. (This time completes the processing.)

Take out the jars and tighten screw bands. Leave to cool, label and store.

Pressure Cooker Method

Type of Fruit	Processing time in minutes at 'low' 2.25kg (5lb) pressure
Apples (quartered) ; apricots and plums (whole), blackberries, loganberries, raspberries, cherries, currants, damsons, gooseberries, rhubarb (in 5cm (2in) lengths)	1 minute
Plums and apricots (halved and stoned)	3 minutes
Pears (eating and cooking) : hard cooking pears can be pressure cooked for 3–5 minutes before packing in jars	5 minutes
Strawberries	Not recommended
Soft fruit (solid pack) : Put the fruit in a large bowl, cover with boiling syrup, (175g (6oz) sugar to 600ml (1pt) water) and leave overnight. Drain, pack and cover with same syrup. Process as usual	3 minutes
Pulped fruit (eg apples) : Prepare as for stewing. Pressure cook with 150ml (¼pt) water at high, 6.75kg (15lb) pressure for 2–3 minutes, then sieve. Fill jars whilst hot and process	1 minute

EASY VEGETABLE GROWING

Martyn T Hall

Spade Work

To grow vegetables successfully a gardener needs to understand his soil. Soil varies widely in its texture—even in the same garden or allotment there can be variations. Soils may be described as light, medium or heavy. When gardeners talk of 'a good loam' they are describing a good, average soil.

A light soil is one where sand particles predominate. Light soils are easy to work but dry out quickly and need plenty of humus. A medium loam is one where the sand and clay particles are in roughly equal proportions. This type of soil will grow almost anything and blessed is the gardener who has it ! A heavy soil is one which has a preponderance of clay. Clay soils are more difficult to work but do not dry out quickly. The best time to break down a clay soil is when the soil is beginning to dry out after reasonable rainfall. Do not trample a clay soil when it is wet or it will set like concrete.

'Topsoil' is the upper, fertile layer of soil ; 'subsoil' is the layer beneath the topsoil and is usually low in fertility. The fertility of subsoils can be increased by double-digging, manuring and liming, but unless you are growing vegetables for exhibition, this deep cultivation is not necessary. It is enough to work the soil to the depth of the spade.

Single digging is the turning over of the soil to a spade's depth. This should be done in autumn or winter, leaving the clods of earth where they fall. Frosts, which cause contraction and expansion of the soil, will break it down for spring sowings.

Clay soils can be improved by winter ridging. To make a ridge, mark out a

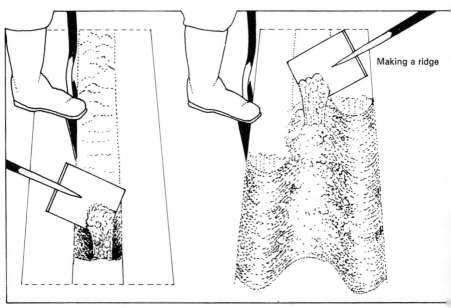

Making a ridge

strip three spadefuls wide. Dig the centre spit (spadeful) over itself, then turn the outer spits over the centre one. This exposes a larger area of soil to the winter weather. In the spring rake the ridges down again.

Before any vegetables are sown, measure up the plot and then make out a crop plan to fit the available space. Keep a copy of this list for future reference. Most vegetables benefit from a change of soil, and it will prevent the build-up of pests and diseases. This is known as crop rotation. A simple form of a three-year crop rotation, dividing the plot into three parts, is given here:

	Part A	Part B	Part C
1st yr	Greens	Potatoes	Other crops
2nd yr	Potatoes	Other crops	Greens
3rd yr	Other crops	Greens	Potatoes

Exceptions to this rule of crop rotation are asparagus and rhubarb which, once planted, should remain there to mature for many years. These are often sited across one end of the plot. As a vegetable plot has to be tailored to the needs of the individual family, each gardener must work out his own system of crop rotation.

Consideration should also be given to the possible limitations of the plot. In a shallow soil, for example, it would be pointless to sow long beetroot, long carrots, or the largest parsnips. Globe beetroot, shorthorn carrots and half-long parsnips would be the varieties to choose. Similarly, if the plot is an exposed one, the tall broad beans and Brussels sprouts may suffer wind damage. In this case, the half-tall varieties of sprouts and the dwarf broad beans would be a better choice.

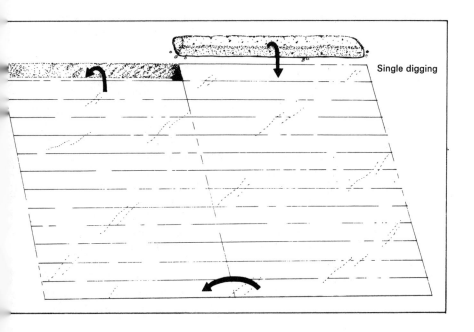

Single digging

Soil Fertility

The importance of building up and maintaining the fertility of the vegetable plot can never be stressed too much. In general, vegetables need a more fertile soil than flowers and some, such as onions and cauliflowers, are gross feeders and will not do their best in a poor soil.

Plants feed on the mineral salts in the soil and take them in by means of tiny root hairs. The essential plant foods are nitrogen, phosphates and potash. Nitrogen is necessary for growth and leaf formation ; phosphates increase root growth and assist ripening, and potash improves the general health and vigour of the plant by promoting root activity. There are other chemicals which are needed only in minute quantities and which are known as 'trace elements'. Iron and boron are two of these. Trace elements are usually present in any good garden soil and do not normally require special attention.

There are two ways of supplying the essential plant foods to the soil. One is by the application of bulky organic manures, such as farmyard and stable manures, which are dug into the soil during autumn and winter. Once in the soil, they are attacked by soil bacteria which break up the vegetable wastes and reduce them to a brown, friable medium called humus. Humus improves the soil structure, releases plant foods slowly, and acts like a sponge to retain moisture.

The other method is to use inorganic manures (fertilizers). These are man-made compounds of mineral salts, scientifically produced and offered in powdered or granular form. They are generally used as 'top dressings' (ie they are sprinkled around the plants and hoed in). Rain washes them down to the roots of the plants. They act quickly but need to be used with care.

The drawback of using fertilizers is that they neither make humus nor improve the soil structure. Used continuously in a soil that is short of humus they tend to leave the soil sticky and intractable. The essential point to keep in mind is that while fertilizers can supplement organic manuring, they cannot replace it.

To keep the soil fertile, some form of organic manuring is essential. Unfortunately, farmyard manure is becoming more difficult to obtain, so you may have to look round for other sources of supply. Horse manure from riding stables, spent mushroom compost, spent hops from breweries, deep litter from poultry houses, seaweed, and sewage are some alternatives. Many local authorities now process their sewage and offer it in an acceptable form.

Every gardener has a good source of humus-making material right on his doorstep. Any organic rubbish forked into a heap will rot down to make compost. Good compost is high on the list of organic manures and is quickly incorporated in the soil.

Kitchen waste, leaves of brassicas and lettuces, straw, green haulms (stems or stalks), weeds (but not the roots of perennial weeds), leaves and lawn mowings can all be used to make compost. The only items which need to be excluded are hardwood hedge-

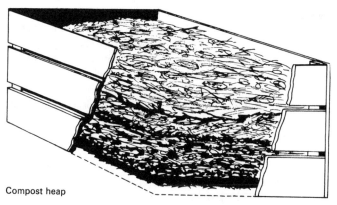

Compost heap

cuttings and green haulms suspected of carrying disease.

To make good compost, a bin of some kind is needed. Proprietary bins are available, but a simple container can be made quite easily by using strong wire netting nailed to corner posts. An alternative to this would be to nail boards to the corner posts. A little gap should then be left between the boards to admit air to the heap, and it would be an advantage if one end could be made detachable so that the contents could be shovelled out more easily. A bin about 122cm × 90cm (4ft × 3ft) is a useful size.

Build up the heap with 15cm (6in) layers of material, mixed for preference, and cover each layer with a sprinkling of a proprietary compost activator, or a dusting of hydrated lime. When the heap is 90–122cm (3–4ft) in height, finish it off with a cap of soil and then leave it to rot down. This process may be completed in as little as three months in spring and summer ; a winter heap takes longer. Where small quantities of animal manures can be obtained, such as poultry or rabbit droppings, it is a good plan to use a layer of these between each layer of greenstuff.

Another method of making humus is by green manuring. This is the practice of growing a green crop especially for digging in, and rape or mustard are the plants most commonly used for this purpose. Ground which becomes vacant during the summer, and which is not needed again immediately, can be sown broadcast with rape or mustard. The plants should be dug in just as they are coming into flower.

Liquid manuring is another method of feeding plants. This should be applied when the soil is damp, at about fortnightly intervals. Proprietary liquid manures can be bought from garden centres or seedsmen. If an old tub is available, a supply can be made by putting a few forkfuls of manure in a hessian sack and suspending it in a tubful of water. Sheep manure is particularly good for this purpose. The 'brew' should be diluted until it is about the consistency and colour of weak tea. Keep the tub covered and make sure that children cannot get into it.

Another method of feeding plants can be effected through their leaves with a proprietary foliar feed, given through a sprayer or a watering-can. It is of special value for well foliated crops.

Basic Tools

The basic tools needed for the cultivation of a vegetable plot may be listed as follows : a spade, fork, rake, hoe, cultivator, dibber, trowel, garden-line and measuring-stick. Stainless steel tools are lighter to use and do not require cleaning but cost more.

Spades come in several sizes. One with a blade about 28cm (11in) long and 20cm (8in) wide is a good, average size.

The digging fork should have four square tines (prongs). There are also forks with flat tines, which are useful for lifting potatoes, as fewer tubers will slip through the prongs. It is not necessary to have both, and if a choice has to be made, the digging fork should be chosen, as this is a more general-purpose fork.

Many of the rakes offered in shops are more suitable for flower borders than the vegetable plot. Soil that is raked down too finely produces more weeds. It is worth looking for a strong rake with a head about 38cm (15in) wide, and teeth about 5cm (2in) apart.

There are several types of hoes. In order to use the draw hoe, it should be extended and then pulled through the soil towards the user ; a Dutch hoe has the reverse action, as the blade is pushed away from the user. A good Dutch hoe is a useful tool, especially if it is the modern kind with a two-edged, serrated blade, but the draw hoe has a wider scope as it can be used for earthing-up and drawing seed drills. (The corner of the hoe is used for this, close up against the garden-line.) The

little onion hoe is also a good buy as it can be used close to the rows. This cuts down hand-weeding.

The cultivator is used for breaking down the soil in spring and also for aerating the soil between rows of plants. It is pulled through the soil towards the user who has to walk backwards. Some cultivators have three spoonlike prongs ; some have five, and there is a more elaborate one with prongs which can be adjusted or removed altogether.

The dibber and trowel perform similar functions. A dibber has a short handle and a pointed end with a steel tip. It comes into its own when making holes for brassicas and leeks. Some gardeners prefer to use a trowel, however, even for leeks, and for moving plants with a good soil ball the trowel is the better tool.

Money spent on a good garden-line is never wasted as a home-made line made from odd pieces of string is never satisfactory. But do take the line indoors when it is not in use—it will last twice as long.

A good measuring-stick can be made quite cheaply at home from a length of lath. A piece 90cm (36in) in length, marked off at 15cm (6in) intervals, is a handy size.

Good tools are worth looking after. Keeping them clean and rubbing them over with an oily rag, when they are not in use, doesn't take long, but prolongs their life and makes all the difference when you next use them.

You will need to add a watering-can or hose to the above list. An old bucket costs nothing and is always useful. A wheelbarrow has many uses and is a good investment.

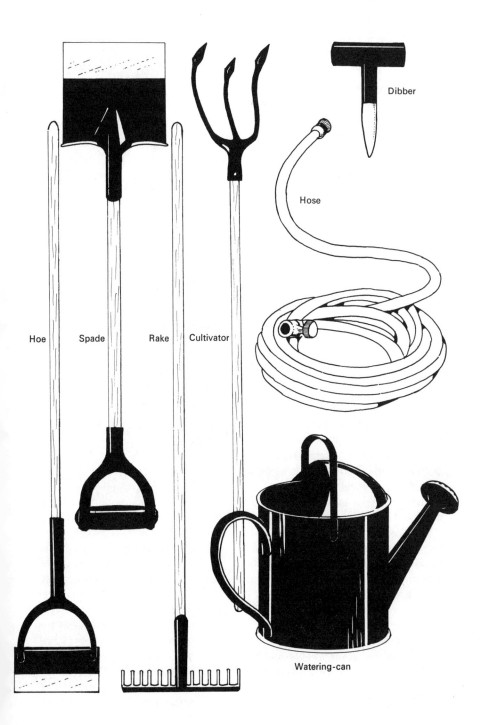

Dibber

Hose

Hoe Spade Rake Cultivator

Watering-can

143

Asparagus

Although asparagus may be considered by some people to be a luxury vegetable rather than a basic one, its cultivation is not as difficult as many people suppose. The main disadvantage of growing asparagus is that it does take up quite a lot of room and will need to occupy that room permanently—a good asparagus bed can crop for twenty years, or more.

The plants can be raised from seeds which are sown in April in drills 2cm (1in) deep and 30cm(12in) apart. The seedlings should be thinned to stand 30cm (12in) apart. In their second season it will be possible to select the best plants for the permanent bed. This is the slowest method; it is more usual to buy two-year-old plants from seedsmen or nurserymen.

Asparagus plants are either male or female. The female plants bear berries; the males do not. It is generally accepted that male plants give a higher yield, but as male and female plants are produced in about equal numbers, some females usually have to be included to make up the required number.

Whether the plants are raised at home or bought in, no planting should be done until the site has been thoroughly prepared. It is worth doing the initial preparation well as there will not be another opportunity. All perennial weeds must be forked out and eliminated. Dig in as much compost or manure as you can spare so that the plants have a good start. In light or medium soils it is worth double-digging the chosen strip

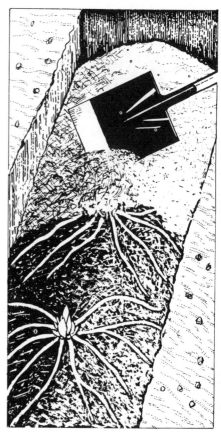

Planting asparagus

which sould be in a sunny, open position. On heavy soils, it is a good plan to make a raised bed with an extra 25–30cm (10–12in) of good topsoil. The site preparation should be completed by February so that the soil has time to settle before planting. A strip 2m (6ft) wide will take two rows 75cm (30in) apart.

To plant asparagus, take out a trench 30cm (12in) wide and 30cm (12in) deep. Put back enough soil in the trench to form a ridge 23cm (9in) high. Sit the plants on this ridge, with the spidery roots down each side of the

Cutting asparagus

middle of April to the middle of June. After this period sticks which appear should be allowed to grow on and form their feathery foliage. This builds up the crowns for the following season. Some twigs pushed in among the foliage, or string run from bamboo canes, will prevent the foliage from being blown down and broken off.

To maintain the bed in good condition, cut down the yellowing foliage each autumn and burn it ; clear the bed of weeds, and then put on an inch or two of good compost. In April top dress the bed with a nitrogenous fertilizer, or agricultural salt, at about 70g per sq m (2oz per sq yd).

The main pest to look out for is the asparagus beetle which appears in July and August. This damages the plants by attacking the young shoots and foliage. Derris or BHC, sprayed or dusted over the bed, will usually control it.

Another trouble which may be encountered is asparagus rust. This fungus covers the stems and foliage with a reddish dust which is followed by black pustules on the next season's growth. Dusting with flowers of sulphur is a good safeguard. If good hygiene is observed by clearing away and burning the dying foliage in autumn, rust should not be a serious problem.

Recommended varieties

Connover's Colossal, the most popular variety

Martha Washington, a more recent introduction that shows some resistance to asparagus rust

ridge, and allow 45cm (18in) between the plants. The crown of each plant, when the trench is filled in, will then be about 8cm (3in) below the soil surface. An important point to remember is that the roots of asparagus should never be allowed to dry out. Keep them covered until planting takes place, then cover them again immediately.

Sticks should not be cut from the bed the first season after planting. In the second year take only one or two sticks from each plant. By the third year the bed will be well established. Cutting takes place from about the

Broad Beans

The bean family is one of the most useful to the vegetable gardener and the broad bean, although not as popular as the runner, is very tasty, especially when served with parsley sauce. It is not demanding in its soil requirements and any good garden soil should grow broad beans.

The best broad beans come from a sowing made in November. Unfortunately, the modern broad bean seems to have lost some of the hardiness of its ancestors and, in most districts, protection in the form of cloches is necessary in the winter months. The other sowing period is from February to April.

There are two types of broad bean, the tall and the dwarf. For some reason the dwarf broad bean has not yet achieved the popularity it deserves. It is especially valuable in gardens which suffer wind damage. The plants branch naturally to give several stems and they crop well.

The tall varieties can be divided into two groups : the longpods and the Windsors. The Windsors are a little shorter in the pod with slightly larger beans. Some people think that the Windsors have a better flavour.

There are two ways of sowing the tall beans. One method, if more than two rows are needed, is to sow them in drills 5cm (2in) deep, with 45cm (18in) between the rows and 20cm (8in) between the beans. The other, and the more usual method, is to sow a double row with a 25cm (10in) gap. To fill up possible spaces, always sow a few extra seeds at one end of the

Dwarf beans

146

rows. For the dwarf varieties allow 30cm (12in) between the seeds and 38cm (15in) between the rows.

It is advisable to stake the tall varieties. This can be done quite easily by pushing bamboo canes into the soil at intervals and then running stout string or garden wire from cane to cane. Plants at the ends of the rows are the most vulnerable. Tie these individually to the encircling string.

Tall beans

When the first pods have set and are forming, pinch out the growing tip of each plant. This turns the plant's energy into the production of pods and also prevents the blackfly from congregating in the soft tip, a favourite haunt.

Picking should begin when the seeds are about as big as a finger-nail. At this stage they are delicious. It is a mistake to leave them too long because once the pods are streaked with black, the seeds have begun to ripen and the skins toughen. Nowadays, as broad beans freeze well, there is no reason why any part of the crop should not be picked at its best.

Blackfly is the most serious menace to broad beans. However, if the plants are sprayed with derris or malathion at the first sign of this pest, or even earlier as a precautionary measure, no real harm should ensue.

Recommended varieties

Windsor : Green Windsor and White
 Windsor are the standard varieties
Longpod : Colossal, Bunyard's
 Exhibition. Aquadulce for autumn
 sowing
Dwarf : The Sutton

Blackfly

French and Haricot Beans

There are two types of French bean, the climbing and the dwarf; of the two, the dwarf bean is more common. It is not as hardy as the broad bean and should not appear above ground while there is any likelihood of frost. This means that, except in milder areas, it should not be sown outdoors before the middle of May.

Although not quite as vigorous as the runner bean, the climbing French bean will still reach a height of 1.5m (5ft) and some form of staking is essential. Tall sticks of brushwood, and pea or bean netting are two methods. Where there is a trellis, or a wire fence of the chain-link type, the beans can be sown about 5cm (2in) deep and 15cm (6in) apart, about 23cm (9in) from the foot of the wire or trellis.

The dwarf varieties are grown in rows 60cm (24in) apart with 15–20cm (6–8in) between the beans. Another way of growing them, if only two rows are needed, is to sow them in a double row, with the two rows 30cm (12in) apart. This is a good method if you wish to use cloches. Sowing under cloches can take place in the second half of April.

French beans are not demanding in their soil requirements and a soil that was manured for a previous crop will be suitable. A sunny, open position is best for them. Their main enemy is slugs, but slug pellets, put down as soon as the plants are breaking through the soil, will give adequate protection.

Although dwarf beans are supposed not to need staking, it is a good plan

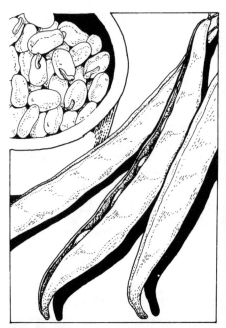

Haricot beans

to push in some twiggy sticks among them to keep them upright. If the plants fall over with the weight of the crop, some of the beans will be at soil level and may be attacked by slugs.

The pods of dwarf beans may be flat, like a smaller edition of the runner bean, or round like a pencil. Whatever form they take they should be gathered young and before the pods become lumpy with seeds. Pick the plants over two or three times each week. Cropping should continue for about six weeks. To prolong the season it is a good plan to make a second sowing in June.

Haricot beans are grown for the seeds, and the plants are left to form seeds from the beginning. There are certain varieties of dwarf beans which are suitable for this purpose, and their cultivation is the same as for dwarf beans.

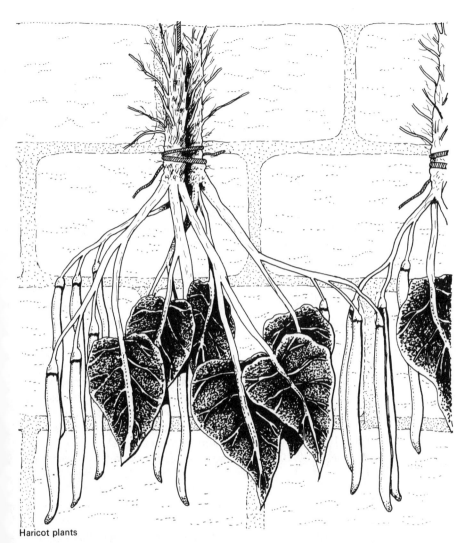

Haricot plants

When the seeds are ripe, the pods will be grey and dry. In a good summer they will often ripen on the plants. In cooler, showery weather, wait until the plants have turned yellow (about late September) then pull them up, tie them in bundles and hang them on a sunny wall to dry. The beans, when shelled out, can be stored in paper bags or in jars. To prevent any mould forming, leave the jars open and give them an occasional shake.

Recommended varieties

Climbing French : Earliest of All. The white seeds can be used as haricots
Dwarf French : Masterpiece, The Prince
Haricot : Comtesse de Chambord, white seeds ; Rembrandt

Runner Beans

The runner bean, like the French bean, is not hardy and cannot be sown outdoors until about the middle of May, or be planted out until early June. It likes a good soil with a moisture-holding root-run, and a sunny position. If you have manure or compost to spare for this crop, it should be dug in during the autumn and winter digging.

There are several ways of growing the runner bean and each has its advantages. The traditional way is to grow the plants up poles or canes

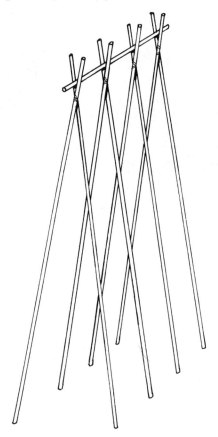

about 2.5m (8ft) long, set out in two rows 60cm (24in) apart, with 30cm (12in) between the poles. The butts should be let into the soil. The poles should be opposite each other and drawn together to cross at the top leaving a V about 20cm (8in) deep. More poles are laid in this V and the whole structure is then securely tied where the poles meet. It is worth making a good job of this as a rickety palisade may blow down in summer gales, and, if this happens, it is difficult to set it up again.

A moist root-run can be assured if a trench about 75cm (30in) wide and a spade's depth is opened out in the autumn or winter. Shovel out the loose soil and then break up the subsoil with a fork. At the bottom of the trench put a layer of newspapers and saturate them with water, then add a layer of manure or compost before filling in the trench.

Another method is to stand poles in a circle about 1–2m (3–6ft) in diameter. Sink the poles into the soil around the perimeter of the circle and then fasten them all together at the top. The advantages of this method are that the wigwams take up less room and, by not presenting an unbroken surface to the wind, are less likely to blow down.

If plants have been raised in boxes in a cold frame or greenhouse, put out one plant against each pole. Otherwise, sow one seed each side of the pole, about 5cm (2in) deep and pull one out if both grow. When the plants have climbed to the top of the poles, pinch out the growing points.

Yet another method is to grow the plants up a trellis or wire boundary fence. It does not matter if the fence is only about 1m (3ft) high. Choose a

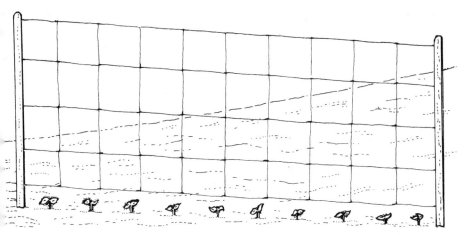

variety of medium height and let it climb the fence (as suggested for French beans). When the plants have reached the top of the fence, they will fall over on the other side and pods will form on both sides of the fence.

Runner beans may also be grown 'on the flat'. In this method the seeds are sown 5cm (2in) deep in drills 90cm (36in) apart, with the seeds 20cm (8in) apart. The plants will then grow together to form a continuous row. If the runners threaten to become entangled in the next row, pinch them back.

A development in recent years has been the introduction of the non-climbing runner bean which makes bushy plants about 45cm (18in) high. The original varieties in this field have been withdrawn because the stock has deteriorated, but other varieties are coming forward and it does seem that this type is here to stay. It is of particular value for getting an early crop under cloches.

The main pests to look out for are slugs and blackfly. Put down slug pellets when the plants are at the seedling stage, and spray with derris or malathion to control the blackfly. Never allow this pest to build up before taking counter measures—attack at the first sign of trouble.

Pick the beans regularly and strip off any older ones which may have been missed at an earlier picking. If seeds are allowed to form, the production of young beans will fall off considerably. If it is intended to save seeds for the next season, set aside a few plants for this purpose.

In hot, dry periods the flowers will sometimes fall off without setting. The cause of this is dryness at the roots, and the remedy is a thorough soaking of the root-run.

Recommended varieties

Achievement, Enorma, Prizewinner, these are all good varieties of long beans

Fry, a new white-seeded variety which has done well in dry summers

Kelvedon Marvel, of medium height, the best variety for growing on fences or along the ground

Beetroot

This is not a difficult root to grow and it will flourish in any good garden soil. Fresh manure is not advisable; a site that was well manured for the previous crop is a good choice. The roots may be long, globe-shaped, or cylindrical. The globe beetroot is by far the most popular.

Long beetroot should be sown in April in drills 2cm (1in) deep and 38cm (15in) apart. To grow long beetroot a good depth of fertile soil is needed—not one freshly manured or the roots may fork. Thin the plants to stand 15cm (6in) apart. Care should be taken when lifting long beet as, if the roots are damaged, they will bleed. Ease them with a fork before pulling them out.

Globe beetroot can be sown from

Globe

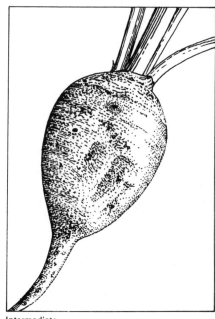

Intermediate

March to July. A March sowing will give tasty young roots for summer salads; a July sowing, provided that the summer is not too hot and dry, will give tender roots in late autumn. There is a tendency with early sowings for some of the roots to 'bolt', ie run up to seed. These roots are hard and woody in the centre and are no use for eating. This tendency is increased if there is any check to growth. Some of the newer varieties do show some resistance to this fault.

Sow globe beetroot in drills 2cm (1in) deep and 30cm (12in) apart, and sow thinly as each seed capsule can give several seedlings. Better and earlier roots can be pulled if some thinning is done. Thin to about 5cm (2in) when they start to show, then take out every other root as soon as it is big enough to use. For good results from July sowings, it is essential to thin

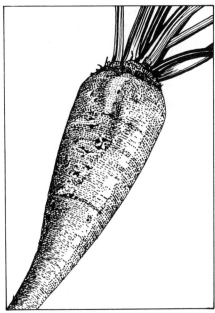
Long

attack the plants in the seedling stage and slugs can be a nuisance, especially in heavy soils. Black cotton, stretched over the seedlings as soon as they are through the soil, will keep the birds away.

Should the roots go brown and rotten inside it will indicate a deficiency of the trace element boron. The disease, which is not a common one, is known as heart-rot, and can be corrected by applying borax at 35g to 17sq m (1oz to 20sq yd).

Recommended varieties

Long beetroot : Cheltenham Green-top
Intermediate : Cylindra
Globe : Detroit, the standard globe ;
    Bolthardy, good for early sowings as
    it has some resistance to bolting

the plants to about 7cm (3in) as soon as they can be handled, as these sowings have less time in which to make good.

For use as a maincrop, globe beetroot should not be sown before the beginning of May. The intermediate or cylindrical varieties are often used as a maincrop because they give a bigger yield.

If at any time the plants do not seem to be making good progress, hoe in a dressing of agricultural salt at about 35g per metre (1oz per yard) run.

The roots can be stored during the winter months in boxes of sand or soil —a layer of beetroot, followed by a layer of soil, and so on until the box is full. For larger quantities make a little clamp in the garden, as described for potatoes (see p 181).

This vegetable is not troubled by many pests but sparrows will often

Brassicas

The brassica family is a very important one. In addition to the vegetables we describe loosely as 'greens'—cauliflowers, cabbages, etc—it includes radishes, turnips, kohl rabi and swedes.

The usual method of growing greens is to sow the seeds in a little nursery bed and then transplant them later. This saves valuable space as an early crop can be taken from the site reserved for greens. If, for example, early peas, lettuces or spinach are sown in rows 60cm (24in) apart, rows of Brussels sprouts can be planted between them.

Greens like a firm, fertile soil and the easiest way of achieving this is to dig in manure or compost during autumn or early winter. Leave the ground rough and then break it down in the spring.

The site for the nursery bed should be an open, sunny one, with some shelter from cold winds if possible. Rake the soil down finely, then take out shallow drills and sow the seeds thinly. Label each variety as it is sown. When the seedlings are large enough to handle, thin them to stand about 2cm (1in) apart. This thinning is often neglected but it does pay as it gives straighter and stronger plants.

When the plants are about 15cm (6in) high they can be moved to their final positions. Dull, showery weather

Transplanting

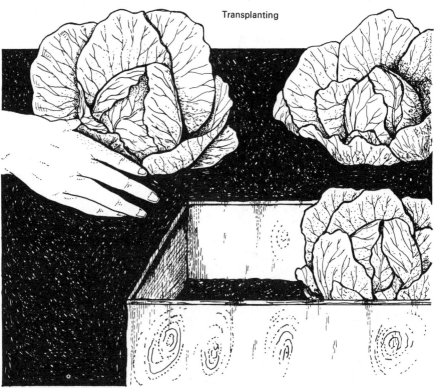

is the best time for transplanting, but unfortunately this cannot be arranged to order ! If the weather is dry, water the seed-bed well a few hours before the plants are moved so that some soil goes with them. Dig the holes to receive the plants, then fill them with water and let it drain away before the plants are put in. Plant them firmly with a trowel or dibber, then water them again.

The pests most likely to prove troublesome are the caterpillars of the cabbage-white butterfly, and the cabbage root-fly. Spraying or dusting with derris will account for the caterpillars ; for the cabbage root-fly it is vital to dust the seed drills with calomel dust and sprinkle a little of it into each planting hole. This should always be done to deter the fly from laying her eggs against the plant stem. The grubs, which hatch out from the eggs, attack the stem below ground and also the roots. The first sign of trouble is plants which wilt badly in bright sunlight. In a bad attack the plants collapse and die. Nothing can be done at the maggot stage except to pull up and burn the affected plants.

The most serious disease of the brassicas is club root, or 'finger and toe' as it is called in some districts. This causes swollen and twisted roots and inhibits growth. There is no cure but it can be controlled by using lime and calomel dust. The lime should be spread on the soil surface in January or February at 70g per sq m (2oz per sq yd). Where the soil has not been limed for some years this amount can be doubled. It helps to prevent a build-up of the fungus if a good system of crop rotation is practised, and greens are not grown on the same site too often.

Club root   Root-fly

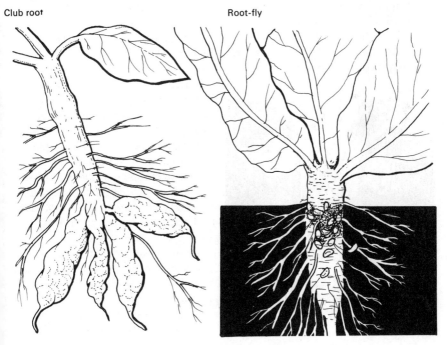

Brassicas
Brussels Sprouts

Because of its long period of cropping, the Brussels sprout ranks high among the brassicas. By using an early and late variety, sprouts may be picked throughout the autumn and winter. Moreover, as they freeze so well you need never be caught out by a glut and you may be able to freeze some for year-round use.

The seeds should be sown in the nursery bed in the second half of March, or early in April. An earlier start can be made if a cold frame or cloches are available. Sow the seeds directly into the frame bed or in boxes 10–15cm (4–6in) deep. An ordinary seed tray is not deep enough to give good root development.

The advice given in the section on pages 154–55 regarding the plants' need for a firm, fertile soil applies particularly to Brussels sprouts. Loose soil is one of the reasons why

Blown sprouts

sprouts 'blow'—ie develop loose rosettes of leaves instead of tight buttons. The advice about pests given on pages 154–55 also holds good.

When planting out, a minimum distance of 60cm (24in) should be allowed between plants and rows, but if space is at a premium, the dwarf or half-tall varieties may be restricted to 53cm (21in) between plants. The tall varieties cannot be expected to give good results under 60cm (24in) and will get more light and air if the distance between the rows can be increased to 75cm (30in).

Some form of staking may be necessary for the tall varieties, particularly those planted in exposed positions. The plants facing the prevailing wind are vulnerable, as are those growing at the corners of the plot. One way of giving them better anchorage is to draw up a little soil around the base of the stems.

When the plants are established, a dressing of a good general fertilizer can be given at 70g per sq m (2oz per sq yd). In the autumn take off any of the lower leaves which have turned yellow and put them on the compost heap.

The cabbage-like head of the plant is also edible and is preferred by some people to the sprouts, but do not take it too early as its real purpose is to protect the developing sprouts. In bad weather, without the protection of the leafy head, the buttons may rot. Late February or early March is a good time to cut out the top ; its removal then will help the topmost sprouts to develop.

Always pick sprouts from the bottom upwards and either cut or snap them off cleanly, close to the stem. In April

any remaining buttons will burst open and send up leafy shoots. These, if left alone will grow on to form flowers and seeds. Cut them and use them when they are a few inches in length. Do not allow the shoots to flower for it is at this stage that the plants are taking most nourishment from the soil.

When the last sprouts have been gathered, chop the plants up with a spade and dig in all the green stuff. The roots take a long time to rot and are better burnt.

Recommended varieties

Early : Early Half-tall, September to Christmas ; Peer Gynt (F1 hybrid), medium height

Late : Citadel (F1 hybrid), medium height ; Cambridge No5, tall

Brassicas Cabbages

Cabbages are easy to grow and are in season all the year round. This makes them one of the most valuable members of the brassica family. Although they appreciate a good, fertile medium they are less demanding in their soil requirements than Brussels sprouts or cauliflowers.

Spring Cabbages

These are sown in July and August for maturing from April to June. It is a good plan to make two sowings—one about mid-July and another three weeks later. If the first sowing fails, there is always the other one to fall back on. The July sowing will form plants to put out in September; from an August sowing plants will be ready for transplanting early in October. Spring cabbages make a good follow-on crop to potatoes.

The smaller varieties should be given 30cm (12in) between plants and 45cm (18in) between the rows; the larger varieties should be 45cm (18in) between plants and 60cm (24in) between the rows. If these distances between the plants are halved, every

other plant can be taken out in March for use as 'spring greens'.

Spring cabbages have a distinctive, nutty flavour of their own and come in at a time when other greens are scarce. They do not suffer from club root (which is not active during the winter months) but may need protection from birds, especially wood pigeons (a net is ideal), and from cabbage root-fly. Fresh manure should not be used and fertilizers should not be given until the spring when a little nitro-chalk —about 70g per sq m (2oz per sq yd)— will give them a boost.

Summer and Autumn Cabbages

These are sown with the other brassicas in the nursery bed in March or April and are planted out in May and June, their season being July to September. They include both round (R) and pointed (P) types. A later sowing about mid-May will prolong the season until October.

The smaller cabbages in this group will need 38–45cm (15–18in) between plants and 53cm (21in) between the

Planting out red cabbage

rows. The larger cabbages should be given 53cm (21in) between plants and 60cm (24in) between the rows.

Round cabbage

Winter Cabbages

The winter cabbages are hardier and slower to mature than the summer ones. They crop from October to February. They should be sown in the nursery bed during April, and be planted out in June or July, 60cm (24in) apart, in all directions. The winter cabbages will stand for some time without splitting. If they are dug up with the roots intact and hung head downwards in a cool, airy shed or cellar, they will remain in good condition for weeks. The variety January King, available from December to February, is worth a special mention as it is in a class of its own. A cross between a cabbage and a savoy it is very hardy and has a good flavour. Some seedsmen list it with the savoys.

Savoy Cabbages

The savoys are the hardiest of all cabbages and can be used from November to April, according to variety. Their leaves are darker than

those of ordinary cabbages and are more crimped and curled. They stand well without splitting.

Sow the seeds in the nursery seed-bed in April for the early kinds and in May for the later ones.

Red Cabbages

Although red cabbages are used mainly for pickling they can also be prepared as a vegetable. They need a long season of growth and should be sown in the nursery seed-bed in March. Alternatively, for a better start, sow a few seeds under a cloche in February. The best red cabbages of all come from a sowing made with the spring cabbages in July or August. Planted out in late September or early October, 60cm (24in) apart, in all directions, they will stand through the winter. Their leaves are tough and birds do not usually attack them.

Recommended varieties

Spring Cabbages : April or Wheeler's Imperial are a good, small variety ; Flower of Spring, a late, large cabbage

Summer Cabbages : Greyhound (P) and Primo (R) are two early, small varieties ; Winnigstadt (P) and Emerald Cross (R) are later and larger

Winter Cabbages : Christmas Drumhead, dwarf and compact ; Holland Winter White and Winter Monarch, two of the best white cabbages for winter use

Savoy Cabbages : Best of All, early and good ; Ormskirk Late, one of the best late varieties

Red Cabbages : Niggerhead, medium size ; Large Blood Red

Brassicas
Cauliflowers and Cauliflower Broccoli

A good, white cauliflower is always a welcome addition to the vegetable supply. Unfortunately, it is not one of the easiest vegetables to grow well. A good, fertile soil is needed, well supplied with humus. A medium loam is ideal, but cauliflowers will do well on heavier soils provided that the drainage is good. They can be divided naturally into two groups : the true cauliflowers which mature during summer and autumn, and the cauliflower broccoli which is in season from February to May, according to the area. These are now usually listed in seed catalogues as 'winter' cauliflowers.

To obtain cauliflowers in June and July it is necessary to raise the plants under glass in a cold greenhouse or frame by sowing in boxes in January or February. An alternative, where cloches are available, is to sow under cloches in September and keep the plants covered throughout the winter. Whichever method is employed, the plants must be well hardened off before they are planted out in the open.

For heading in late summer and autumn, the seeds should be sown in the nursery seed-bed along with the other brassicas. Varieties maturing in August and September can be sown in April, but those for October and November heading should not be sown until about the middle of May. The early varieties should have 45cm (18in) between the plants and 53cm (21in) between the rows ; later

varieties 53cm (21in) between the plants and 60cm (24in) between the rows.

In transplanting cauliflowers be careful to minimize the check to growth. If the soil is dry, water the seed-bed well a few hours before the plants are lifted so that some soil can be taken with the roots. Cauliflowers which suffer a bad check are liable to retaliate by producing their curds prematurely when they are no bigger than egg-cups. This practice is known as 'buttoning'.

A check to growth may also occur if the plants dry out. Keep them well supplied with water in dry weather. Feeding with liquid manure is always a good thing.

Cauliflower broccoli are hardier and generally easier to manage than the true cauliflower, but the curds can be damaged by frost. For this reason, except in frost-free areas, there is not much point in going for the earliest varieties which head in January and

Buttoned cauliflower

Protecting curds from frost

February. For most parts the season is from March to June.

These cauliflowers need a long period of growth and the seeds should be sown in April or May, for transplanting in June or July. They can often be used as a follow-on crop to potatoes or early peas. If this is done, simply prick the soil over, a few inches deep, with a fork and then rake it down again. A sprinkling of a general fertilizer can be given—not exceeding 70g per sq m (2oz per sq yd)—but no other feeding, as the object is to grow a plant hardy enough to stand the winter. Give the plants 60cm (24in), all ways.

The curds of cauliflowers can be yellowed by bright sunlight or blackened by frost. Snap a few leaves over the developing curd of summer cauliflowers when it becomes visible in order to protect it. The inner leaves of cauliflower broccoli fold over to protect the curd, but if there is a likelihood of frost before the curds are ready for cutting, it is always a good plan to snap one or two of the outer leaves over as well.

Recommended varieties

June and July heading :
    Early Snowball, Dominant
August and September : All the Year Round, South Pacific
October and November : Autumn Giant, Canberra
March and April : Leamington, St George
May and June : Royal Oak, Late Queen

Brassicas
Sprouting Broccoli
Calabrese and Kales

Sprouting Broccoli

This brassica does not form a central head but a number of sideshoots, each of which carries a small flower like a tiny cauliflower. It is available in two forms, purple and white, and crops during March and April. The white form is believed by many gardeners to have better flavour than the purple, but it is not quite so hardy.

Seeds of sprouting broccoli should be sown in the nursery seed-bed in late March or April, for transplanting to stand 60cm (24in) apart in all directions. A soil in good heart in an open, sunny position should be chosen, but not one freshly manured as the plants need to be grown hard to stand through the winter. There is no need to wait until the flower head shows; the shoots can be taken as soon as they are long enough to pick.

Calabrese

Another form of sprouting broccoli is known as calabrese. This is an all-green type which matures from October to December. Some varieties have a large, central head, rather like a cauliflower, which is followed by sideshoots. In others the head is smaller, with more sideshoots. Calabrese freezes well, and large quantities of it are now being grown for the frozen-food trade.

To grow calabrese sow the seeds in April and then move the young plants into their final quarters in June or July. Give them 45cm (18in) between

Sprouting broccoli

plants and 60cm (24in) between the rows. They can often be used as a follow-on crop to earlier vegetables. Where this is done put down a general fertilizer at about 70g per sq m (2oz per sq yd) and prick it into the top few inches of soil with a fork.

Kales

Last but not least among the brassicas are the kales, the hardiest members of the family. Although they will naturally do best in a good, fertile soil, they are not as demanding in their soil requirements as Brussels sprouts or cauliflowers. They, too, can be used as a follow-on crop to earlier vegetables.

Cutting calabrese heads

Scotch kale

Sow the seeds in the nursery seed-bed during April or early May and plant out in late June or July. There are several types of this vegetable, some with densely-curled, dark-green leaves, and others with plain leaves. The dwarf Scotch kales should be given 45cm (18in) between plants and 60cm (24in) between the rows; the others should be 60cm (24in) apart in all directions. An exception to this is Hungry Gap kale which needs rather different treatment as the seeds should be sown in June or July in the bed where the plants are to mature. Sow in shallow drills 60cm (24in) apart, and then thin the seedlings to stand 30cm (12in) apart. This is the hardiest of all the kales and the latest to mature.

Recommended varieties

Sprouting Broccoli : Early White, Late White ; Early Purple, Late Purple

Calabrese : Green Comet (F1 hybrid), large central head, followed by sideshoots ; Autumn Spear, an abundance of green shoots

Kales : Scotch (tall and dwarf), densely curled ; Thousand-headed, plain leaves ; Pentland Brig (F1 hybrid), a cross between the curly and plain-leaved types

Carrots

Most vegetable gardeners want to grow carrots, but it must be admitted that this is not one of the easiest vegetables to grow successfully. Few gardeners have ideal carrot soil, which is a light to medium loam, well worked to a good depth and moisture retentive. However, much can be done by taking a little extra trouble and using the right varieties. Light soils can be enriched by digging in manure or compost during the winter months, and heavy soils can be lightened with the addition of coarse sand or weathered ashes forked into the top 15cm (6in) of soil. On soils which do not have a good depth of fertile soil, grow only the stump-rooted varieties.

Carrots can be sown at any time from March to July, or earlier than March if there is a cold frame or cloches to give protection. For the earliest sowings, use the shorthorn or early stump-rooted varieties, and come back to them for the July sowing which is designed to give young carrots for pulling in autumn.

Maincrop carrots for storing should not be sown earlier than the middle of

Thinning seedling carrots

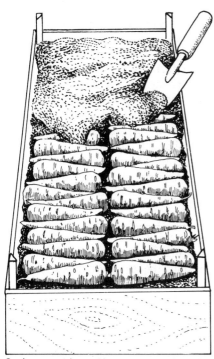
Storing carrots in sand box

May, up until early June, as these later sowings have more chance of missing the destructive carrot-fly. Where there is sufficient depth of soil to grow long carrots, these give the heaviest crops of all.

Sowing of all varieties should be done in drills not more than 13mm (½in) deep and 25–30cm (10–12in) apart. Sow *thinly*. Some thinning may still have to be done, for if the seedlings are crowded in the row, many of them will never make usable roots, and it is better to remove them in the early stages. Thin the early varieties to about 2cm (1in) and the maincrops to 5–8cm (2–3in), and put the thinnings on the compost heap. Never leave them lying about on the soil as the carrot smell may attract the fly.

The carrot-fly is the scourge of carrots. This little creature lays her eggs along the carrot rows. From the eggs hatch little maggots which burrow into the soil and then tunnel into the developing roots. In a severe attack the roots can be ruined. The presence of the grubs can be detected by changes in the foliage which loses its green lustre and turns a dull, reddish brown. Unfortunately, by that time not much can be done. Control lies in keeping the fly away. One method of control is to dust the seed-drills with a good seed dressing or Gamma/BHC dust, and to repeat this when the seedlings are a few inches high. Bromophos is another preparation recommended as a control.

In an open autumn carrots will continue to grow until November. While they can be left in the ground all winter, it is better to lift and store them. Heavy rains may cause the roots to split and they will be a prey to slugs, millipedes or wireworms. They store well in layers, head to tail, in boxes of sand or soil, or in a little clamp in the garden.

Recommended varieties

Early carrots : Early Horn, Early Nantes
Maincrop carrots : James Scarlet
    Intermediate, Chantenay Red Cored
Long carrots : St Valery, Autumn King

Celery and Celeriac

Trench celery needs a rich soil, well supplied with humus, and plenty of water. Unless these conditions can be given, it is better to stick to the self-blanching celery, which is easier to grow but not such good quality.

Celery and celeriac need a long period of growth and the seeds should be sown in a seed-pan during February. A gently-heated greenhouse is ideal for raising celery plants, but if this is not available put the seed-pan in the sunny window of a warm room, and turn the pan daily when the seedlings have appeared. When they have formed their first true leaves, prick them off into boxes and put them in a cold frame or under a cloche. By June or early July they will be ready for transplanting.

For trench celery, take out a trench 45cm (18in) wide and a spade's depth. Shovel out the loose soil and then break up the subsoil with a fork. Put in a good layer of manure or compost, then return most of the soil, leaving the

trench a few inches deep. As the soil is returned, mix in some bonemeal or weathered soot (ie soot which has been stored for several months).

When the plants are ready for moving, put them out in the trench in two rows 23cm (9in) apart in all directions. The plants should be opposite each other in the rows, not staggered. From then on, until earthing-up begins, see that they never lack water. It is difficult to overwater celery.

Trench celery needs blanching before it can be eaten, and this work is done in several stages by drawing soil up round the stems. When the plants have made good growth (usually about mid-August) cut off any suckers, yellow leaves and small leaves that would be buried by the soil, then draw the stems together and make a loose tie with soft string. Holding the plant with one hand, take the soil from the sides of the trench and sweep it up round the stems. Take care that the soil does not fall into the hearts of the plants, or they may rot. Repeat this

Celery plants in trench

process every two or three weeks until about the end of September when most of the growth will have been made.

After the final earthing, only the tips of the plants should be visible above the bank of soil. Pat the sides of the bank smooth with the back of the spade. In three or four weeks blanching will be completed. To dig the sticks, start at one end of the double row and remove the bank until the whole of the stick is visible, then thrust the spade well down under the root.

An alternative method which can be recommended is to wait until most of the growth has been made and then tie cardboard collars round the plants before earthing them up. This keeps the sticks cleaner and makes it more difficult for slugs to get at them. It is best to use corrugated cardboard.

There are white, pink, and red varieties of trench celery. The white is not quite so hardy as the other two and should be eaten first.

Self-blanching celery, as the name implies, does its own blanching. To do this successfully it should be planted in blocks and not in long rows. Put the plants out 20cm (8in) apart, in all directions. The plants on the edges of the block will need some help and this can be given, either by earthing them up, or by packing boards, straw, or short litter against them. This type of celery is less hardy than trench celery and generally needs to be used up by Christmas.

Celeriac, or turnip-rooted celery, forms a swollen root which has the true celery flavour. It may be used grated in salads or as a vegetable. It does not need blanching. The plants go out in rows 45cm (18in) apart, with 30cm (12in) between the plants. The only attention necessary is to cut off any suckers or lateral shoots from the roots as they swell. The roots are hardy and can be left outside.

The two pests of the celery family are slugs and the celery-fly. To combat the slugs sprinkle slug pellets around the plants, and include some in the soil when earthing-up. Grubs from the eggs of the celery-fly burrow into the leaves, leaving shiny, blistery trails. This saps the strength of the plants. Spray with Lindex or malathion to control them.

Recommended varieties

Trench celery : Giant Red, Giant White, Clayworth Pink
Self-blanching: Lathom Self-blanching
Celeriac : Globus

Trench celery with cardboard collar

Leeks

The leek is a useful vegetable as it comes in during winter and early spring. It is easy to grow and not prone to pests or diseases. It likes a soil enriched with humus, and given this will do well in heavy or light conditions.

Leeks can be bought at planting time from nurserymen or garden centres, but they are quite easy to raise from seeds. These should be sown in a seed-bed in late March or early April. Sow the seeds thinly in shallow drills 25cm (10in) apart.

Planting out can be done from June to August, and this means that leeks are often used as a follow-on crop to earlier vegetables. If the ground was manured for a previous crop, it will be enough to fork it over and add a general fertilizer at 70g per sq m (2oz per sq yd). If it was not manured, then dig it over and put in some well rotted manure or compost, burying this in the bottom of each trench as leeks are deep rooting.

The plants can be moved when they are about 15cm (6in) high. Ease them first with a fork, then pull them up and sort them. Reject any plants which are not straight, and any which have a short stem. Trim the leaves of the chosen plants by about half, and the roots likewise. This makes for easier planting.

To plant leeks, make a hole deep enough to take the plant up to its lowest leaves, drop it in, trickle a little soil over the roots, then fill the hole with water. The remainder of the hole will fill in when hoeing takes place. Allow 20cm (8in) between the plants. The distance between the rows will depend on whether the plants are to be earthed-up or not. They can be planted as close as 30cm (12in), but if soil is to be drawn up to them to give a greater length of blanched stem, a minimum of 45cm (18in) will be required. Choose a dry day in October to do the earthing and draw the soil up under the lowest leaves.

The two main periods of growth are in autumn and early spring, but unless the weather is severe, leeks will make some growth all through the winter. By May any remaining plants should be dug as they will then begin to produce their seed heads.

Leeks are perfectly hardy and can remain in the ground all winter. The only problem may be that during severe frost it will be difficult to dig them. This can be avoided if one or two rows are mulched with peat or straw which will absorb most of the frost.

Although leeks *may* be attacked by the onion-fly or onion white rot (see Onions), they rarely are. If they are not grown on the same site too often they are generally free from pests or diseases, which is another point in their favour.

Recommended varieties

The Lyon, Musselburgh, Marble Pillar

(*From the top*) planting; watering; earthing up to blanch stems

Lettuces, Outdoor Cucumbers and Gherkins

Lettuces

There are three types of lettuces in general cultivation : cabbage, cos, and non-hearting. Lettuces with a cabbage-like head may be either smooth, or crisp and curled. Cos lettuce has oval leaves which fold over to make a pointed heart. The non-hearting lettuce forms a loose head of curly leaves which can be picked as required.

Apart from the winter months, when a heated greenhouse is needed, it is not difficult to grow lettuce. The introduction of improved varieties and the use of cloches, which are excellent for lettuce, has extended the season at both ends. And the lettuce is not particularly fussy in its soil requirements. It does not mind a heavy soil provided that the drainage is good. On light, hungry soils it may bolt in dry weather (go to seed prematurely), but this tendency can be overcome by forking good compost or peat into the top few inches of soil.

Early lettuces can be obtained by raising the plants in boxes in a cold frame or under cloches. If cloches are placed in position some weeks beforehand to warm the soil, a sowing can be made outdoors in January or February. Lettuces are hardier than is often supposed. The seeds should be sown in shallow drills 25–30cm (10–12in) apart. Outdoor sowings without protection can be made from March to July.

Lettuces for maturing during the summer months should be sown in April and May. This is also the main season for sowing cos lettuce.

In July, sowings can be made for autumn use, and for these we turn back to the early varieties. Tom Thumb, a small cabbage lettuce, can be sown well into August and will still mature before winter, especially if it is cloched in September.

Certain varieties can be sown in August for overwintering which will mature in early spring. Their success will depend to a large extent on the severity of the winter. A sunny position, sheltered from cold winds, should be chosen for them.

A better and more certain way of obtaining lettuces in spring is to sow them in September and cover them with cloches a month later. Make a preliminary thinning to 5–8cm (2–3in) when the plants are big enough to handle, then thin them again in February, this time to 12–15cm (5–6in). The February thinnings can be transplanted to give a later row. In April, take out every other plant for early use.

Most lettuces should be thinned out to stand 25–30cm (10–12in) apart, but Tom Thumb and Little Gem do not need more than 15cm (6in). Lettuces maturing during July and August will do better if sown in the lee of taller crops which will give them some shade for part of the day.

Birds and slugs are the worst enemies of lettuce, but bird damage can be prevented by stringing black cotton over the plants. Botrytis may cause a problem in frames or under cloches. This disease, known also as 'brown rot', causes the plants to rot off at soil level. The best safeguard against it is to give plenty of ventilation so that a good circulation of air is maintained.

Ridge Cucumbers and Gherkins

The outdoor or ridge cucumber can be raised in pots in a cool greenhouse by sowing two seeds, 13mm ($\frac{1}{2}$in) deep in a pot about the middle of April. If both seeds grow, pull one out. The plants may also be raised in a similar way in a sunny window. By early June, when the risk of frost has passed, they will be ready for planting out.

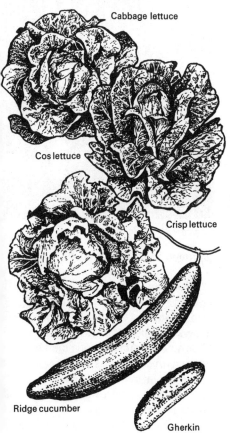

Cabbage lettuce

Cos lettuce

Crisp lettuce

Ridge cucumber

Gherkin

An alternative method is to sow the seeds directly into the soil during the middle of May. Sow three seeds in a triangle and thin them to the strongest plant. The planting sites should be prepared by digging holes 45cm (18in) square and 30cm (12in) deep. Half-fill these with manure or good compost, then return the soil. This will leave the plants on a slight mound. The prepared sites should be 75cm (30in) apart.

When the plants have made three pairs of leaves pinch out the growing points. This will make them produce lateral shoots on which the fruits form. It is not necessary to remove the male flowers. The crop will be largely at the mercy of the weather, but, if barn cloches can be used to cover the plants for at least part of their growth, the chance of success will be much greater.

The cultivation of the gherkin is the same as that of the ridge cucumber. Pick the fruits when they are a few inches long and the plants will go on producing for weeks.

Recommended varieties

Lettuces : (cabbage varieties unless otherwise stated)
For use in summer and autumn : All the Year Round, Buttercrunch, Webb's Wonderful, Unrivalled, Tom Thumb, Lobjoits Green Cos, Little Gem (small cos)
For overwintering without protection : Arctic King, Valdor
For overwintering with protection : Suzan (also listed as Hilde), Premier, Winter Density (cos)
Ridge Cucumbers : Baton Vert, Burpless
Gherkins : Venlo Pickling

Onions

Onions like a rich, firm soil. A medium to heavy loam suits them best, but they will do well in lighter soils provided that there is a good reserve of humus.

There are three main ways of growing onions : growing from seed in August for overwintering ; growing from seed in early spring, and growing from onion sets.

The August sowing should be sited on a strip which was manured for the previous crop, eg early potatoes. No fertilizer should be given at this stage as sappy growth is not wanted. Simply fork the soil through, a few inches deep, then rake it down again and sow the seeds in drills about 13mm ($\frac{1}{2}$in) deep and 25–30cm (10–12in) apart. Keep the plants clean by hoeing and weeding whenever possible. In the spring thin the seedlings to 10cm (4in) apart, or 15cm (6in) if larger bulbs are needed, and use the thinnings as 'spring onions'. Liquid manure, at fortnightly intervals, is a good help when the bulbs begin to form.

Care should be taken in choosing varieties for this sowing as some varieties are quite unsuitable. The new Japanese onions are rapidly gaining favour and have so far withstood British winters successfully.

For sowing in spring the ground should be dug and manured in autumn or early winter so that it has time to settle down before sowing. In March or early April (March, if possible), rake the soil down into a fine tilth. Larger bulbs can be obtained by sowing in boxes in a lightly heated greenhouse in January, or in a cold greenhouse in

Planting sets

February. These plants can be put out in April.

Onion sets are tiny bulbs in an arrested state of development which are planted 10–15cm (4–6in) apart, in rows 25–30cm (10–12in) apart, and this is now the most popular method of growing onions. The easiest way of planting them is to draw out shallow drills and then make a little depression with the tip of the trowel. Push the soil back so that the bulbs are just covered.

Spring onions   Globe onion

This method avoids trouble from the birds, which are likely to pull the bulbs out again if any part is showing.

The popular salad onions can be sown in rows 15cm (6in) apart in August and September for spring use, or March to May for summer use. These should be pulled up in the green state. Pickling onions should be sown thickly in a broad row 15cm (6in) wide in April. Salad and pickling onions do not need a rich soil.

The worst onion pest is the onion-fly, which lays her eggs against the young plants. White maggots come from the eggs and burrow into the bulbs. Yellow, sickly-looking foliage is a sign of their presence. There is no cure at the maggot stage. Calomel dust, sprinkled up the sides of the rows at the seedling stage, helps to keep the fly away. August-sown plants and sets, although not immune to this trouble, are less likely to be attacked.

Yellow, sickly plants may also be a sign of onion white rot. In this disease a white mould attacks the base of the bulb. Affected plants should be pulled up and burnt, and onions should not be grown again on that site for several years. Fortunately, the disease is not widespread.

Onions are ready for harvesting when the tips of the leaves turn yellow and then flop over. Ease the bulbs with a fork before pulling them out, then dry them thoroughly in the sunshine. An onion rope can be made by hanging up a length of stout string and then tying the onions to it, beginning at the bottom and working up. Alternatively, store them in shallow boxes in a light, cool place.

Recommendeded varieties

August sowing : Reliance, Solidity ;
   Japanese varieties : Empress Yellow,
   Imai
Spring sowing : Ailsa Craig,
   Bedfordshire Champion
Sets : Suttgarter Giant, Sturon
Salad onions : White Lisbon
Pickling onions : Paris Silverskin

173

Parsnips

The parsnip is a good winter vegetable, hardy, and easy to grow. It also makes good wine. It will grow in most soils but, like most roots, should not be grown in freshly manured soil.

It is sometimes recommended that parsnips should be sown in February, but the ground is often too wet for this. A March sowing is just as good and even April sowings, if made in the first half of the month, will give roots large enough for kitchen use.

Sow the seeds in shallow drills about 13mm ($\frac{1}{2}$in) deep and 38cm (15in) apart. There are two methods of sowing. One is to trickle the seeds all the way along the drill and then thin the plants to 15cm (6in) apart when they are big enough to handle. In the other method, known as 'station'

sowing, a few seeds are sown at 15cm (6in) intervals. The seedlings from these are thinned to leave the strongest plant at each station.

The advantages of the second method are that less seed is required and that there is room to sow a few radishes between the clusters of parsnip seeds. This is to mark the rows for hoeing. Parsnips are slow to germinate and take weeks to come through. The radishes come through first and, by marking the rows, enable hoeing to be done before weeds get the upper hand.

Keep the plants clean by hoeing and weeding ; no special cultivation is needed. As the tops attain their full growth, light will be excluded from between the rows and no further weeding will be necessary.

The roots are ready for digging when the foliage has died down. There is no

'Trickle' sowing

'Station' sowing

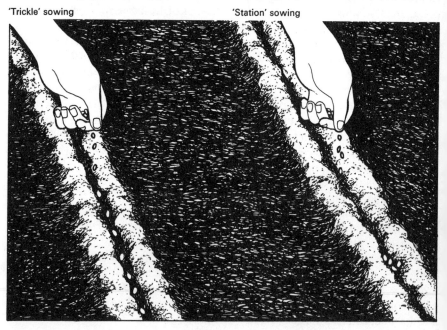

point in digging them earlier than this for most gardeners agree that the roots are sweeter when they have been touched by frost. To get them out intact dig out a spadeful of soil from against each root, then put the spade into the hole and thrust it well down and under.

Parsnips are completely hardy and can be left in the ground all winter. Should severe weather threaten to make conditions impossible for digging, lift a few roots and store them in a box of sand or soil. By the end of March or early in April the plants, being biennial, will begin to make fresh growth. It is time then to dig up any roots which are left and put them, with soil mixed among them, in a shady corner until they can be used up.

The only trouble likely to be encountered with parsnips is canker. This fungus disease causes the roots to crack, usually at the shoulders, and then produce brown patches which may go rotten. There is no cure. There is some reason to believe that April sowings are less likely to be attacked. Where the disease is prevalent—but many gardeners never see it—it is worth sowing late and growing a variety that has some resistance to canker.

Recommended varieties

Avonresister, a small, conical root which has some resistance to canker
Improved Hollow Crown, long, well-shaped roots
Offenham, stump-rooted, suitable for shallow soils

Digging parsnips

Peas

Peas will grow in most soils provided that they have a good humus content. Where the ground was dug and manured during the winter, no other preparation will be necessary, except to give a dressing of lime over the digging at about 70g per sq m (2oz per sq yd). Peas like lime.

There is a wide range of varieties to choose from, dwarf, medium and tall. The dwarf varieties are the most popular, no doubt because they are the least trouble.

Sowings can take place in October or November, and from March to the end of June. In most areas the autumn sowing will need some protection. A row of cloches is ideal. Where cloches can be used, a February sowing is also possible. For these sowings it is customary to use a round-seeded variety rather than a wrinkled one. The round-seeded peas are hardier than the wrinkled ones but are not of such good flavour.

For sowings in March and April choose an early, wrinkled variety. Maincrop varieties are sown in May. For the June sowings, which have only a limited time in which to mature, return to the early varieties.

There are two methods of sowing. One is to take out a drill about 5cm (2in) deep with the corner of a draw hoe and sow the seeds thinly along the bottom of the drill. The other is to scoop out a trench about 5cm (2in) deep with the spade and sow the peas in three lines, with all the peas being about 5cm (2in) apart.

For the tall varieties it is best to take out a trench 38cm (15in) wide. Break up the subsoil and put in a layer of manure or compost before returning the soil. Do this work several months in advance of sowing. Although the tall peas are more trouble, they are worth a place as the peas are large and of superb flavour. April and May are the months for sowing.

The distance between the rows of peas should be about the same as their height, eg plants 45cm (18in) high will need that distance between the rows. However, where space is precious (as it is for most of us) some savings can be made. Varieties 75cm (30in) in height will do well enough with 60cm (24in) between the rows, and those 122–152cm (48–60in) in height can be given 107cm (42in) between the rows. Summer lettuces can be intercropped between the rows of tall peas and will benefit from the shade given by the taller plants.

Although dwarf peas are supposed not to need staking, it helps to keep them cleaner and easier to pick if twiggy sticks are pushed in on each side of the row when the plants are about 15cm (6in) high. For the tall varieties some form of support is essential. Brushwood is ideal but difficult to obtain. Large mesh netting for supporting peas and beans is a good substitute. When netting is used for peas, run it up *both* sides of the row so that the peas climb up inside the netting and grow through it. This makes it impossible for summer winds to blow the plants off the netting. Make sure it is firmly fixed.

Birds love the tender green shoots of peas and can soon play havoc with a crop. Strands of black cotton,

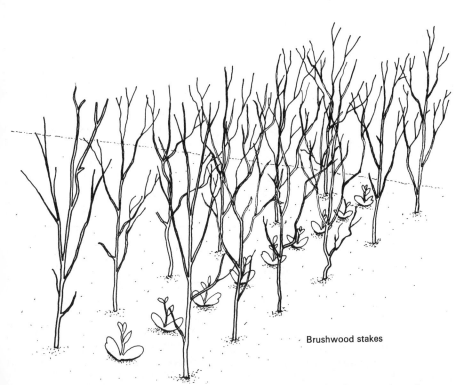

Brushwood stakes

suspended just above the seedlings when they come through, will prevent this damage. Run further strands across as the peas grow. The other menace at the seedling stage is the pea weevil, which bites holes in the young leaves. This can be controlled by spraying or dusting with derris.

Grubby peas are the work of the pea moth. They can be prevented by spraying or dusting with derris when the flowers appear, and again about ten days later. Do this in the late evening so that the bees are not harmed.

When picking peas take care that the bines are not twisted or broken. If this happens the upper pods will not fill. The bine should be held in one hand while the pods are picked off with the other.

When the crop has been gathered, run the hoe along the row to cut off the haulms, which can then be put on the compost heap. The roots of peas are rich in nitrogen and should be left in the soil.

Recommended varieties

(The height of the variety is given in brackets. All have wrinkled seeds unless otherwise stated.)

October/November sowings : Feltham First (round seeded), 45cm (18in)

March/April sowings : Kelvedon Wonder, 45cm (18in) ; Early Onward, 60cm (24in)

April/May sowings : Onward, 60cm (24in) ; The Lincoln, 60cm (24in) ; Miracle, 137cm (54in) ; Lord Chancellor, 122cm (48in)

June sowings : Little Marvel, 45cm (18in)

Potatoes

Cultivation

Potatoes can be grown in most soils. Light soils need the addition of plenty of humus, or the plants may die during a dry period. Heavy soils can be made more open by the addition of strawy manure or rough compost. Potatoes like a loose medium into which they can thrust their stolons (underground shoots on which the tubers form).

Early potatoes are planted in March and April and crop from June to August. Late varieties are planted in April and May and mature from September to October. If the vegetable plot is a small one it is wise to concentrate on the earlies.

Potatoes are propagated by planting a tuber of the previous year's growth. These are referred to as 'seed' potatoes. They may be either 'once grown', ie tubers saved from your own crop, or 'new' seed, ie new Scotch or Irish stock bought through a seedsman.

Unfortunately, the potato is subject to a number of virus diseases which are spread largely by greenfly. The professional seed-growing areas are at a high altitude where greenfly cannot work, and these stocks are certified 'virus free'. It is reasonably safe to save some tubers from the new seed of the earlies, which have a shorter growing period, but risky to save them from the later varieties.

Whether the seed tubers are new or once grown they should be 'chitted' before being planted. This is done by taking a shallow box and tilting it at one end. The tubers are then stood on end in the box with the 'eye' end uppermost.

When filled, the boxes should be stored in a light, cool and frost-proof place. Strong, young shoots will grow from the eyes. Chitting gives the tubers an early start and enables any dud tubers to be picked out before planting. Once-grown tubers can be set up as early as January or February (these give the earliest crops) ; new seed as soon as you have bought it.

There are several methods of planting. One of the most popular is to put your garden-line down across the plot and, with the back of the spade close up to the line, chip out a trench 10–15cm (4–6in) deep. Plant the tubers upright in the bottom of the trench, and fill it in with the soil thrown forward from the next trench.

Another method is to plant with the trowel. Draw out shallow drills where the rows are to be, make holes with a trowel and drop the tuber in. The advantages of this method are that any manure or greenstuff which has been dug in is not disturbed, and that

Planting in trenches

uniform planting is assured because the holes can be adjusted to the size of the tubers.

A more modern method is to use strips of black polythene 60cm (24in) wide. The tubers are planted just beneath the soil surface and the polythene is laid out above them. Soil on the edges of the polythene keeps it in place. When the shoots can be seen pushing at the polythene, slits are made with a knife and the shoots are drawn through. Using this method there is no need for hoeing or earthing-up as the polythene acts as a mulch. The tubers form beneath the sheet or just inside the soil.

Early varieties should be planted with 30cm (12in) between the tubers and 60cm (24in) between the rows. Late varieties need 38cm (15in) between the tubers and 60–68cm (24–27in) between the rows.

Potatoes are not frost hardy and, if frost threatens any shoots which have come through, they should be covered with newspapers, plant-pots or cloches. If the worst happens and the growth is blackened by frost, the tubers will send out fresh shoots, but the crop will be later and possibly smaller.

When hoeing the young plants, do not hoe too deeply or some of the underground stolons may be cut off. When the plants are about 15cm (6in) high, they should be earthed-up. This is done by standing between two rows, facing the row to be earthed. Reach out over the row with the hoe and, with a steady chopping movement, draw the soil up under the leaves of the plants. Turn at the end of the row and do the other side. This leaves the tubers in a ridge. The object of earthing-up is to prevent the tubers from pushing up into the sunlight. Tubers greened by the sun are unfit for human consumption.

No further cultivation is necessary with the possible exception of spraying the late varieties against blight. This fungus disease produces browny-black patches on the leaves, and these spread quickly, destroying the haulms. The spores, if washed into the soil, spread disease to the tubers. Blight is at its worst in damp, humid weather in July and August. If its presence is known or suspected in the area, spray the plants thoroughly with a copper-based solution such as Bordeaux mixture.

Recommended varieties

Earlies : Arran Pilot, white kidney ;
  Home Guard, white oval ; Pentland
  Javelin, white oval
Lates : Majestic, white kidney ;
  Pentland Crown, white oval ;
  Desiree, red kidney

Planting in holes

Potatoes and Jerusalem Artichokes

Harvesting and Storing Potatoes

Early potatoes are dug as required while the haulms are still green. If any part of the crop is not dug at this stage it can still be used after the haulms have died off, the only difference being that the tubers will no longer scrape.

Late varieties are not harvested until the haulms have died. This process begins with a yellowing of the lower leaves, followed by the gradual browning of the leaves and stems.

To lift the tubers, put the fork in at the side of the ridge—not across the ridge and between two roots or tubers may be speared. Thrust the fork well down and under, then lift the root

and throw it forward. Shake off the tubers and spread them out to dry, then fork through the place where the root has been in case any stragglers have been missed.

Leave the tubers on the soil for an hour or two to dry, then pick them up and rub the loose soil off them. The ware (eating) potatoes should be put into deep boxes or paper sacks. Plastic sacks are not suitable. Tubers too small for table use must also be picked up or they will turn up again as self-sets.

To keep through the winter months the tubers must be stored in a dark, cool and frost-proof place. Garden sheds are seldom frost-proof; if tubers have to be stored there, provide extra coverings during frosty spells. A few weeks after harvesting, take the tubers out into the light and sort them through again. Any tubers which may have been

Lifting potatoes; (*insert*) cross-section of clamp

180

carrying disease when they were lifted will have deteriorated still further, and can now be spotted and picked out.

If the crop exceeds several sacks it will be worth making a clamp in the garden. This provides ideal storage conditions and saves indoor space. The only materials needed are straw, hay, or dried bracken.

To make the clamp, tread the soil firm and then put down a layer of straw several inches thick. Pile the potatoes out on to the straw and build them up into a conical heap, making it as compact as possible. Now cover the heap with about 15cm (6in) of straw and then mark out a circle about 25cm (10in) from the straw. This is the ledge on which the soil will be built up.

Dig the soil out from beyond the circle and pack it up layer by layer on the cone, following the curve of the heap as it goes up. Cracks and hollows are filled in with loose soil from the bottom of the trench, which should be extended outwards, not downwards, as subsoil should not be used. Leave a tuft of straw sticking out at the top so that air can get into the heap. Later, when wintry conditions arrive, pull this out and fill in the hole.

When a supply of tubers has been taken out, make sure that the heap is adequately sealed up again. Do not attempt to open the clamp during frosty weather. By late March the tubers will have started to sprout. It is time then to break up the heap, rub off the sprouts, and take the tubers indoors.

Jerusalem Artichokes

Another vegetable which produces tubers is the Jerusalem artichoke. The tubers are smaller than those of the potato and have no starch content. As they are not affected by frost they can remain in the ground all winter.

Select tubers of even size and shape (an initial supply can be bought from seedsmen) and plant them 10cm (4in) deep in February or March, with 38cm (15in) between the tubers and 75cm (30in) between the rows. The stems reach a height of 2.5–3m (8–10ft) and need supporting with wires and stakes. Because of their height the plants make

Jerusalem artichoke

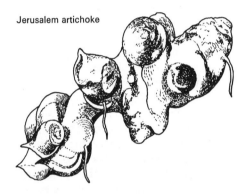

an excellent windbreak. When the foliage has been blackened by frost digging can begin. The tubers are not subject to virus diseases, and selected tubers from one's own crop can be used year after year.

Radishes

Summer Radishes

The summer radish matures more quickly than any other vegetable. In ideal conditions—warm, showery weather—the roots can be ready for pulling in three to four weeks. They like a fertile soil but not one freshly manured. As most of the growth is made in the top few inches of soil, it is a good plan to enrich this by forking in a little organic fertilizer, eg hoof and horn, or fishmeal.

If the soil is light and dries out quickly, fork in some well-moistened peat to make the soil more moisture retentive. In dry periods water the plants well so that there is no check to growth. The best radishes are always those that have been grown quickly.

There is never any need to reserve space for radishes as this is the ideal intercrop. Sow them between the rows of slower-growing crops such as peas or beans, on ground reserved for brassicas, or on any strip that will not be needed for a few weeks.

Summer radishes may be either of finger length or turnip-rooted. Where a frame or cloches are available, sowings can be made as early as February. Outdoor sowings should be made from late March or April, and then throughout the spring and summer. Sow little and often—it is easy to get too many radishes !

Most of the trouble encountered in growing radishes can be traced to two faults : sowing too deeply or too thickly. My own experience has convinced me that the best method of growing radishes is to sow them thinly

French Breakfast radish

Globe radish

Long white radish

on the soil surface in a band about 15cm (6in) wide. A good raking will put most of the seeds under the soil.

The only pest likely to be a nuisance is the flea-beetle, which eats holes in the young leaves. At the first sign of trouble dust the plants with derris or a proprietary flea-beetle dust.

Pull the roots as soon as they are large enough to eat. If they are left too long they become 'hot' and 'woody'. Take care when picking so that the other plants are disturbed as little as possible. Most sowings will give several pickings. After this, the residue is unlikely to be worth eating ; run the hoe through them, weeds and all.

Winter Radishes

Winter radishes are not as popular as summer ones, but are useful for winter salads. They make large roots which can be left in the ground all winter.

They are a good follow-on crop as they do not need to be sown until July or August. Sow the seeds in drills 25cm (10in) apart and thin the seedlings to stand 10–15cm (4–6in) apart. No special cultivation is required.

Recommended varieties

Summer radishes : French Breakfast, (long) red, with white tip ; Icicle (long), all white ; Sparkler and Cherry Belle (both turnip-rooted)
Winter radishes : China Rose, rose skin, white flesh ; Black Spanish, black skin with white flesh (roots may be either long or round)

Sowing radishes

Rhubarb

If given good treatment, rhubarb will crop freely for many years. As the roots are perennial a permanent site must be found for them. For convenience of access, the most favoured situations are across one end of the plot or down a pathside, and there is no objection to this provided that the site is in full sun. Because the plants will be there for many years, the ground should be well prepared, and this is one occasion where double-digging will be of benefit. A strip 5.5 × 1.5m (18 × 5ft) will take six plants, which is ample for the average family.

To double-dig the chosen strip, take out a trench 60cm (24in) wide, shovel out the loose soil, then break up the subsoil with a fork. Put some manure or good compost in the trench, then fill it in with the topsoil taken out from the next strip. The last trench is filled in with the soil from the first one. As each lot of topsoil is put back, mix in some bonemeal at 140g per sq m (4oz per sq yd). Do this work some weeks before planting so that the soil has time to settle down.

The quickest way of obtaining rhubarb is to buy one-year-old roots and plant them in November, February or March. Dig a hole with the spade and plant each root so that the crowns (growing points) are about 5cm (2in) below the soil surface.

Do not pull any sticks the first season after planting, and pull only lightly during the second season. The leaves, as they die off in autumn, give their support to the crowns, and, by building up strong crowns, a more productive bed is assured. For the same reason no crown should ever be cropped too severely, and pulling should cease at the end of June. Stalks which form after then should be left to feed the crowns.

Rhubarb may also be grown from seeds which are sown in April in drills 2cm (1in) deep and 38cm (15in) apart. Thin the seedlings to stand 30cm (12in) apart. They will vary widely in quality, and it will be necessary to leave them for a second season in order to pick out the best and strongest roots. No stalks should be taken from these, but they may be pulled from the rejected plants.

To maintain the bed in good condition, rake off the dead leaves each autumn and then spread a layer of good compost over the bed.

Seed heads take the strength from the plants and should be cut out as they appear. If, after a long period, the stalks become weaker and thinner it will be a sign that the roots need lifting and dividing. Dig them out, select the best and youngest crowns for replanting (they will be on the outside) and throw the old roots away.

Mild forcing of the roots can be done by covering the whole bed with a 15cm (6in) layer of straw in January. Another method is to cover selected roots with old buckets or tubs so that light is excluded and a little extra warmth given, but do not choose the same roots each year.

Recommended varieties

Champagne Early, Victoria, Glaskin's Perpetual

Rhubarb crown

Pulling rhubarb sticks

Shallots and Garlic

Shallots

There is an old gardening tradition that shallots should be planted on the shortest day and harvested on the longest. This does not always work, but it does give an indication of how hardy the shallot is. It can, in fact, be planted from December to March.

The shallot is one of the easiest vegetables to grow. The type of soil is not important, but it should be healthy. A strip that was dug and manured in the autumn is ideal.

An initial supply of bulbs can be obtained from any good seedsman or garden centre. There are two types, red and yellow, and for most purposes there is little to choose between them. The yellow shallot is a little larger and is generally preferred for exhibition purposes. For future crops, simply pick out firm bulbs of medium size from the current crop.

Plant the bulbs in rows 30cm (12in) apart, with 20cm (8in) between the bulbs. The best method of planting is to make a small hole with the point of the trowel, and sit the bulb in the hole with about one-third of it showing above ground. Birds may cause a nuisance by pulling the bulbs out again, but this can easily be prevented by running some black cotton over them or covering them with pea guards. When the tips of the bulbs show green they will have rooted and there should be no further trouble.

Although the bulbs are not damaged by frost, it will sometimes lift them a little; if this happens firm them in again. Keep them clean, but do not hoe too close to them or too deeply around them. Each bulb will split up to form a cluster of new bulbs.

By the end of June or in July,

Shallot bulbs planted in rows

according to the seasonal weather, the tops will turn yellow and flop over. The bulbs can then be lifted. To harvest them ease them with a fork, then pull them out and leave them on the ground to dry. Do not split them up at this stage. In warm, dry weather they can be dried off without difficulty; in cool, showery weather the roots may take hold of the soil again. To prevent this, remove them to a hard surface or put a few cloches over them. When the bulbs are quite dry and the tops withered, break up the clusters and rub off any loose skin.

Store the bulbs by spreading them out thinly in a light, cool and frost-proof place. The best method is to ask your greengrocer for a few shallow tomato trays and store the bulbs in these.

Garlic

Garlic is not difficult to grow. It likes a light to medium loam in good heart, and in full sun. A garlic bulb, as every garlic user knows, is made up of a number of segments or cloves. If these are planted in February, 5cm (2in) deep, with 20cm (8in) between the cloves and 30cm (12in) between the rows, they will grow on to form bulbs. No special cultivation is required. If flower heads form, pinch them out.

About the end of July the foliage turns yellow, and this is the sign to lift the bulbs. The harvesting and storing process is the same as for shallots.

Recommended varieties

Shallots : Giant Red, Giant Yellow
Garlic : Italian ; the easiest method is to
buy a bulb from the shop in the
ordinary way and use this.

Easing shallot bulbs

Garlic and shallot

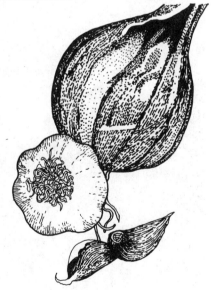

Spinach and Spinach Beet

Spinach beet

Spinach between
rows of peas

Spinach

Spinach is known to the housewife as a plant rich in iron, and to the gardener as the vegetable which holds the record for bolting ! Summer spinach is easy to grow, but it does like a soil well supplied with humus which will retain moisture. On light, hungry soils the bolting tendency is increased.

The plants are usually grown as an intercrop between rows of slower-growing vegetables such as peas or beans. The seeds of summer spinach are round, and it is sometimes referred to as round-seeded spinach. Sow the seeds from March to June in drills 13mm ($\frac{1}{2}$in) deep. As the period of harvesting is relatively short sowings every two or three weeks are needed to keep up a supply.

When the plants are large enough to handle, thin them to stand 8cm (3in) apart, and then take out every other plant when it is large enough to use. Mature plants can be picked over several times by taking the largest leaves first. Cut, or pinch them off, close up to the stem.

Dryness at the roots is another reason why the plants go to seed, so make sure they never lack water. Plants maturing during July or August will welcome the shade given by taller crops.

Winter spinach is also known as Prickly Spinach. This description is applied to the seeds, not the plants. It is hardier than the summer type and does not go to seed as quickly.

A strip of ground that was well manured for a previous crop is the best choice. As the seeds are not sown until August or September it is customary to use this as a follow-on crop to earlier vegetables. Sowings made at this time will give pickings from November until early April. Sow the seeds in rows 13mm ($\frac{1}{2}$in) deep and 30cm (12in) apart, and thin to 20cm (8in) apart. In February a little nitro-chalk at about 35g per metre run (1oz per yard run) will help to boost production.

Take only the largest leaves from each plant and do not take too many from one plant at a time as growth is slower during the winter months. The plants are hardy, but a better and cleaner crop will be otained if they are covered with cloches early in October.

Spinach Beet

This plant, which is also known as Perpetual Spinach, is an excellent spinach substitute. The leaves are larger and fleshier than those of the true spinach and the plants, being biennial, do not go to seed until their second year. Each plant forms a root like a beetroot, but it is grown for the leaves, not the root. When the larger leaves are removed, others grow to replace them.

Sow the seeds in drills 13mm ($\frac{1}{2}$in) deep and 38cm (15in) apart, and thin the plants to 20cm (8in) apart. A sowing can be made in April for summer use, and another in July or August for use in spring and early summer.

Recommended varieties

Summer Spinach : Viking, Long-
  standing Round
Winter Spinach : Greenmarket, Long-
  standing Prickly
Spinach Beet : usually listed as Spinach
  Beet or Perpetual Spinach

Sweet Corn

The plants do best in a medium loam, well supplied with humus. Heavy soils are not as suitable as they take too long to warm up. If manure or compost cannot be spared, choose a site that was well manured for the previous crop, and supplement this with a general fertilizer at 70g per sq m (2oz per sq yd), applied when the soil is worked down.

There are several ways of starting off the plants. If a cold greenhouse or frame is available, they can be raised in 9cm (3½in) pots, two seeds being sown in a pot. If both grow, pull one out. Sweet corn is only half-hardy and cannot be planted out while there is a risk of frost.

Another method, suitable for the cloche owner, is to sow two rows 38cm (15in) apart under barn cloches in April, and keep the plants covered until June. For an outdoor sowing without protection, sow the seeds about the middle of May, 5cm (2in) deep, with 30cm (12in) between the plants and 38cm (15in) between the rows.

The plants do not like root disturbance and if transplanting has to be done it should be done as carefully as possible. Peat or cardboard pots which break up after planting are often used for sweet corn.

Hoe carefully, as the plants are not deep rooting, and water well if the weather is dry. Moisture can be conserved after watering if a mulch of peat or lawn mowings is put down between the rows. In July and August the plants will respond well to foliar

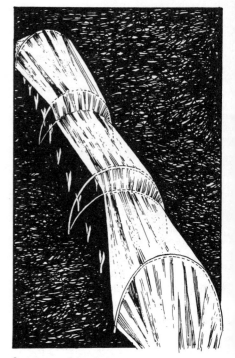

Sweet corn under cloche

feeding.

It helps to anchor the plants if a little soil is drawn up around the base of the stems. As they are subject to wind damage some kind of staking is advisable. One method is to use stout bamboo canes for each row, and run garden wire between them. Individual plants can then be tied to the wires.

The plants are decorative, and unusual, in that each plant carries both male and female parts. Fertilization takes place when the pollen from the male 'tassels' at the top of the plant is caught by the female 'silks' at the end of each immature cob. Each silk is a tuft of fine, silky hairs which turn brown as the cob ripens. Planting a number of short rows to form a block will make fertilization more effective

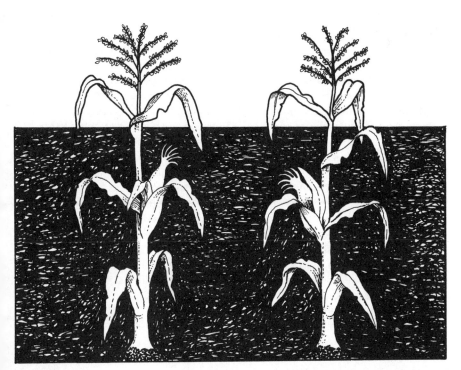

Sweet corn plants

and will also make staking easier.

Part of the art of growing sweet corn lies in knowing when the cobs are ready for gathering. The browning and withering of the silks is one guide. The most reliable way of judging the correct moment for harvesting is to turn back a little of the sheath until the grains are visible and then pierce a grain with a thumb-nail. If the liquid that comes out is watery, leave the cob a little longer ; the ideal stage for eating is when the liquid is milky. Detach the cob with a quick twist and cook as soon as possible after gathering.

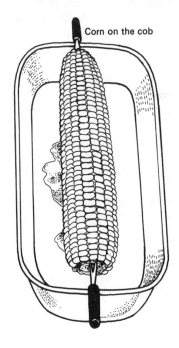

Corn on the cob

Recommended varieties

John Innes Hybrid (F1 hybrid),
    Earliking (F1 hybrid), Golden
    Bantam

Outdoor Tomatoes

To some extent, success with outdoor tomatoes must always be dependent on weather conditions, but the introduction of new varieties and the bush tomato, coupled with the use of cloches, have made it less of a gamble than it used to be.

A medium loam in good heart suits them well enough, but the type of soil is actually of less importance than the site, which should be a sunny one, preferably with some shelter from cold winds. A south-facing wall or boarded fence is ideal, as heat will be reflected back on to the plants.

Plants may be bought in, if desired, but the choice of varieties is limited. Choose plants which are short jointed and of a good, deep colour. The plants can be raised without much trouble if a cool greenhouse is available. Sow the seeds in a seed-pan early in April, and prick them off into 9cm ($3\frac{1}{2}$in) pots when the first true leaves have formed. Keep them well to the light and harden them off thoroughly before planting out. Gardeners without a greenhouse can raise enough plants for a family by starting them off in the sunny window of a warm room. Turn the pots daily to keep the plants from growing to one side.

Unless the plants can be put out under frames or cloches, transplanting cannot take place until the risk of frost has passed. In most districts this will be early June. Put them out 45cm (18in) apart, with the soil ball covered by about 13mm ($\frac{1}{2}$in) of new soil.

It helps the plants to get off to a good start if they can be given some protection from cold winds for the first few weeks after planting. Strips of plastic joined together or plastic bags cut open and secured to bamboo canes, make an effective screen.

Outdoor tomatoes are of two types—cordon and bush—but it should be remembered that any tomato plant, if left to its own devices, will make a bush. Growing the plants as cordons (ie keeping them to one main stem) is done to produce better and earlier fruits. The side-shoots, which form in the axils of the leaves, should be pinched out as they appear. When each plant has set four or five trusses (branches) of fruit, pinch out the growing point.

Bush plants under barn cloche

Bush tomatoes, on the other hand, do not need any training except perhaps to cut out superfluous shoots. They are excellent for growing under barn cloches.

Cordon varieties can be fed with a proprietary tomato fertilizer once the bottom fruits have set. Bush tomatoes do not need feeding ; on too rich a diet they tend to produce foliage at the expense of fruit.

Covering the plants with frames or cloches, if only for a few weeks until they grow too big, is of great benefit, and similar protection at the end of the season will assist ripening. Cordon varieties should be cut from their stakes in September and laid on clean straw or black plastic. Bush plants, pulled down with fruit, can have cloches put over them. Ripening will then continue into October. After that, pick all the fruit and take it indoors. Many will still ripen if they are kept in a basket in a warm living-room or kitchen. Cover them with a cloth.

Outdoor tomatoes are not subject to as many pests and diseases as their indoor cousins. Slugs may be troublesome, especially with the bush varieties. Potato blight can be deadly and spraying should be done, as for potatoes.

Recommended varieties

Outdoor cordons : Outdoor Girl, Marmande
Bush tomatoes : French Cross (F1 hybrid) and Sleaford Abundance (F1 hybrid) are two varieties that give heavy crops of good-quality fruit

Pinching out side-shoots

193

Turnips, Swedes and Kohl Rabi

Turnips

Turnip varieties can be divided into two groups : the early summer ones, and the later ones which can be stored for winter use.

The summer varieties need a soil with a good humus content which will not dry out too quickly. Medium to heavy loams usually fill this need. On light soils these turnips can prove difficult, especially in a hot summer.

Sow the summer varieties from March to June in drills 13mm ($\frac{1}{2}$in) deep and 30cm (12in) apart, and thin the seedlings to stand 10–15cm (4–6in) apart. It is better to make several small sowings than one large one ; the roots can then be used before they become too big.

Turnips for winter storage should be sown towards the end of June or in July. These should stand 15cm (6in) apart and will crop from October onwards. They can be used as a follow-on vegetable. To prepare a bed for them apply a dressing of a general fertilizer at 70g per sq m (2oz per sq yd) and prick it into the top few inches of soil.

In November the turnips can be lifted for storage. Cut off the tops an inch or two from the crown, trim the roots a little, and then store the turnips in boxes of dry sand or soil.

Swede

Milan White

Swedes

Swedes may be sown in May or June. They need similar conditions to turnips. Sow them thinly in drills 38cm (15in) apart and thin out to 20cm (8in). They are hardier than turnips and can stay out all winter. The garden swede is a little smaller than the field swede.

In the spring any swedes which are left will make new tops. These are rich in iron and can be cut for use as a vegetable. Where they are appreciated a sowing can be made especially for this purpose. This sowing need not be made until August and need not be thinned.

Kohl Rabi

Where turnips prove difficult it is often recommended that kohl rabi should be grown instead. This is good advice as this vegetable is less demanding in its soil requirements and will grow in any good garden soil. But it is also well worth growing as a vegetable in its own right. It has a nutty, turnip-like flavour and its popularity is increasing. The plant is rather curious in that it forms the edible root above the ground. The root is, in fact, the swollen stem of the plant which bulges out like a ball. It is at its best when it is between golf- and cricket-ball size.

Kohl rabi may be sown from March to early August in shallow drills 38cm (15in) apart. Thin the plants to stand 15cm (6in) apart. There is a white form and a purple form of this vegetable.

Being brassicas, turnips, swedes and kohl rabi can all be attacked by club root (see Brassicas, page 154). It is wise, therefore, to keep them clear of badly-infected soil and change their site each year. The flea-beetle may

Kohl rabi

plague them when they have just broken through the soil, but this can be dealt with by dusting the seedlings with derris or a flea-beetle dust.

Recommended varieties

Summer turnips : Milan White, Snowball
Winter turnips : Manchester Market, Golden Ball
Swedes : Purple Top
Kohl rabi : White Vienna, Earliest Purple

Vegetable Marrows, Courgettes and Pumpkins

Marrows and Courgettes

Nowadays the large marrow is out of favour and the trend is for smaller fruits. Courgettes, now so popular, are simply baby marrows cut when they are very small.

The vegetable marrow can be grown in most soils. Light soils will need enriching with manure or compost to help them retain moisture. Heavy soils should be opened up with strawy manure or rough compost to improve the drainage and to prevent water from gathering round the roots of the plants.

Plants can be raised by making a

sowing in pots in a frame or cool greenhouse in April. Push two seeds down on edge in a 9cm (3½in) pot and pull the weaker seedling out if both germinate. Marrows are only half-hardy and cannot be planted out until the risk of frost has passed. They do not like root disturbance and should be moved with care. Peat or cardboard pots, which break up after planting, should be used for them. The object of this method is to gain a few weeks of growing time.

An easier method is to push in the seeds where the plants are to grow. This can be done during the middle of May, planting three seeds in a triangle, 10cm (4in) apart, then selecting the best plant for growing on; allow 122cm (48in) between the plants.

Marrows and courgettes

Beyond seeing that the plants are kept clean, and that they do not lack water during dry periods, no special care is needed. Fertilization should occur naturally with outdoor plants, but if the flowers fall off without setting, hand fertilization can be done by stripping a male flower of its petals and pushing it into the heart of a female flower. The females are easy to recognize as they have an embryo marrow behind the flower.

Some varieties produce long vines (trailing shoots) on which the fruits form. The bush varieties grow in a circle. It is not always realized that the trailing varieties will climb. This makes them suitable for planting at the foot of a fence or trellis. Some of the vines may need to be tied up, and hanging fruits should be supported or their weight may pull the vines down again.

Cut the fruits when they are large enough to use and others will follow. For use as courgettes the fruits need not be more than 10–15cm (4–6in) long. Some varieties are better than others for producing courgettes, but their cultivation is exactly the same as for ordinary marrows.

Pumpkins

Pumpkins are grown in the same way as marrows, but need to be 2m (6ft) apart. The fruits of pumpkins should be left to ripen and then cut around the end of September. Limit each plant to two or three fruits so that they reach a good size.

Surplus marrows may also be left to ripen on the plants. If the ripe fruits of pumpkins and marrows are stored in a dry, warm place they will keep sound for several months.

Pumpkin

Recommended varieties

Marrows : Long White Trailing ; White Bush ; Long Green Trailing ; Green Bush ; Table Dainty, a trailing green marrow of medium size

Courgettes : Zucchine (F1 hybrid), green bush ; Golden Zucchine (F1 hybrid), yellow bush

Pumpkins : Hundredweight, the standard variety

Herbs

Because they are found so often in vegetable gardens or on allotments, there are five herbs that can fairly be described as basic herbs. They all do well in a good, medium loam and a sunny position, and will succeed also in heavier soils provided that drainage is good. They are chives, parsley, sage, thyme and mint.

Chives

This plant resembles spring onions both in appearance and in flavour. It sends up a profusion of slender leaves which can be cut off about 5cm (2in) above soil level. New shoots soon appear. The foliage dies down in winter and reappears in spring. If the clumps are not cut attractive blue flowers are formed. An initial supply can be obtained by growing seeds in April. Thereafter , it is only necessary to divide the clumps as needed in autumn or spring.

Parsley

The best time for sowing parsley is in February and March, and again in July. Parsley is a biennial and goes to seed in its second year. Germination is very slow (it is said that parsley goes nine times to the devil before coming up !) and it is a good plan to sow a few radish seeds with the parsley so that the row can be picked out for weeding. Thin the plants to stand 25–30cm (10–12in) apart. This gives finer plants and better leaves. If the plants are covered with a cloche or two in the autumn, fresh parsley can be picked all through the winter. Some people are

Parsley

convinced that pouring boiling water on the newly-seeded bed makes the plants come up faster.

Sage

The best sage for most purposes is the broad-leaved sage. This is a shrubby, perennial plant about 45cm (18in) high, with grey-green leaves. Cuttings of broad-leaved sage root readily, if planted in May. After a few years the plants tend to get leggy and should be replaced with rooted cuttings. The narrow-leaved sage bears a purple flower and can be grown from seed.

Thyme

A good thyme bush will be about 30cm (12in) high and as much as 90cm (36in) across. The common thyme is the most popular. It can be grown from seeds, sown in the spring. The other method of propagation is to draw soil up all around a plant and peg the thyme into the soil. New roots soon form. The plant has a delightful fragrance when the leaves are bruised and is quite hardy.

Mint

There are several forms of mint, but spearmint is the most common. Mint is an invasive plant which grows by thrusting out its roots into the surrounding soil. New shoots are sent up from the joints of the roots. Start off with a few roots and plant them in early spring about 5cm (2in) deep. The easiest method of planting is to take out a shallow trench with the spade, spread the roots out along the trench and then cover them. Mint tends to grow outwards, leaving the middle of the bed bare, and as it has to be hand-weeded it is a good plan to make a fresh bed every few years. Some people keep it within bounds by growing it in an old bucket or tin bath sunk into the soil. It will grow in partial shade.

Mint is subject to a fungus disease called rust which produces brown spots underneath the leaves. The best cure is to burn the foliage off in the autumn by forking dry straw or litter among the stems so that the flames sweep through quickly.

Thyme

Mint

MAKING YOUR CHILDREN'S CLOTHES

Gail Fox

Introduction

In the past, children's clothes were difficult to make as they were really replicas of grown-up clothes in miniature and very intricate in design. They were more often than not uncomfortable to wear as well, as the fabrics were too heavy and coarse, irritating a child's delicate skin.

Today, the picture is totally different. The clothes are very simple in style and easy to make. The major pattern companies, McCall's, Vogue, Butterick, Style and Simplicity, have an excellent variety of children's designs to choose from, covering all aspects of clothing which are suitable for children of all ages from newborn babies and toddlers to older children. Until recently fabrics were a problem, but now fabric manufacturers have realised that the type of materials, colours and designs offered to grown-ups were unsuitable for children. There is a wide variety of exciting and pretty fabrics just right for children's wear available in the shops.

This book is designed to give helpful hints and information on sewing children's clothes and saving the pennies. Careful planning when creating a child's wardrobe, by choice of fabrics and colour co-ordination, is the secret of success, enabling you to clothe your child as you would wish while keeping within your budget. By making them yourself, you will also be able to afford many more clothes for your child which will give the garments a longer lease of life as they will suffer less wear and tear. With the advent of marvellous electric sewing machines, children's clothes can be made up very quickly indeed as the machines do most of the work for you. However, not all of us are lucky enough to possess one, so techniques of sewing by hand are included here as well. The end results will be just the same but will take a little more time and patience. I hope the book will encourage sewing beginners as well. Once you understand the basic sewing techniques and terminology you will see how simple it is and sewing will become a pleasure rather than a chore—and you will save money at the same time.

Choose the correct size of pattern by consulting the Standard Measurement Chart at the back of the pattern catalogues and always have a fitting before finally machining up the outfit. Check that your fabric is suitable for the design by consulting the fabric recommendations on the back of the pattern envelope. Extra fabric will be required for matching checks, stripes and one-way designs depending on the size of the repeat.

Before starting to machine, always check the tension and stitch length on a test sample of the fabric and ensure that you have the correct needle : for stretchable knitted fabrics use a ball-point needle ; for delicate fabrics, eg lawn, batiste, lightweight cottons, use a fine sharp needle ; for heavier fabrics you will need a stronger needle.

Select your thread : use a synthetic thread for synthetic fibres ; cotton for pure cotton and lightweight wools and mercerised cotton for heavier weight, natural fabrics ; or use a multi-purpose thread such as Drima or Dewhurst Star. Use a special thick top-stitching thread for top-stitching or the effect of the stitching will be lost. Always choose the thread carefully, choosing a slightly darker shade than the fabric as the thread will come up lighter as it comes off the full reel.

Machine seams from the top towards the hem. On curved seams, such as armholes and cuffs, machine from the inside. When joining a gathered skirt or frill to the main part of the outfit, machine with the gathers uppermost to keep them smooth. Always machine fabrics with a pile, such as velvet and corduroy, 'with' the pile to avoid the foot marking the fabric.

In order to protect the pile when working with slippery fabrics or with velvet, it is a good idea to place tissue paper between the two layers before machining the seam. When using fabrics which can stretch out of shape, tack tissue paper underneath. The tissue can easily be torn away after machining.

There are some marvellous quick and easy sewing aids on the market such as hemming web, so you can just iron your hem into place, buttonsnaps which avoid the labour of making buttonholes, and self-adhesive fastenings. Decorative elastic is available in various widths perfect for waistbands, cuffs and around the bottom of jackets.

Fitting

The fit of a garment has great bearing on the finished appearance of an outfit. It is the difference between clothes looking home-made and the professional touch. Careful measurement beforehand can save a lot of heartache. Children are impatient and not prepared to stand still for lots of adjustments to be made. Accurate notes at the beginning should ensure that only one fitting is needed, when the garment is tacked up, before the final machining or sewing.

Children's wear does not need the tailored fit of grown-up attire. Clothes tend to hang loosely from the shoulders, controlled either with a tie belt or an elastic casing to give them any slight shaping required. Therefore the shoulder, chest and neckline fit, together with the finished length, are the most important factors. Patterns should be selected by the breast/chest measurement as other areas are easy to adjust once this fit has been accomplished.

Children's patterns come in various figure types: toddlers, children, girls and boys. It must be remembered that the sizes refer to the child's measurements and not to his age. To ascertain one's choice of size and type of pattern, take the following measurements and compare them with the Standard Measurement Chart found at the back of pattern catalogues. Firstly it is important to locate the waist. This can be difficult as children are fairly straight up and down. But it will be needed not only as a measurement in itself but also to calculate the finished length of clothes Mark the waistline by tying a piece of string or narrow ribbon around it and take the following measurements:

Overall height standing against a wall without shoes
Breast/chest placing the tape measure under the arms straight across the back and front
Waist over the top of the tie
Back waist length from the 'bump' at the base of the neck—ie the vertebra at the top of the spine— to the waist tie

To measure the finished lengths of the clothes, take the back length of dresses from the base of the neck; skirts, pants, and shorts from the waistline tie over the hip; and sleeve length from the tip of the shoulder to the wrist.

Toddlers' and children's breast and waist measurements are usually the same although the clothes vary in length. Toddlers' patterns begin at a smaller size and are graded for a figure between a baby and a child, so clothes are shorter and pants have extra ease to go over nappies. Girls' patterns are designed for a girl who has not begun to mature but has acquired a waistline. Boys up to a 65cm (25½in) chest come into the children's category. For boys' sizes 7–12 (see the measurement chart at the back of the catalogues), who have not reached the age of adolescence, you will also need the following measurements:

Around the bottom of the neck
Around the largest part of the hip between the waist and crotch
Shoulder length from the bottom of the neck to the top of the shoulder
Outside leg from the waist to finished

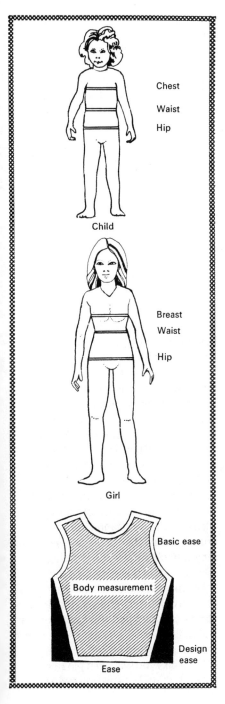

Chest

Waist

Hip

Child

Breast

Waist

Hip

Girl

Basic ease

Body measurement

Design ease

Ease

length
Inside leg from crotch to finished
length
Crotch depth, which is the difference
between the inside and outside leg
measurements.

Ease

Having bought your pattern, compare
the child's measurements with the
tissue by measuring from seamline to
seamline, so if any adjustments are
necessary these can be made to the
tissue before cutting out your fabric.
It is most important to remember that
all patterns have a certain amount of
ease built into the design to allow for
natural movement and the tissue
should be slightly larger than actual
measurements to account for this.

The amount of ease will vary
according to the type of fabric
recommended for the design listed
on the pattern envelope (knitted
fabrics have less ease because of their
natural elasticity than woven fabrics)
and the type of design.

Room should also be allowed if
sweaters, etc are to be worn under the
outfit and body measurements should
be taken over the top of these garments.
Ease will also be greater in all-in-one
outfits, such as jumpsuits and
dungarees, to avoid your child being
rubbed or cut painfully when moving.
Careful note should be taken of the
front and back crotch lengths.

Patterns designed for stretch fabrics
normally carry a guide to show how
much elasticity there should be in the
material. As the amount of stretch does
vary in different fabrics, it is essential
that the correct one is chosen, or the
design will become distorted.

Basic Wardrobe

Layette for a Newborn Baby

Baby clothes should be light, warm and loose fitting so that the child's limbs are not constricted. Babies have very delicate skins so fabrics must be fine and soft to avoid irritation. As their clothes will be washed frequently, choose easy-care materials such as lightweight cotton, batiste, voile, challis, lightweight wools, cotton flannel, cotton knits and soft towelling. If possible, ensure that the clothes are washed in pure soap rather than in strong detergents which again may irritate delicate skin. Do not choose harsh colours which will detract from the baby's tiny features and pale complexion. White and cream are an obvious choice, but if you would like to use other colours, pick mute shades of blue, lemon and pink, avoiding harsh colours at all costs. Elaborate trimmings are not advisable as they have the same unkind effect as strong colours. Keep clothes very simple, highlighting edges with blanket stitch, fine narrow lace, or scallops, which will give a pretty finishing touch. Only use simple embroidery stitches such as satin, chain, and lazy daisy, which don't look fussy on small clothes.

You will find excellent layettes for your baby in the major pattern companies' catalogues which you can make up while waiting for the birth. In general, it is worth remembering that raglan sleeves and sleeves cut in one with the garment are a good idea as they give extra room around the upper arm. Choose clothes which hang loosely, either gathered into the neck or into a high yoke to give lots of room for movement.

Basically, you will need a long dress and coat which can also be used for the baby's christening ; a bonnet or hat to keep the head warm ; an all in one cover-up, clothing hands and feet, with a hood for the head ; a nightgown, a dressing gown, a bib, a matinée jacket, a short day dress for a girl, and a small jacket and pants to go over a nappy for a boy ; bootees, mittens, a vest and a shawl. I have not mentioned nappies as they can be made from 1 sq m (1 sq yd) of towelling, but it is probably quicker and easier to buy them.

Basic Wardrobe for Young Children

For children whose clothes are going to have to suffer more wear and tear than babies' clothes, it is a good idea from a budget point of view to include quite a few separates. These can be worn with different shirts and sweaters so you can swing the changes to get several different looks from a few basic clothes. Keep one outfit for 'best', a dress for a girl and a suit for a boy, which is not going to end up covered in mud, or with the pockets torn off during robust play, just when you are in a hurry to go somewhere special. Also give them a change from school uniform when they come home so that they can relax and let off their high spirits without fear of getting dirty.

When deciding on a basic wardrobe choose colours carefully so that they can be co-ordinated and a new jumper will not necessarily need to have a new skirt or trousers to go with it.

For a girl, you will need pinafore dresses, skirts, blouses and sweaters,

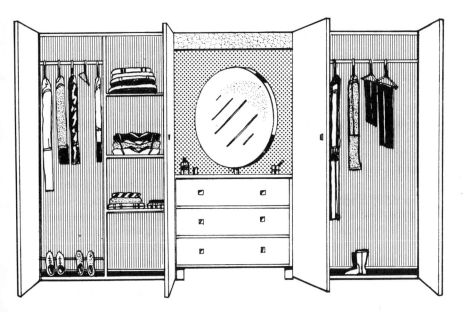

day dresses and perhaps a long party dress, a nightie and a dressing-gown. For a boy you will need one good suit, a tie, trousers, shorts, a casual jacket, shirts and sweaters, pyjamas and a dressing gown. Dungarees, jumpsuits, jeans and T-shirts can be worn by either sex. A coat will be needed, and an anorak or poncho, a mackintosh, socks, shoes and wellingtons.

School uniforms are expensive to buy and it is well worth while checking with your child's school to see if they have chosen a pattern and fabric for their uniform which you can then make up far more cheaply yourself.

Hardwearing and easy-care fabrics are a must for children's clothes as they spend so much time in the washing machine. Now there is a wide choice of fabrics on the market at economic prices suitable for children's wear, ranging from lightweight cottons, lawn, batiste, gingham, synthetic

blends and mixtures to duck, drill, gaberdine, denim, corduroy, wools, wool blends, and their synthetic counterparts which all come in a variety of colours and designs.

For a tall, thin child, choose clothes which give an illusion of extra width such as smock dresses, empire-line or waisted dresses with gathered skirts, skirts with frills, short puff sleeves or long full sleeves gathered at the sleevehead. Bold prints and checks and horizontal stripes are very suitable.

For a plump child, choose a straighter silhouette such as A-line dresses flaring from a high yoke or from the shoulders and set in sleeves. Small prints and checks and lengthwise stripes are the most suitable.

Waterproof fabric for raincoats and ponchos is not widely available in this country. However, most good dry cleaners will proof the clothes for you after you have made them up.

207

Pattern Markings and Terminology

The major pattern companies all have clear markings on the design tissue to ensure the garment goes together correctly and easily. A clear understanding of this terminology will aid quick and easy making up of a garment.

The Selvage Edge

This is the narrow woven strip on either side of the width of the fabric.

Fabric Grain

It is most important that your fabric grain is perfect to ensure that the garment hangs properly when completed. If the material is off-grain and not straightened out before cutting the pattern pieces, the fabric will pucker and bulge and never hang correctly. The grain is the direction in which the threads of the fabric run. In woven fabrics, the lengthwise grain comprises the threads running parallel to the selvage and the crosswise grain comprises the threads running across the fabric, under and over the lengthwise threads at right angles. In knit fabrics, the vertical rows of loops are the lengthwise grain and the crosswise grain runs perpendicular to this, as in woven fabrics. To cut on the bias, first find the true bias of the fabric by folding the material diagonally so that the crosswise threads are parallel to the selvage. The grainline will be shown on the tissue by a thick arrow with points at both ends. Whether the tissue is to be placed on the lengthwise or crosswise grain or bias of the fabric will also be indicated.

If your fabric is off-grain, there are two ways to correct this. With the help of a friend, hold one end of the fabric and pull the material on the true bias in the opposite direction to the higher off-grain edges. Keep stretching in this way along the selvage edges until the crosswise threads are at ninety degrees or perpendicular to the lengthwise threads. If the fabric is too thick and strong to straighten in this way, as wools would be, it has to be pulled and blocked into shape while pressing the material using a damp pressing cloth or steam iron.

Fabric Layouts

When laying out your pattern pieces, study the instruction sheet carefully to see whether the fabric is laid out flat in a single layer, whether the two selvage edges should be together giving a lengthwise fold, or whether the fabric is folded on the crosswise grain giving a crosswise fold.

Notches

Notches are triangular markings which are vital to ensure that the correct pieces go together and to avoid mistakes, such as a sleeve being put in the wrong way round. You may also be required to gather between two

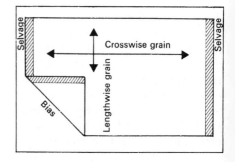

notches or ease in the fabric. Transfer these markings either by cutting out the notches outside the seam allowance—two or three notches can be cut together as one shape—or by making small snips in the seam allowance.

Small and Large Dots

These are also very important guidelines during construction. They mark points in a seam to show how far it should be sewn up, such as to the bottom of the zip opening, or to where a pocket is to be inserted into the seam allowance. They are used as markers for gathering and often matched up with seams, especially when setting in a sleeve to match the sleevehead with the shoulder seam. They mark darts and the positioning of pattern pieces such as patch pockets. These markings should be transferred to the fabric by making two tacks to form a cross. Use double strands of thread and leave fairly long tails of thread at either end of the stitch. You can also use proper tailor's tacks. Work these stitches with tacking thread of a different colour from the fabric so that they will show up clearly.

Seam Allowances and Cutting Lines

The seam allowance is clearly shown on designs from all the major pattern companies. This is normally 1.5cm ($\frac{5}{8}$in) and shown as a broken line inside the thick cutting-line. When checking your measurements against the tissue to see if any adjustment is necessary, remember to measure from seamline to seamline and not between the cutting-lines. Most

modern sewing machines will have a space gauge beside the foot which helps you keep an even seam. If there is no seam allowance inside, only a single line, check to see whether this line should be placed on a fold and do not cut it. Transfer the seam allowance to your fabric, making a series of tacks using double strands of thread and leaving fairly long tails, or make tailor's tacks.

Darts

A dart will be shown by dots at intervals along two broken converging lines ending in a point with a single dot. Darts control fullness and give shape to garments to make them fit. These markings should be transferred to the fabric using tacks with long tails of thread at either end of the first and last stitch for the broken lines. Double tacks forming a cross should mark the dots or use tailor's tacks with different coloured thread.

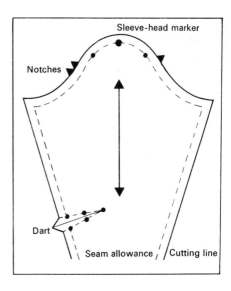

Sleeve-head marker

Notches

Dart

Seam allowance / Cutting line

Pattern Markings and Terminology

Right and wrong sides

The right and wrong sides of the fabric are usually differentiated by shading. This is most important if the material is printed only on one side. A pattern piece, to be placed face down on the fabric, will also be marked by shading so check carefully with the sewing directions on the instruction sheet to find out what sort of markings they have used.

Grading

When you have two or more layers of fabric, and possibly interfacing too, the seam has to be graded to reduce the bulk and prevent an unsightly ridge forming and showing through to the right side of the garment when the seam is pressed. The layers of fabric have to be cut away in differing widths with the widest layer next to the outside fabric and the interfacing trimmed as close as possible to the seamline.

Interfacing

Interfacing is used to give a crisp finish to garments and keep them in shape. It is used in collars, cuffs, openings which have to bear the strain of fastenings and waistbands. Interfacings vary in weight and construction and it is important that you choose the sort compatible with your fabric. Woven interfacings should be used for woven fabrics. Use transparent interfacings for sheer fabrics. There are also lightweight, medium and heavy qualities and a special thick interfacing for waistbands. For stretchable knitted fabrics use a non-woven interfacing with a flexibility to complement the fabric and prevent puckering while still providing the necessary stability. Both woven and non-woven interfacings come in iron-on versions, which is a great time-saver, but do be careful that your fabric is suitable and will not shrivel away when a hot iron is applied. Interfacing is also used on hems of very stretchy knits to prevent the fabric from puckering. When applying by hand, tack into place on the wrong side of the fabric 1.3cm ($\frac{1}{2}$in) in from the raw edges and hem stitch along a foldline.

Transferring Markings on to the Fabric

It is extremely important that all markings on the tissue—darts, notches, dots, seam allowances, pleats and tucks—are transferred on to the fabric before the tissue is removed. There are several ways to do this including tacking, as already described. Two other quick and easy ways are to use either pins and tailor's chalk or dressmaker's carbon and a tracing wheel.

The former method can be used on most fabrics as the chalk marks come off easily when the outfit is washed or dry cleaned. With the tissue facing upwards, insert pins through the markings and continue straight down through the layers of fabric. Carefully turn the tissue and fabric over so that all the pins are pointing straight up in the air. On a hard, flat working surface draw lines connecting the pins with a ruler and tailor's chalk. Turn the piece

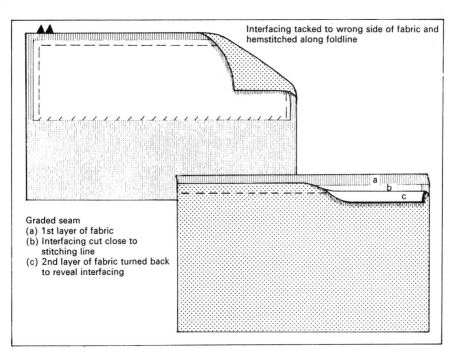

Interfacing tacked to wrong side of fabric and hemstitched along foldline

Graded seam
(a) 1st layer of fabric
(b) Interfacing cut close to stitching line
(c) 2nd layer of fabric turned back to reveal interfacing

over with the tissue facing upwards and gently remove the pattern piece pulling the pins through the tissue so that they remain in the fabric. Draw in the lines connecting the pin heads.

When using dressmaker's carbon and a tracing wheel, the markings have to be transferred to the wrong side of the fabric. This method cannot be used on transparent or very pale fine fabrics as the carbon lines would show through to the right side. They do not wash out. Select light-coloured carbon paper for dark fabrics and vice versa for light-coloured fabrics. To mark two layers of fabric at the same time, cut a strip of carbon 7.5cm (3in) wide by 25.5cm (10in) long and fold it in half with the carbon side exposed. Put the bottom half under the top layer of fabric and the other between the top

layer of fabric and the tissue. Draw along the markings with the tracing wheel using a ruler where necessary.

With and Without Nap

A fabric with nap has a one-way design, pile, nap or shading such as corduroy, velvet and fur, and all the pattern pieces must go in the same direction. Test which way the pile runs by gently rubbing your hand over the surface of the fabric. Velvet should be cut with the pile running towards the top of the outfit and corduroy and fur with the pile going towards the hem. A fabric without nap is one with a design going either way and without pile, nap or shading so pattern pieces can go in opposite directions, which often saves on the amount of fabric required.

Hems

The hem, normally the final part of
construction, should not be finished in
a rush at the last minute. In a way it is
almost the most important aspect,
making the difference between a
perfectly finished garment and one
which looks home-made. It is difficult
to persuade a child to stand straight
and still, and it is worth a bribe so you
can mark the hem accurately using a
ruler and tailor's chalk or pins, the
secret of a successful, even hem rather
than one which dips and sways.

Always allow the garment to hang
for at least twenty-four hours before
turning up the hem in case the fabric
should drop, making the hem uneven.
Make sure the child is standing on a
hard, flat surface and wearing any
bulky clothes which will usually be
worn underneath. Turn up the hem on
the marking-line and pin into place
with pins perpendicular to the folded
edge, removing any marking pins as
you go.

Tack evenly, close to the folded edge.
Take out the pins and press the hem on
the inside on the folded edge. Cut the
hem to an even width.

With very stretchy fabrics and
loosely-woven knits it can be a good
idea to interface the hem to give it extra
stability. Cut the interfacing on the bias
5mm ($\frac{1}{4}$in) wider than the finished
hem and mark a line 2cm ($\frac{3}{4}$in) in from
one of the long edges. Place this line
to the foldline of the hem on the
wrong side of the fabric and sew into
place 5mm ($\frac{1}{4}$in) below the foldline,
catching the top edge of the interfacing
to the garment seams. Turn up the hem

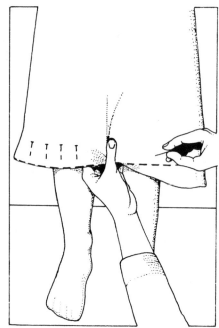

Turn up hem on marking line

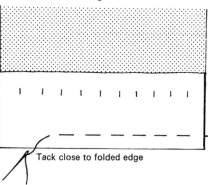

Tack close to folded edge

Trim hem

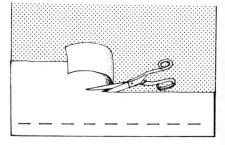

on the foldline and sew into place.

If the upper edge of the hem is wider than the garment, which can easily happen in children's clothes when a large hem is being allowed to account for growth, the extra fullness can be shrunk out. Run a gathering thread round the hem just below the top edge. Turn up the hem and pin to the seams, pulling up the thread in between to fit and adjusting the fullness evenly. Put thick paper between the hem and the garment fabric and press with a steam iron on the inside. The paper will prevent a mark appearing on the right side of the garment.

As children seem to shoot up at a rate of knots, always allow as deep a hem as possible and slip stitch by hand so that it can be let down easily. Do not machine the hem as this may leave a mark on the fabric when you try to let it down. If the style of the outfit allows it, make a double hem. Make the first hem as described, then turn up the amount of the hem again and slip stitch into place.

Hems

There are several kinds of hems and which one you choose really depends on the type of garment and weight of fabric, as the object is to make the hem as invisible as possible.

A regular or dressmaker's hem is suitable for most fabrics and styles. First neaten the raw edge by the method most suited to your material (see the section on seam finishes). Tack the hem in place, 1.3cm ($\frac{1}{2}$in) below the upper edge. Turn the fabric back on this stitching-line and sew, picking up a thread of the garment and making a small diagonal stitch into the hem. Do not pull the stitches too tight as this will make the hem pucker. When the hem is completed, take out the tacking threads and press it from the inside.

If the fabric is likely to fray, the edge of the hem can be encased in bias seam binding. With right sides together, stitch the binding to the top of the hem and if necessary, trim the seam to 3mm ($\frac{1}{8}$in). Fold the tape over the top of the raw edge of the hem and press.

Join the binding to the hem, stitching along the seamline on the right side. Fold the hem back to just below the stitching-line and sew into place with invisible stitches as before.

Very fine, delicate fabrics, such as baby clothes, should be finished with a tiny rolled hem. Using a machine or continuous running stitch, sew round the garment 3mm ($\frac{1}{8}$in) from the bottom edge, trimming the fabric close to the stitching-line. Roll the edge of the fabric between your thumb and first finger to cover the raw edge and secure with tiny hemming stitches. Alternatively, a very narrow hem can be made which is useful for shirts and blouses as well as in places where a normal hem would be too bulky. First turn under 3mm ($\frac{1}{8}$in) on the raw edge and stitch close to the edge. Fold under the same amount again and sew into place with tiny hemming stitches.

A useful hem for children's clothes which are going to spend most of their time in the washing machine is a turned and stitched hem, but this can only be applied to fabrics which do not show through to the right side. Make an even row of tacking stitches 6mm

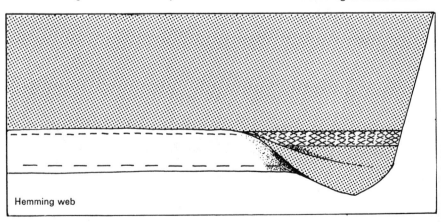

Hemming web

($\frac{1}{4}$in) below the top edge of the hem and turn under the raw edge on the stitching-line. Machine close to the folded edge, press and remove the tacking threads. Turn up the hem and tack into position. Sew the hem into place with invisible stitches.

A smooth and simple finish can be used on shorts and blouses made in fabrics which do not fray. Either machine around the bottom 1.3cm ($\frac{1}{2}$in) from the raw edge and trim the fabric with pinking shears 6mm ($\frac{1}{4}$in) below the stitching-line and leave flat or turn up the trimmed edge on the stitching-line and sew into place close to the folded edge.

Felt, of course, is a marvellous time-saving fabric for skirts and capes if your child is not going to outgrow the garment before it wears out. As the fabric does not fray, there is no need to neaten the seams or turn up the hem. Simply cut the skirt to the desired finished length taking care to keep it even.

There are two quick and easy ways of turning up a hem if it is likely that the clothes will be worn out before they become too short. Using either of these methods it is almost impossible to let down a hem at a later date. Either a strip of hemming web can be placed between the hem and the garment, which will stick the two together when they are ironed, or a hem can be turned up and top stitched into place giving a decorative finish to the garment. Neaten the raw edge and turn under 1.5cm ($\frac{5}{8}$in) hem. Tack and machine two rows of top stitching, the first 6mm ($\frac{1}{4}$in) from the folded edge and the second 6mm ($\frac{1}{4}$in) above this. Remove the tacking stitches and press.

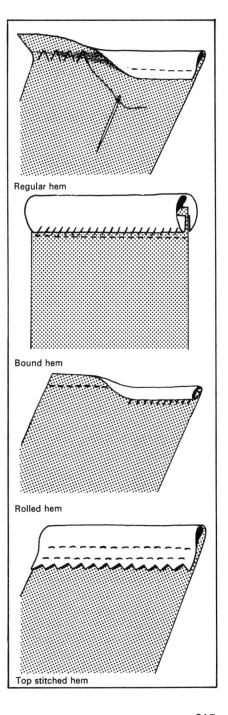

Regular hem

Bound hem

Rolled hem

Top stitched hem

Trousers

Trousers, like skirts, are very useful separates for a child's wardrobe as they can be worn with different shirts, blouses, T-shirts and sweaters, giving various looks from one basic garment.

The fit of trousers so that they hang correctly and are neither too loose nor too baggy is most important. The measurements you will need are waist, hip, thigh, inside and outside leg and the crotch length. The waist should fit comfortably and remember to allow enough ease on the hips and thighs so that the child can bend and sit down. The crotch length is most important and should be taken sitting down. Measure from the waist to the middle of the crotch both from the front and from the back, taking the tape-measure through the child's legs. Although the crotch length on the pattern may be the same as the overall crotch measurement, children tend to have round tummies and the front crotch length should be lengthened to account for this. On the other hand, if the child has a large behind the back crotch will have to be extended. Obviously, the crotch does not want to be hanging down around the knees but *do* allow enough ease for natural movement and for your child to sit down without being cut in two.

Probably the most sensible waists for children's trousers are made either with an elastic casing or with a waistband made of decorative elastic, which will stretch as the child begins to grow. With an elastic casing, the elastic can always be removed when the waist becomes too tight, and a longer length can be inserted.

To make the casing, allow a 2cm ($\frac{3}{4}$in) turning at the top edge of the trousers. Turn under 3mm ($\frac{1}{8}$in) to the wrong side on the top edge and press. Turn under a further 1.5cm ($\frac{5}{8}$in) and press. Stitch close to the folded edge at the top and then stitch again close to the bottom edge leaving a 2.5cm (1in) gap to insert the elastic through. Cut a length of 1.3cm ($\frac{1}{2}$in) wide elastic so that it fits comfortably around the waist plus an extra 1.3cm ($\frac{1}{2}$in). Attach a safety pin to one end of the elastic and thread it through the casing. Overlap the ends of the elastic by 6mm ($\frac{1}{4}$in) on each end and sew together securely. Hem the remainder of the casing to close the gap.

When using decorative elastic to control fullness at the waist, cut a length to fit comfortably around the waist plus an extra 2cm ($\frac{3}{4}$in). Turn in the ends by 3mm ($\frac{1}{8}$in) to neaten. If the opening is at the centre front, have the left side of the elastic level with the left side of the opening and the right side extending by 1.3cm ($\frac{1}{2}$in) for a girl and vice versa for a boy. Attach to the right side of the trousers with the bottom of the elastic just covering the seam allowance. Machine on the seamline and sew hooks and eyes or snaps on the underside of the overlap to close the waistband.

To elasticate trouser waistband: turn down top of trousers to inside and stitch to form casing, leaving a gap in the centre back to insert elastic

217

Trousers

If a self-fabric waistband is preferred to give the trousers a more tailored look, cut a rectangle of fabric on the lengthwise grain so that it fits comfortably around the waist plus an extra 4.5cm (1¾in). It should be twice the finished width of the desired waistband with an added 3.2cm (1¼in). Cut out a piece of interfacing the length of the fabric but half the width. Pin the interfacing to the wrong side of half the waistband, tack 1.5cm (⅝in) in from the edges and slip stitch to the centre. Turn up 1.5cm (⅝in) on the other long edge and press. For girls' trousers, place right sides together and pin the interfaced side of the waistband to the trousers extending the left hand side by 1.5cm (⅝in) and

the right end by 2.8cm (1⅛in) beyond the zip opening. Reverse this procedure for boys' trousers. Stitch into place taking a 1.5cm (⅝in) seam. Trim the interfacing close to the stitching-line and grade the seam allowances. Press the seam towards the waistband. Fold the waistband in half lengthwise with right sides together and sew the short sides taking a 1.5cm (⅝in) seam allowance. Clip the corners diagonally and grade the seam allowances. Turn the waistband to the right side and pull out the corners gently with a pin. Turn under 1.5cm (⅝in) on the remaining long edge and hem into place on the seamline. Press and close the waistband with hooks and eyes or snaps sewn under the overlap.

Trousers with an elastic casing obviously do not require a zip as they can easily be pulled on and off. This is

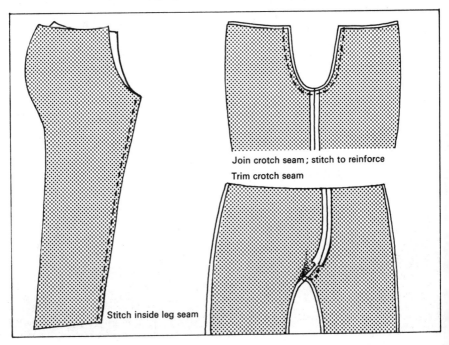

Join crotch seam; stitch to reinforce

Trim crotch seam

Stitch inside leg seam

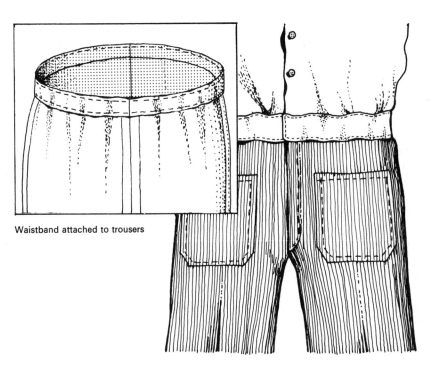

Waistband attached to trousers

another point in their favour when teaching your child to dress on his own as then he will not have to fiddle with awkward fastenings. If a zip is required this can be inserted either in the side seam, in the normal way, or in the centre front with a mock fly opening (see page 243).

When making up the trousers, first sew up the inside leg seam, press open and neaten. Match up the inside leg seams and join the crotch seam. Reinforce the curved part of the seam which goes between the legs, with a second row of stitching over the first extending a little way on either side. Trim this part of the seam to within 3mm ($\frac{1}{8}$in) of the reinforced stitching, and press open the remaining parts of the seam. Sew up the outside leg

seam last so any last-minute adjustments can be made and a zip can be inserted if required.

A very large hem would be too bulky for trousers, so a turn-up can be made which can easily be let down when the child begins to grow. Cut the trouser legs 10cm (4in) longer than the finished length. Neaten the raw edge and turn up the 10cm (4in) to the wrong side. Hem into place by hand and press on the lower edge. Turn up 5cm (2in) to the right side of the trousers and press. Catch stitch the underside of the turn-ups to the side seams to hold them in place.

Seam Finishes

It is most important, especially in children's clothes, that the inside of the garment is finished off neatly and the seams are as flat as possible so that there are no rough edges and bulky seams to rub and chafe delicate skins. As children's clothes spend a good deal of time in the washing machine, neatening edges will prolong their life by preventing the fabric from fraying until the seams disintegrate.

There are several ways of neatening seams but each one should be neatened as you go along. Do not wait until the garment is finished because it will be very difficult to neaten a seam completely once it is joined to another garment section. First press the seam open and then choose one of the following methods according to the weight of fabric being used and the amount it frays.

The simplest and quickest way for fabrics which do not fray is to trim the seam with pinking shears. This will give a notched edge to the fabric, but you must be careful to cut in a straight line to keep the seam even. If the fabric will fray only slightly, pinking shears can again be used, but first run a line of stitching 6mm ($\frac{1}{4}$in) in from the edge along the seam and then trim.

Fabrics which fray a great deal can be neatened either by hand or by machine. Set the machine to a small zig-zag stitch and sew close to the edge of the seam allowance. Neaten by hand with overcast stitches. First run a row of machine stitches or sew by hand with small running stitches along the seam 3mm ($\frac{1}{8}$in) in from the raw edge.

Oversew the raw edges with overcast stitches along the stitching-line at 6mm ($\frac{1}{4}$in) intervals. The edges can be neatened either on their own on an open seam or overcast together if the seam is to be pressed to one side.

On a seam which is to be pressed to one side, if the fabric is not prone to fraying, a double-stitched seam can be used by running a second row of stitches close to the original seam through both layers of fabric and then trimmed close to the second line of stitching. This is a very good finish for garments which are going to be washed frequently.

On fine delicate fabrics which fray easily, run a row of machine stitches or small running stitches by hand along the length of the seam 3mm ($\frac{1}{8}$in) in from the raw edge. Turn under the

Machine stitched and trimmed with pinking shears

Machine stitched with zig-zag

Seam finishes

Overcast by hand

fabric on the stitching-line to the wrong side and stitch again close to the folded edge.

For thick fabrics which fray and are too bulky to be turned under, such as wools, the edges can be blanket stitched by hand. Make a series of even, straight stitches and catch the working thread under the point of the needle so that it forms a loop which is pulled flat along the raw edge. These fabrics can also be neatened by binding the edges with bias binding. Fold the bias binding over both sides of the raw edge, encasing it in the binding, and machine or hand-stitch with small running stitches along the narrow side of the binding.

Neaten delicate transparent fabrics with a tiny rolled hem. Press both sides of the seam allowance together and trim to 1 cm ($\frac{3}{8}$in). With your fingers roll the edges together to the seamline so that the raw edges are encased. Sew into place with a whipping stitch keeping the stitches evenly spaced. Do not pull the thread too tightly as this will cause the seam to pucker.

The French seam is used on fine, delicate fabrics which fray and is especially common on blouses and lingerie which are in constant contact with the skin. Basically, it is a double seam with one seam encased inside another. Begin with the fabric's wrong sides together and make the first seam 1 cm ($\frac{3}{8}$in) in from the raw edges. Trim the seam to 3mm ($\frac{1}{8}$in) and press open. Turn the fabric over and with right sides together press flat at the seamline. Make a second seam 6mm ($\frac{1}{4}$in) in from the folded edge covering the raw edges of the first seam.

A final method of neatening on lightweight fabrics which fray is to bind one side of the seam allowance over the top of the other. Trim one side of the seam allowance to 3mm ($\frac{1}{8}$in). Stitch under 3mm ($\frac{1}{8}$in) on the raw edge of the other side and fold it over the top of the trimmed seam allowance and sew into place on the original seamline.

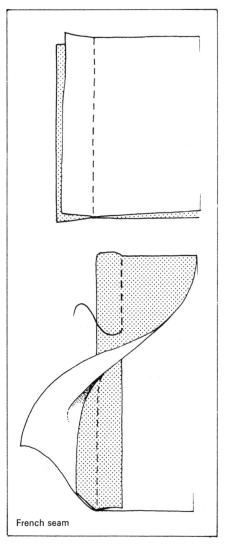

French seam

221

Making Clothes Last Longer

Simple Adjustments and Alterations

As children grow so quickly, clothing them can be quite a problem. If you make the clothes a size too big, your child is swamped until he grows into them and then it seems only two minutes before the clothes are too small. Easy adjustments can be made, as the child begins to grow, if simple allowances are included when the garment is first made up.

A very deep or double hem is ideal as mentioned in the sections on hems. On a waisted or empire-line dress, the adjustment can be made where the skirt is joined to the bodice. Lengthen the bodice allowance by approximately 5cm (2in), join the skirt in the correct position and leave the extra fabric on the inside. It can then be let down when required.

If you are lining a garment and have allowed extra length, do not forget to lengthen the lining as well so that both can be let down at the same time.

A good idea when constructing the garment is to make an inverted pleat at the sides or in the centre front. This is really a box pleat in reverse and is made on the wrong side of the fabric by turning two knife pleats away from each other. (Knife pleats are described in the section on pleats.) Not only does this sort of pleat have a slimming effect, but it will stretch as the child begins to grow and can be let out completely to give extra width to the garment.

Skirts and dresses can easily be lengthened by adding a pretty frill, either in the same fabric, if you have any left over, or in a contrasting band. Simply measure the width around the lower edge of the garment and note the amount by which you wish to lengthen it. Depending on the desired fullness of the frill, cut a straight piece of fabric either one and a half times or twice the length of the hem plus 3.2cm ($1\frac{1}{4}$in). To the depth required for lengthening add 3.2cm ($1\frac{1}{4}$in). If necessary, piece the fabric to give the required length. Neaten the raw edges. Fold the fabric in half lengthwise with right sides together and machine along the short side taking a 1.5cm ($\frac{5}{8}$in) seam. Press the seam open. Run two rows of gathering along one of the long edges and pull up the threads to the width around the lower edge of the garment. Having let down the existing hem, join to the gathered edge of the frill right sides together, taking a 1.5cm ($\frac{5}{8}$in) seam and distributing the gathers evenly. Press the seam up towards the main part of the garment. Turn up 1.5cm ($\frac{5}{8}$in) on the lower edge and hem stitch into place.

Trousers can also be lengthened in this way by cutting a piece of fabric the length of the bottom of the trouser leg plus 3.2cm ($1\frac{1}{4}$in) by the amount to be lengthened in depth plus 3.2cm ($1\frac{1}{4}$in). Neaten the raw edges. Fold the fabric strip in half lengthwise with right sides together and machine along the short side taking a 1.5cm ($\frac{5}{8}$in) seam. Press the seam open. Let down the existing hem on the trouser leg and join the fabric to the trousers right sides together taking a 1.5cm ($\frac{5}{8}$in) seam. Press the seam towards the original trouser leg. Turn up 1.5cm ($\frac{5}{8}$in) on the lower edge and hem stitch into place.

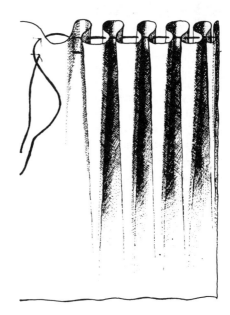

(*Right*) Insert two rows of gathering thread
(*Below left*) Inverted pleat
(*Below right*) Skirt lengthened by adding frill,
seen from wrong side

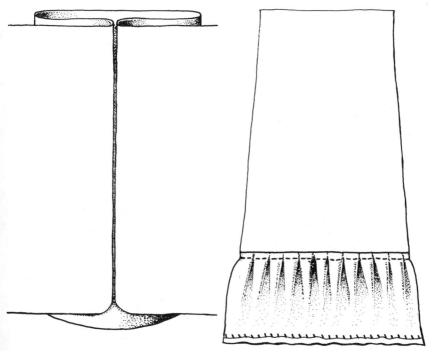

Making Clothes Last Longer

Another way to revitalise clothes which have become too short is to shorten them still further.

Trousers can be turned into 'plus twos'. Cut off the trouser legs 3.2cm (1¼in) below the knee. Neaten the raw edge and turn up 1.5cm (⅝in). Machine or hand sew with a continuous running stitch 3mm (⅛in) in from the edge to form a casing, leaving a 2.5cm (1in) opening. Measure the width around the child's leg and cut a piece of elastic this length plus 1.3cm (½in). Attach a safety pin to one end of the elastic and insert it through the casing. Overlap the ends of the elastic by 6mm (¼in) and sew them securely together. Stitch the gap in the casing.

You can also shorten a dress to prolong its life. Cut it to just below the waist plus 1.5cm (⅝in). Neaten the raw edge and turn up a 1.5cm (⅝in) hem. Tack and sew into place with tiny hemming stitches. Press and remove the tacking stitches. The dress can then be worn as a top with trousers or skirts.

Children's clothes which have become too tight can be let out by inserting godets into the side seams. A godet is a shaped piece of fabric which is inserted into a fitted garment to allow fullness from a given point. In a dress this can be used to give extra width across the chest, waist and hip and in a skirt to give extra width over the hip. Open up the side seams in the existing garment to just below the armhole or waistband. Cut out a triangular piece of fabric, grading to a point at the top, but remember to allow for a seam at either side and a hem at the bottom. Insert the godet, joining it to the original seams, neaten and press. Turn up the hem and sew into place. A godet can be made from the leftover fabric of the original garment or from a contrasting fabric provided it is compatible in weight otherwise it will pull the garment out of shape.

When a simple dress which is gathered on to a yoke becomes too short, it can be revitalised by turning it into a skirt. There are two ways of doing this but first remove the yoke. Then you can either adjust the gathers, pulling up or letting out as the case may be, to fit the child's waist comfortably. Undo the side seam and insert a zip. Join the gathered skirt to a waistband of self-fabric, if you have any left over, or of a contrasting fabric compatible in weight. Or you can let the

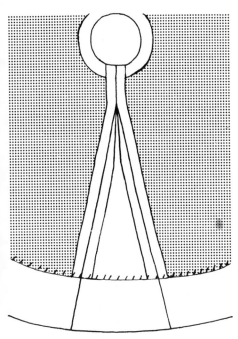

Godet in side seam

gathers out completely and turn the top edge to the wrong side, machining top and bottom to form a casing. Thread the elastic through the casing to fit your child's waist comfortably and this will form a pretty, gathered skirt.

Mending

Children's clothes have to stand up to a tremendous battering. When your child is not busy growing out of them, he will probably seem to delight in wearing them out very quickly indeed. He will go out to play or off to school in brand new clothes, looking all spick and span, and as if by magic, almost overnight, holes and thin patches appear. A stitch in time saves nine may be an old adage, but darning and patching play a very important part in the life of children's clothes.

Darning and Patching

Darning

Small holes and patches which have become thin during wear can be repaired by darning. You will need a darning needle which stretches from one side of the darn to the other, with an eye large enough to thread the wool through without separating the strands. A darning mushroom is useful to insert under the material as this will ensure a flat darn. Use a slightly finer wool than that of the garment and for fabrics other than wool use the corresponding thread (eg cotton for cotton). To make the repair less noticeable, it is best to darn from the wrong side, but with garments, such as vests, worn next to the skin it is more comfortable if the darn is worked from the right side to avoid irritation.

In areas where the fabric has become thin but has not actually worn away into a hole, such as elbows, knees and heels, use a strengthening darn. The darning stitches must extend outside the weak part into the surrounding firm material, which will take the strain, and be worked evenly to retain elasticity. Start at the bottom left hand side just below the weak area, in the firm material, running the first line of stitching over and under the alternate fibres of the material in a vertical line and extend the stitches into the firm material at the top as well. Leave a tiny loop at the end of the row to allow for shrinkage during washing and to maintain elasticity. Repeat the stitching in the opposite direction but start one fibre higher so that the under loop of the first row becomes the upper of the

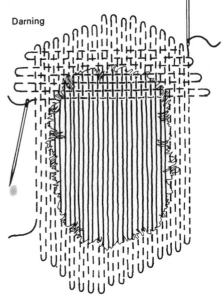

Darning

next and vice versa. Repeat these alternating rows extending into the firm material at each side of the darn. If an actual hole appears in the fabric or it is very thin, further rows of darning stitches will be necessary. These should go horizontally over and under the vertical lines already worked and be kept close together.

Patching

A patch should be used to repair an area which is too large to darn. It should be made from a fabric which is compatible with the original material to avoid pulling the outfit out of shape, and, unless used for decorative purposes, should be as invisible as possible. If the garment has faded slightly during wear, the fabric for the patch can be washed in a mild bleach so that it will tone in. When a printed fabric is used, try to match it up exactly with the design of the garment.

Cut a square or oblong, according to the shape of the hole, large enough to cover the gap and the weak fabric surrounding it. Turn in the edges of the patch by approximately 1 cm ($\frac{3}{8}$in) to the wrong side. Pin the patch to the right side of the garment, matching the fabric pattern, and tack into place. Remove the pins and hem or machine on the edge of the patch. Turn to the wrong side of the garment and trim the raw edges of the tear to 1 cm ($\frac{3}{8}$in) in from the sewing-line. Oversew the edges to neaten and prevent them fraying but do not catch up the fabric of the patch or the stitches will show through to the right side.

If the garment is made from a plain fabric, and there is no worry about matching up the design, the patch can be applied from the wrong side of the outfit. Prepare the patch as before. Pin, tack and sew the patch into position underneath the hole. On the right side turn in the raw edges of the tear and sew the folded edge to the patch with tiny hemming stitches.

Patches can now be fashionable and fun, so why not make them an obvious decorative feature by using a contrasting fabric. For instance, you can buy packs of pretty squares from Laura Ashley shops. Applying leather patches to jacket elbows or jersey elbows gives a grown-up look, which little boys will love. Also available is a wide range of novelty patches with motifs which can either be ironed on or sewn into place. A patch is quick and easy to apply with iron-on hemming web. Not only will hemming web save time, by sticking the patch into place, but it will also bond the ragged edges around the tear and prevent them from fraying. Patches can also be highlighted by hand-sewing them into place with a decorative blanket stitch in a contrasting, but not clashing, coloured thread.

When clothes are first made up, it can be a good idea to patch up areas which are going to be under the most strain, thus strengthening them to begin with.

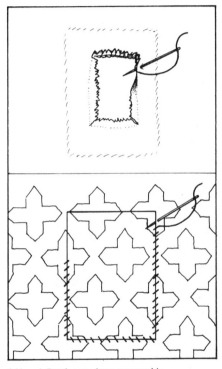

(*Above*) Patch seen from wrong side
(*Below*) Patch seen from right side

Patchwork

Patchwork takes a little time and patience but it is a great money-saver because patches can be made up from small pieces of left-over fabric. It is very enjoyable too, as you can give full vent to your creative flair and imagination. Matching is not really necessary unless you have a specific design or colour scheme in mind. Patches can be different shapes and sizes and the more fabric designs used the brighter and jollier the finished effect will be. It is a very pretty idea for simple children's wear such as skirts, tops and aprons and makes an attractive design for holdalls for shoes, laundry, toys, school books, pencils, crayons and paints. Patchwork is a lovely way, too, to brighten up the nursery in the form of cot covers or bedspreads and cushions. Packs of regular-shaped patches can be obtained from Laura Ashley shops which produce prints ideal for children's clothes.

There are really only two basic points to watch out for when making up patchwork. One is to ensure that the patches are of the same weight of cloth to avoid the patchwork being pulled out of shape, and the other is to avoid fabrics which fray easily otherwise the edges of each patch must be neatened first. Decide on the amount of material required and, as with quilting, make up the patchwork before cutting out each section.

Begin by tracing the patchwork shapes on to heavy card. Cut these out and use them as patterns from which to cut your patches. When cutting remember to leave a 6mm ($\frac{1}{4}$in)

seam allowance around each fabric shape, which will be required for joining the patches together. You will need a large, smooth surface on which to work. The floor is often the best place of all. It is easiest to work in long strips, stitching the patches together and pressing the seams open to keep the work flat. Join the strips together and press open the long seams. Continue joining the strips until you have sufficient area for the work you have planned. Pin the relevant pattern pieces to the fabric and cut as you would an ordinary fabric.

The fabric can be lined. This is particularly necessary with bedspreads and clothes worn next to the skin. Cut out the lining the same size as the patchwork plus a 1.5cm ($\frac{5}{8}$in) seam allowance. With right sides together machine around three sides, taking a 1.5cm ($\frac{5}{8}$in) seam. Trim the seam, cut corners diagonally and clip curves. Turn through to the right side of the fabric and turn in the seam allowance. Then catch stitch the opening on the fourth side together.

If you are making patchwork cushions it may be a good idea to insert a zip, or two strips of self-adhesive fabric, into one of the seam allowances so that the cushion can easily be removed before washing or dry cleaning the patchwork.

Patchwork quilts also look most attractive in children's bedrooms. Just make up the amount of patchwork to cover the area required and use it as the top fabric. It can be quilted in the same way as a regular fabric (for directions see the section on quilting).

(*Right*) Join patches together in a strip;
Join strips together
(*Below*) Finished patchwork quilt

Fur and Synthetic Fabrics

Fur

There is a wide and exciting variety of fake furs on the market suitable for children's jackets, coats, caps and mittens. They are fun to wear as well as a good way to keep warm and snug in winter. The fabric can also be used for making up soft toys such as teddy bears and other toy characters, like The Wombles, which are produced by pattern manufacturers but which are so expensive to buy ready-made. Fake fur is not nearly as difficult to work with as many people imagine provided a few golden rules are remembered.

Fur is a with nap fabric and the pile goes in one direction, so you must ensure that all the pattern pieces are laid out the same way, with the pile of the fur going down towards the hem. Place the pattern pieces out singly on the wrong side of the fabric and mark the shapes with tailor's chalk. Obviously, because of the bulk of the fabric, it would be difficult to place a pattern piece to a fold. Instead, lay out the pattern piece and pin along the foldline with the pins parallel to this line. Mark around the tissue, turn exactly on the pinline and mark the other half of the garment section. Cut out each pattern piece individually with a sharp razor blade or the point of very sharp scissors. Be careful to cut the backing only, which will help prevent the fur from shedding.

As the fabric is so thick, it would be very difficult to tack sections together. The pieces should be pinned to each other at 1.3cm ($\frac{1}{2}$in) intervals, with the pins going horizontally across the seam to ensure that there is no movement under the machine. Before beginning to sew, comb the fur away from the seam edges. However, if some strands become caught in the seam, pull them out gently on the right side with a pin. It is important always to use a synthetic thread and if you are using a machine set it for a medium length stitch. To be certain that you have the correct stitch length and tension setting, it is a good idea to test on a small sample of the fabric before finally machining.

Synthetic Fabrics

Synthetic fabrics tend to collect a great deal of static electricity and it may help if you wash the material in an anti-static conditioner before making up in order to avoid the fabric clinging in the wrong places causing the seams to pucker. For knitted

Fur jacket

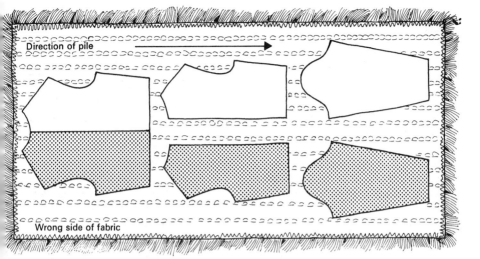

'With nap' layout for fur jacket

synthetic fabrics, use a ball-point needle which will go between the fibres of the material and prevent snagging or tearing. Some synthetics are likely to ladder in one direction and this should be checked by gently pulling the cut edge. If laddering occurs, ensure that the pattern pieces are laid out with the laddered edge to the hem and strengthen the raw edge with a machine zig-zag stitch. With very stretchy fabrics, tissue paper can be tacked to the underside of the seam. This will help to hold the shape and it can easily be torn away after machining. If the fabric is very slippery, tissue paper can be inserted into the seam, between the two layers of fabric, and again it can easily be torn away after stitching.

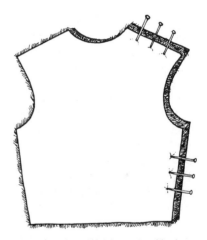

Pin seams at 1.3cm ($\frac{1}{2}$in) intervals with pins at right angles to seams

Quilting

Anoraks and quilted jackets are expensive to buy and even ready-quilted fabric is quite costly in the shops. However, it is quite simple to quilt your own. Quilting is just the stitching together of two layers of fabric with a layer of filler between them. It should be remembered that the fabric must be quilted before cutting out your garment.

Firstly, lay out your pattern pieces on the fabric to ensure that you have a rectangle of fabric with 5cm (2in) to spare around the edges, which will be taken up as the fabric is quilted. Remove the pattern pieces and press the fabric flat. Cut a rectangle of the filler the same size using either polyester or cotton wadding 28g (1oz) in weight or, for a lighter padding, use one or two layers of flannelette or non-woven interlining. Cut a further rectangle of very light-weight batiste for the backing and press flat.

Mark the quilting lines diagonally on the outside of the fabric with sharpened tailor's chalk, beginning across one corner and continue to mark the diagonal lines 3.2cm (1¼in) apart. Then repeat the procedure from the opposite direction.

Place the filler on top of the backing and then put the top fabric over the filler, with the outside of the fabric uppermost, and pin the three layers together. Tack the layers together by hand with large stitches, working diagonally from corner to corner, starting from the centre and sewing towards the edges to prevent the fabric from slipping. Leave the pins in place.

The fabric is now ready for quilting.

To ensure the stitch length and tension are correct, first practise stitching on a test sample of the three layers. Then with the tension press adjusted and the stitch length set, start from a centre marking line and stitch slowly from one edge to the other, guiding the fabric in front and behind the sewing foot to smooth the fabric outwards away from the foot. Stitch the rows in alternate directions to keep the fabric in place. Work very slowly when crossing previous rows, stretching the fabric slightly to avoid puckering; and prevent the fabric from hanging off the back of the machine. If necessary, cut the tacking threads while stitching is in progress in order to keep the fabric smooth. When the whole piece is quilted ensure that all the tacking threads are removed.

The pattern pieces can now be laid out and cut in the normal way. After sewing sections together, remove the

Marking quilting lines

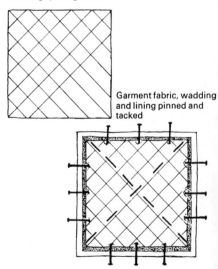

Garment fabric, wadding and lining pinned and tacked

232

wadding from the seam allowances to avoid bulky seams. When pressing use a steam iron to prevent the quilting becoming flattened.

Remnants

The remnant counter provides many bargains ideal for children's clothes because their small, simple outfits rarely take more than 1.20m ($1\frac{1}{4}$yd) of 90cm (36in) wide fabric and frequently use up less. You may find as well that a child's garment can be made out of fabric left over from your own clothes, especially if you lay the two patterns out together and intersperse the pattern pieces.

A favoured look today is to make up an outfit in more than one fabric, teaming up prints and plains, combining two or even three prints together, and co-ordinating matching large and small prints. This is a marvellous way to use up small pieces of fabric by making them into contrasting yokes, collars, cuffs,

pockets or frills, all of which can look most effective.

In fact, there are many ways in which remnants can be useful, pretty and money-saving at the same time. Use them to make up hats, caps, mittens, bibs or purses ; or make them into attractive bags to hold toys, shoes, laundry, nightdresses, pencils and paints, thus encouraging your child to be tidy. And they are perfect for dolls' clothes.

Sew along quilting lines

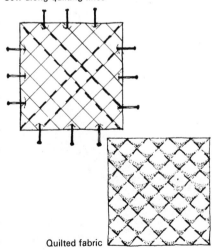

Quilted fabric

Decorative Finishes

Decorative embroidery, trimmings, appliqué and iron-on transfers greatly enhance the prettiness of children's clothes, especially when used on plain fabrics. But when they are already included on ready-to-wear clothes they usually send the high price still higher. However, the stitches are basically simple and can easily be done by hand, with a little time and patience, if you are not lucky enough to own one of those marvellous modern sewing machines which will do the work for you.

Decorative Embroidery

Elaborate embroidery would be too heavy and fussy for children's clothes so choose simple motifs and designs. Freestyle embroidery is probably the most popular and commonly used for children's clothes, the stitches being worked over an iron-on or traced transfer. Many paper patterns include iron-on transfers for embroidery and a

selection of transfers can be bought from specialist needlework shops. If you wish to be more creative you can trace your own design.

For embroidering, you will need a crewel needle for fine and medium-weight threads and fabrics, and a chenille needle for heavier weights ; a sharp pair of scissors with pointed blades, and a thimble to protect your middle finger when working. There are various types of embroidery thread to choose from according to the type of design and fabric being used. It is important, though, to use a yarn which is compatible with the fabric. Stranded embroidery cotton is very useful as the strands can be separated and used either singly or in groups depending on the desired effect. An embroidery ring may be needed, to keep the fabric smooth and taut, if you are using closely-worked stitches which might pucker.

Transfers

Iron-on transfer designs are generally impressed on the fabric by placing the transfer face down on the fabric and applying a hot iron for a few seconds to release the ink. The backing paper can then be gently pulled away. However, the manufacturers' instructions should be followed closely as they can vary.

Home Designing

There are several ways to impress a tracing of your own design on to a fabric. The easiest way to trace is to use carbon paper—yellow or light blue for dark fabrics and black or dark blue on light-coloured fabrics. Place the carbon paper face down on the fabric,

then put the drawing or tracing of the design on top and secure in place. Take a pencil with a sharp point and draw over the lines being careful to press only on the design lines or the carbon may smudge the fabric. Remove the carbon and drawing and place a sheet of tissue paper over the impression on the fabric. Press with a warm iron to fix the design on to the fabric and prevent the colour from coming off on the embroidery threads.

Another method is to trace the design on to firm tracing paper. Mark the lines of the design with a needle, pricking small holes about 1.5mm ($\frac{1}{16}$in) apart. Remove any roughness from the back of the design by rubbing it with fine sandpaper. Place the design on to the fabric, using weights to keep it in place. Rub french chalk for dark fabrics and powdered charcoal on light colours through the holes. Take the tracing off and blow away any surplus powder. Then paint over the dotted lines with water colour, using dark or light paint depending on the colour of the material.

With fine transparent fabrics, such as nylon or voile, the design can be traced directly on to the material. Place the design under the material and hold firmly in position. Trace with a soft pencil or water-colour paint and then iron the impression under a piece of tissue paper to prevent the colour from coming off on to the embroidery threads.

Embroidery Stitches

Embroidery stitches are generally worked from left to right. There are many, many embroidery stitches and there are lots of publications giving an in-depth study of the subject. Described below are some basic stitches which are easy to do and their simplicity of design makes them ideal for children's clothes. They look just as attractive when used on their own, or combined as part of an overall design.

Stem Stitch

This is basically an outline stitch and can be used singly for flower stems or can be made to fill in a shape by working rows of the stitch close together. Take even, slightly slanting stitches over the outline and work from left to right with the thread coming

out on the left-hand side of the previous stitch.

Running Stitch

This stitch is easily recognisable from everyday sewing, but ensure that the top stitches are of equal length and the under stitches about half the length of the upper ones. This stitch can be used very effectively as a border around the bottom of skirts, dresses and jackets by looping a contrasting coloured thread through the upper stitches, but do be careful not to catch the fabric.

Scroll Stitch

This can make a very pretty border. Again working from left to right, loop the thread to the right and then back to the left on the fabric. Take a small slanting stitch to the left under the line of the design inside the loop and pull

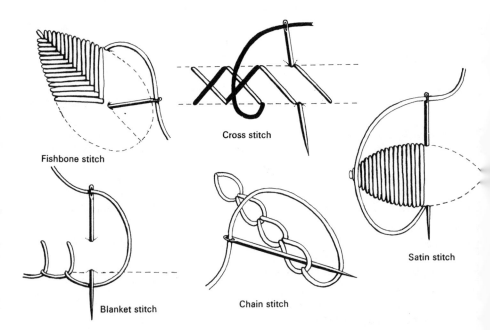

Fishbone stitch

Cross stitch

Satin stitch

Blanket stitch

Chain stitch

236

the thread through over the top of the loop. Space the stitches evenly.

Straight Stitch

These stitches are the basis for several different designs. They can be used as a series of single, regular stitches spaced out to give a shape or they can vary in size. If the straight stitches are worked closely together covering a shape, they are known as satin stitch. A large or irregular shape can be filled with straight stitches of varying sizes known as long and short stitch. If a shaded effect is desired, alternate long and short stitches around the outline of the shape and then work the filling rows of stitches to give a smooth look.

Fishbone Stitch

This is useful for filling small shapes such as leaves. Take a small straight stitch along the centreline of the shape

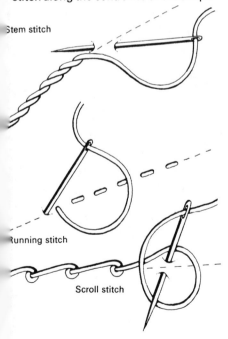

Stem stitch

Running stitch

Scroll stitch

and end with the needle on the left hand side of the stitch. Take a sloping stitch to the centre at the foot of the first stitch. Make a similar sloping stitch from the right hand side of the first stitch just below the first sloping stitch so that it overlaps at the centreline and continue working from alternate sides until the space is filled with overlapping sloping stitches.

Cross Stitch

This is very easy and attractive. Make a series of sloping stitches from left to right keeping them the same length and equidistant. Then repeat the stitches from the opposite direction to form the cross.

Blanket Stitch

This is often used as a decorative form of top stitching to attach patches and appliqués and it is equally useful for neatening raw edges. Make a straight stitch vertically and repeat with even stitches catching the working thread under the needle as it emerges at the top to form a loop. Pull the thread up so that the loop is level either with the edge of the fabric or with the top of the stitches if it is being used as a border.

Chain Stitch

This is another basic stitch upon which other designs are formed. Hold the thread where it emerges with the left thumb and make a small loop returning the needle to this spot and insert again bringing it out at a short distance ahead with the loop under the needle. Repeat and the stitch will form a chain. Lazy daisy stitch is worked in the same manner, but the head of the loop is secured with a small stitch.

Trimmings

Gaily-coloured braids, ribbons, rick-rack and lace give a pretty finishing touch to children's clothes. Children are easily bored with clothes and adding trimmings is a good way to give clothes a different look and a new lease of life.

Soutache and other narrow braids are attached with a single row of stitching either by hand, or by machine using a braiding foot. Test on a sample of the fabric first and, if the braid begins to pucker, place tissue paper under the fabric before machining. This paper is easily torn away after the stitching is completed.

With wider, flat braids both edges have to be stitched into place. Stitch around the outside edge first and then along the inner edge. Some trimmings can be damaged by machine stitching, so test first. If the trimmings are unsuitable for machining, they should be applied by hand using a back stitch. To ensure a smooth, flat finish when going around a square corner, it is necessary to mitre the trimming. Stitch on the outside edge to the point of the corner, then back stitch and clip the threads. The loose end of the trimming is folded back over the stitched part. Note the width of the trimming and transfer this measurement to the inside of the stitching-line, marking the point with tailor's chalk on the trimming. Stitch diagonally from the corner to this point, then press. Pull down the free end of the trimming and it will go neatly around the corner. Press again and continue to stitch the rest of the outside edge. Complete

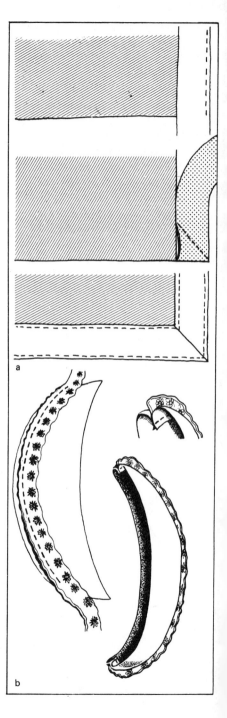

a

b

by sewing along the inside edge.

Rick-rack makes a pretty piping and an attractive edging on an outfit. When used as a piping first turn under the edge of the fabric to the wrong side and press. Lap the folded edge over the rick-rack to the centre of the trimming, covering half of it. Stitch very close to the edge of the fabric, exposing the remainder of the rick-rack to form the piping. When used as an edging both sides of the rick-rack show. Fold under the seam allowance of the fabric to the wrong side and press. Position the rick-rack on the right side of the fabric with the centre of the trimming to the foldline. Stitch along the foldline through the centre of the rick-rack. Bands of rick-rack in one or more colours can also be used to form a decorative border around the bottom of skirts. To ensure the trimming is level, first mark the position of the bands using a measure and tailor's chalk. Measure the length required plus 6mm ($\frac{1}{4}$in). Turn under each end of the trimming by 3mm ($\frac{1}{8}$in) to neaten. Place the rick-rack over the chalk mark and stitch through the centre of the trimming.

Lace makes a very dainty trimming and small amounts can turn a simple style into a pretty dress for parties. You can even make your child's christening robe or bridesmaid's dress. Choose a narrow, fine lace with a small design for collars, cuffs and pockets. A wider lace may be used around the bottom of a dress. Wide, coarser lace is a perfect way to lengthen a cotton skirt giving it a pretty, peasant look.

Lace can be sewn by hand or machine, but a fine thread and fine, sharp needle must be used in order to make the stitching line as inconspicuous as possible. If you wish to have a gathered lace edging, this can either be bought pre-gathered, or you can gather it yourself by pulling up a thread in the upper edge to the required amount of fullness. Secure the end of the thread by winding it around a pin and adjust the gathers evenly.

When attaching lace trimming to the bottom of a dress or skirt, pin the right side of the lace to the right side of the finished hem, keeping the edges of the lace and the hem level with each other. Sew the two together with small whipping stitches. When joining the lace by machine, put the wrong side of the lace to the right side of the fabric with the edge of the lace 3mm ($\frac{1}{8}$in) above the hem. Machine along the edge of the lace using a zig-zag stitch.

Use gathered lace trimming for collars and cuffs, inserting the lace between the top and the facing. Pin and tack the straight edge of the lace to the right side of the collar and cuff over the seamline and, if possible, level with the raw edge of the fabric. If the lace is too narrow move it slightly closer to the seamline. On a collar, taper the ends of the lace so that they do not overlap when the garment is worn. With the ruffled edge of the lace towards the centre of the collar or cuff, pin to the facing, right sides together, tack, remove pins and machine on the seamline. Trim the seam, clip curves and cut corners diagonally. Turn the section through to the right side showing the lace edging.

(a) Trimming a square corner
(b) Attaching lace trimming to a collar

Appliqué

Appliqués are fun and make a cheap and cheerful way to brighten up children's clothes. Motifs can be added to pockets, collars and around the hem to form a decorative border. You can buy appliqué patterns or trace your own designs. Appliqués can even be made from scraps of left-over fabric. One or more fabrics may be used for highlighting features in the design, such as eyes on an animal motif or flower stems and petals. Felt is an ideal fabric to use as it does not fray so the edges don't have to be neatened. So, when working with this fabric, ignore the following references to seam allowances as they are totally unnecessary.

Appliqué can be done by hand or machine. If working by hand, stitch around the outline of the design. Cut out the shape, leaving a 3mm ($\frac{1}{8}$in) seam allowance outside the row of stitching. Turn under the edges to the wrong side on the stitching-line, tack and press. Pin the appliqué into position and attach, using a decorative blanket stitch or hemming stitch. Remove the pins and the tacking thread. The appliqué can also be machined into place stitching on the edge instead of hand-sewing.

In general, when applied by machine, allow a 6mm ($\frac{1}{4}$in) seam allowance around the edges. Pin or tack the motif into position and machine stitch on the seamline. Trim the fabric close to the row of stitching and machine the raw edges with a very small zig-zag stitch. For extra interest, the appliqués can be applied with brightly coloured or contrasting threads.

There are two quick and easy short-cuts to appliqué. The first of these is to buy some of the very attractive four-colour iron-on transfers featuring a variety of motifs, initials and embroidery. These are easy to apply by simply placing the transfer face down on the fabric and pressing with a hot iron. The transfer is left to cool and the backing paper removed. However, it is essential that the manufacturer's instructions are followed carefully as they can vary. Also check that your fabric is suitable and will not shrivel up under the heat of the iron. Alternatively, you can apply your own motifs by inserting a strip of hemming web between the appliqué

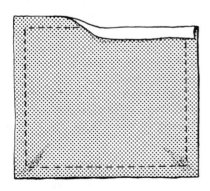

and the fabric and ironing into place. Appliqués are not only decorative in their own right, but they also make very useful and attractive patches for covering holes or thin, worn material.

Decorative zips are great fun on children's clothes as they are sewn on the outside of the garment and act as attractive trimmings. Machine the seam to the bottom of the zip and tack

(*Opposite*) Turn edge of fabric under Sew into place with blanket stitch

up the remainder of the opening on the seamline. Press the seam open. On the outside of the garment place the zip face up with the centre of the teeth over the seamline and the top of the zip 2.2cm ($\frac{7}{8}$in) below the top edge of the garment. Tack into position and turn under the raw edges of the tape at the bottom of the zip, to face the fabric. Sew by hand or machine, using a zipper foot, close to the teeth. Remove the tacking and press. Sew again down the outside edge of the zip.

Zips

Zips are easy to put in provided that a few golden rules are followed. They can be inserted either by hand or by machine, but if a machine is used a zipper foot will be necessary. Zips should always be put in by hand when using fabrics with a pile or nap so that the surface of the material is not distorted. It is also better not to machine them in if working with slippery materials, very fine delicate fabrics or knits which may pucker. Check that you have the correct length of zip. A child's measurements may be fine for the pattern size for the chest, waist and hips but if he is shorter in height the zip opening might need to be shorter too. If possible, insert the zip into the garment section before the outfit is completed as it will be easier to handle.

There are several methods of putting in a zip. The easiest method is the one where the two sides of the opening meet together over the centre of the zip. Machine the seam to the bottom of the opening. Tack up the remainder of the seam and press the whole seam open. On the wrong side of the fabric, centre the zip over the opening, face downwards towards the seam, with the zip head 2.5cm (1in) below the top edge of the outfit. Tack the zip into place down both sides. Turn to the right side of the fabric and hand-stitch or machine with a zipper foot 6mm ($\frac{1}{4}$in) from the edge of the opening down one side, across the bottom of the zip, and up the other side. Press and remove the tacking stitches.

Separating zips are a marvellous way to fasten children's jackets, coats, tops and skirts. Children can operate them easily on their own so that they can quickly dress themselves instead of tussling with awkward buttons and having to wait for their mother to give them a helping hand. Turn under the seam allowance or facing on the foldline down either side of the opening, tack and press. With the zip closed, pin the right side of the zip to the wrong side of the opening, the edges meeting over the centre of the zip teeth. Open the zip and tack each side into place, turning in the tabs at

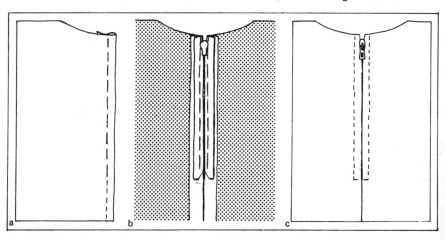

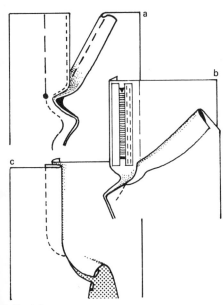

Mock fly
(a) Front seams extended; (b) Apply zip to left fly front; (c) Right front lapped over left and stitched

the top of the zip to face the fabric. Turn to the right side of the fabric and sew by hand with continuous running stitches or by machine using a zipper foot 6mm ($\frac{1}{4}$in) from the opening edges, catching in the tabs. Remove the tacking stitches and press.

Young boys love to feel grown-up and have clothes just like daddy's. In trousers, zips can be inserted down the centre front to give a mock fly opening. Extend the centre front seams by 2.5cm (1in) from the top of the opening to 5cm (2in) below the bottom of the zip, marking the centre fronts with tacking stitches or tailor's chalk. Put the zip with the slide 2.2cm ($\frac{7}{8}$in) below the seam allowance on the waist and mark the position of the

(*Opposite*) (a) Seam machined and tacked (b) Zip tacked to inside (c) Zip stitched into place

zipper top stop. Remove the zip and stitch up the centre front seam from the marking finishing 3.8cm (1$\frac{1}{2}$in) away from the edge of the inside leg. Neaten the extension edge on the left front by stitching 6mm ($\frac{1}{4}$in) from the edge tapering the stitches towards the bottom. Turn the fabric under to the wrong side on the stitching-line and edge stitch in place. With the zip closed, pin it to the left, front face upwards, having the outside edge of the right zip tape 1cm ($\frac{3}{8}$in) inside the raw edge and the slide 2.2cm ($\frac{7}{8}$in) down from the top edge. Machine stitch using a zipper foot close to the outside edge of the left tape and place a second row of stitching 6mm ($\frac{1}{4}$in) inside this. Still keeping the zip closed, pin it to the right front with the outer edge of the tape 1cm ($\frac{3}{8}$in) inside the raw edge. Stitch into place close to the outer edge of the tape and again 6mm ($\frac{1}{4}$in) in from this stitching-line. Clip diagonally across the left front to the bottom of the zip. On the right side of the garment turn under the right front on the centre front marking, tack into place and press. Match up the centre fronts with the right front overlapping the left. Tack along the line 2.5cm (1in) inside the folded edge through all the layers curving the stitching at the bottom towards the crotch, but be careful not to catch in the extension on the left front. Machine along the line of tacking on the right side only and remove the tacking stitches. Turn over to the inside of the garment and catch stitch the lower edges of the front extensions together. Join to the waistband in the normal way, matching up the ends with the folded edges of the fly front extensions.

Buttons and Fastenings

Buttons should be chosen with care so that they add a decorative finishing touch to a garment apart from their obvious practical use as a fastening. Tiny round pearl buttons and loops give a dainty look to a small girl's blouse or dress and, when used on a boy's shirt, turn it into a perfect pageboy's outfit. Brightly coloured and novelty buttons with motifs give a young look, ideal for children's clothes. Pick out one of the colours in a patterned fabric or choose a contrasting colour for the buttons and top stitching thread on plain materials. Metallic buttons on a blazer and mock leather buttons on a tweed coat or jacket look very smart and make the child feel very grown-up to have an outfit just like his parent's.

If you wish the buttons to match the material, but have difficulty in matching the colour, button trims covered with self-fabric are the answer. These come in various shapes and sizes and different weights : either metal for heavier fabrics or plastic for lightweight materials. The latter are perfect for children's clothes as they will not rust when subjected to constant washing. Covered buttons need not look old and fuddy-duddy either if you choose ones with decorative rims.

Snap fasteners and button trims with snaps underneath help to make a quick and easy-to-fasten outfit for busy mothers who haven't the time to spare for working buttonholes. Manufacturers now produce these in different sizes with a very modern and young look and include some super metal ones which give an authentic look to denim outfits. Another quick fastening method makes use of decorative zips, which are sewn on the outside of the garment, becoming an attractive feature of the outfit while avoiding time-consuming buttonholes.

Velcro, which is a self-adhesive fastening, can also be used in place of zips and buttons. Simply sew two strips to either side of the opening, press together to close and pull apart to open. Snaps, zips and Velcro, which are so easy to open and close, are also ideal fastenings for teaching children to dress themselves. Small fingers may find buttons fiddly and difficult to fasten and need their mother's help.

If you want buttonholes, they can be made either by hand or by machine. A quick way to fasten buttons, if you do not have a machine, is to make loops instead of buttonholes. The loops can be self-fabric made into a rouleau strip or they can be made from purchased cording or soutache braid. To make a self-fabric loop, cut a piece of material on the bias twice the finished width of the loop plus 1.3cm ($\frac{1}{2}$in) seam allowance. With the right sides together, fold the material in half lengthwise and machine along the long edge taking a 6mm ($\frac{1}{4}$in) seam. Trim very close to the stitching. Attach a strong thread to one end and insert through a darning needle. Turn the tube through to the right side with the aid of the needle and press. Cut the strip into loops so that they fit comfortably over the button and allow a seam allowance. Oversew the raw edges to neaten. Tack into position on

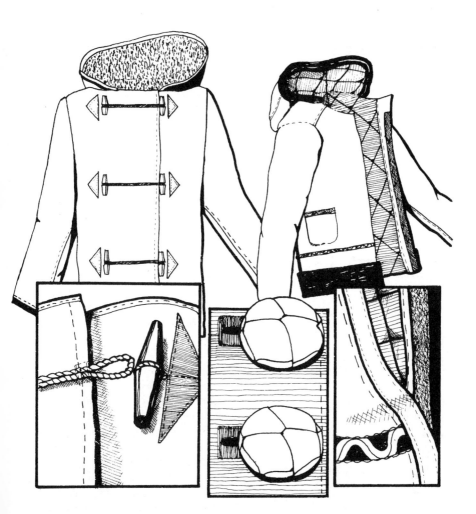

the right side of the garment. Join the facing to the garment over the top of the loops, right sides together, so that when the facing is turned through to the wrong side, the ends of the loops are encased. If you have insufficient self-fabric to make the loops, they can be worked using buttonhole twist or silk thread. Attach two or three strands of thread close to the edge of the fabric opening, forming a loop large enough to slide comfortably over the button. Bind the strands together using a buttonhole stitch.

Buttonholes

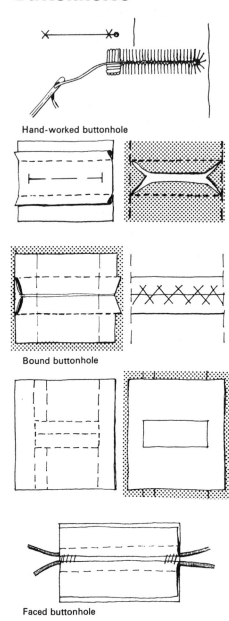

Hand-worked buttonhole

Bound buttonhole

Faced buttonhole

Three methods of making buttonholes

To make a buttonhole by hand, first position the button on the fabric half its diameter in from the edge of the opening and mark the width of the button at either side. Make an eyelet hole with a stiletto at the end of the buttonhole, nearest the opening edge, which will hold the shank of the button. Allow approximately 3mm ($\frac{1}{8}$in) ease for the button to slide through comfortably. Using sharp, pointed scissors cut a slit to the inside mark to form the opening. Overcast the edges or sew, with continuous running stitches, around the opening to strengthen. Working from right to left sew with buttonhole stitches using buttonhole twist. These stitches are basically blanket stitches worked very closely together. The opposite end to the eyelet should be finished off with a bar tack. Make a few vertical straight stitches the width of the buttonhole and surrounding buttonhole stitches and bind these together. When a very strong buttonhole is required, as on coats and jackets, work the buttonhole stitches over a cord.

A bound buttonhole takes a little more time and patience but gives a neat finish and stands up well to wear and tear. There are several ways to make this sort of buttonhole. One method is to use a fabric patch, turned through to the inside. Cut a piece of fabric on the lengthwise grain 2.5cm (1in) longer than the width of the buttonhole by 3.8cm (1$\frac{1}{2}$in), and mark the centre of the patch with a row of tacking stitches. Fold one edge of the patch 6mm ($\frac{1}{4}$in) from the centre mark and tack on the foldline. Sew a tuck 3mm ($\frac{1}{8}$in) from the folded edge and remove the tacking. Repeat this procedure on the other side of the centreline so there is a 6mm ($\frac{1}{4}$in) space between the stitching-lines of the tucks. With right sides together centre the patch over the buttonhole position on the garment matching the centre tacking-line on the patch with the buttonhole marking. Tack the tucked piece to the main fabric along the centreline of tacking. Mark the ends of the buttonhole with tailor's chalk and sew along the stitching-lines on the tucks between these points. Cut a 6mm ($\frac{1}{4}$in) slit on the centreline of the buttonhole on the inside of the garment and then cut diagonally into each corner. Turn the tucked piece to the inside through the opening. Turn the garment over to the right side and fold the front edge back over the buttonhole exposing the triangular ends. Sew these ends to the tucks across the strip on the chalk marks indicating the ends of the buttonhole. Catch stitch the edges of the tucks together on the outside and cut the corners of the patch in a curve. Press the buttonhole from the inside. Join the facing and tack around each buttonhole to hold it securely in position. Mark the corners and centre of the buttonhole with pins and cut the facing as for the buttonhole opening, making a horizontal slit at the centre pin. Cut diagonally from the slit to the corners and turn in the edges to the facing. Sew to the stitching-line with very small hemming stitches. Remove the tacking and catch stitching and press. The buttonhole will now be the same on both sides.

Thick, bulky fabrics have to be fastened with a faced buttonhole and strengthened with fine cord. Cut a piece of fabric 3.8cm (1$\frac{1}{2}$in) larger all round than the size of the buttonhole and mark the centreline as before. With right sides together, centre the patch over the buttonhole marking on the garment, and tack into place. On the wrong side stitch around the buttonhole 3mm ($\frac{1}{8}$in) from the edge. Cut a 6mm ($\frac{1}{4}$in) slit on the centreline and cut diagonally into the corners. Turn the strip through the opening to the wrong side and press. Cut out two pieces of fabric 3.2cm (1$\frac{1}{4}$in) wide and fold each over fine cord 2.5cm (1in) longer than the buttonhole, stitching into place close to the cord. Sew these pieces together leaving a space in the centre the same size as the buttonhole. Centre the strips under the faced opening in the garments. Slip stitch the edges of the opening to the stitching-lines and across the ends of the corded strip, pulling the stitches tight so that they disappear into the fabric. Join the facing as before.

Buttons should be sewn into place using double strands of strong thread or buttonhole twist. If the button is not manufactured with a metal shank, a thread one can be formed while sewing the button into place. Anchor the thread on the wrong side of the fabric and take one stitch through the button. Insert a thick pin or matchstick under this stitch and continue to sew over the top. When completed, remove the pin or matchstick and pull the button to tighten the threads. Wind the thread around the strands under the button several times to form a shank. Secure the thread on the wrong side. The button can be attached by sewing through another small button on the inside of the fabric.

Gathering and Shirring

Gathering, shirring, smocking, tucking and pleating are all decorative ways of controlling fullness. Not only do they look very pretty on children's clothes but they are very practical as their elastic properties enable the clothes to stretch as the child begins to grow.

Gathering

Gathering is one of the most popular and simple ways to control fullness. It is used on lightweight materials including very fine wools. Gathering stitches must be even. When seams must be crossed, clip the seam allowance first so that the stitches can go between the clipped edges. The amount of fabric to be gathered

Gathering

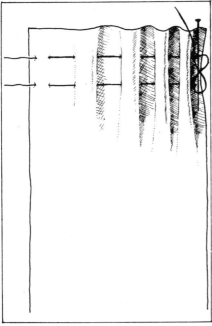

should be about one and a half times the finished width of an outfit—or twice the finished width if you prefer a very full garment.

The quickest and easiest way to gather is by machine. Wind the bobbin with thick thread or buttonhole twist and use a regular thread on top of the machine. Set the machine to the longest stitch and sew the first row of stitching on the seamline, leaving a long thread at each end of the row. Machine a second row of stitching 6mm ($\frac{1}{4}$in) inside the seamline, again leaving long threads at either end. Secure the threads firmly at one end, winding them around a pin. From the other end pull up the bobbin threads to the required width, and secure. Adjust the gathers evenly. To give a neat, flat finish to the gathers, stroke them down with a large needle, such as a darning needle, above and below the gathering threads about 1.3cm ($\frac{1}{2}$in) each way, taking care not to snag the fabric.

To gather by hand, make two rows of small running stitches, one under the other. The stitches must be perfectly even and the best way to do this is to make the stitches on the right side twice the size of the stitches on the under side. Anchor the thread at the beginning of the row with a series of small back stitches and continue with the running stitches to the far end. Pull up the thread to the required width and secure with back stitches. Adjust the gathers evenly. However, if the fabric is too delicate for stroking, make the rows of gathering wider apart, leaving about 6mm ($\frac{1}{4}$in) between them.

Gathering up a long length of

fabric can be a bit of a problem. It is difficult to get the gathers even, if they are all together. The best way is to divide the fabric to be gathered into four sections and then divide the rest of the garment to which it will be joined into quarters as well. Gather the four sections separately and pin to the corresponding quarter of the garment fabric. Pull up the gathering threads to fit, and adjust the gathers evenly.

Shirring

Shirring is the use of three or more rows of gathers to control fullness. A regular thread can be used and pulled up, as in gathering, but for children's clothes it is better to use thin elastic which will give extra stretch to allow for growth.

Only use the elastic thread on the bobbin, either by winding the bobbin

Shirring

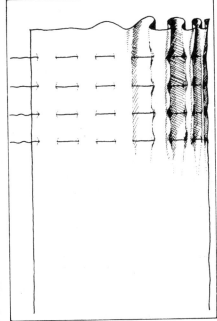

by hand without stretching the thread or by machine without using tension. Use the correct thread compatible with the fabric on top of the machine and a medium-size needle. Set the machine to the longest stitch length and test on a sample piece of the fabric to ascertain the correct amount of fullness. Machine in straight lines keeping the rows equidistant, about 6mm ($\frac{1}{4}$in) apart. It is important to stretch the fabric flat for each row of stitching. Therefore, if a large area such as a bodice, is to be shirred, the fabric must be worked before the garment section is cut out. Press with the tip of the iron only, being careful not to place the iron flat over the fullness as this would destroy the raised effect.

Smocking and Tucking

Smocking

Smocking looks most attractive on small children's clothes. The actual stitch is easy but great care must be taken in preparing the fabric first. The best materials to use are small checks, such as gingham, or narrow stripes, which will act as guidelines. With plain fabrics, the guidelines must be marked out with small dots, evenly spaced at approximately 6mm ($\frac{1}{4}$in) intervals in absolutely straight lines. Iron-on transfers which are great time-savers, are now readily available but, even so, care must be taken to ensure that they are stamped on straight. Before marking, lay out the fabric and secure firmly to keep it flat and taut.

With the dots in place, take a long thread and fasten securely at the beginning of the first horizontal row of dots. Gather along the line going from dot to dot and leaving a length of thread at the far end. Repeat this procedure for all the rows. Pull up the threads and secure every two rows by wrapping the threads around a pin. This will give the material a regular, pleated effect.

Begin at the right hand side and sew the first two pleats together level with the first row of horizontal stitches. Then, working across the fabric, sew the second and third pleats together, half-way between the two rows of stitching. Return to the top row of stitching and sew together the third and fourth pleats. Repeat the process to the end of the row and secure the thread. Go back to the right hand side of the top of the second line of horizontal stitching and start again, sewing as before. If you wish, you can use different coloured threads. This gives a very pretty effect.

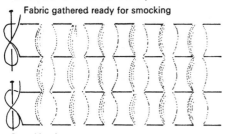

Fabric gathered ready for smocking

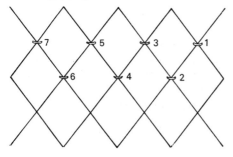

Smocking in progress

Tucking

Tucking controls fullness by gathering the fabric up into a series of flat folds which are stitched into place. Tucks vary in size according to the type of garment. Pin tucks are the smallest and prettiest tucks, being approximately 3mm ($\frac{1}{8}$in) to 6mm ($\frac{1}{4}$in) wide. They are used on fine delicate fabrics and are perfect for the bodice of a small child's dress or on a shirt. Tucks would obviously be wider on skirts and loose-fitting tops and dresses. In general, the amount of material required is three times the width of the tuck to allow for both sides of the tuck and the fabric it covers. However, if the tucks are spaced apart with the space

in between the tucks equal to the width of the tuck, only twice the amount of fabric will be required.

The easiest way to prepare the fabric for tucking is to make a gauge out of cardboard or thick paper, cutting notches to mark the width of the tuck (1) and the space between the tucks (2). Transfer these markings on to the fabric. Place the two outer marks of the width of the tuck together and press along the foldline. Pin and tack the tucks across the area to be tucked and then sew firmly into place, either by hand using a small running stitch, or by machine. Pin tucks, on the other hand, should be stitched normally close to the folded edge.

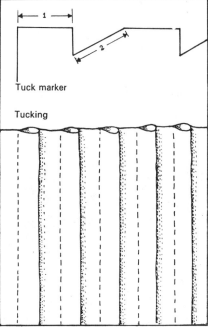

Tuck marker

Tucking

Pleats

Marking-up fabric

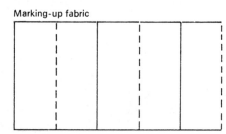

Knife pleats

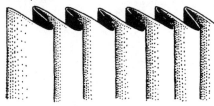

Box pleat

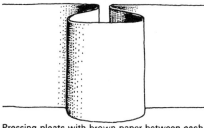

Pressing pleats with brown paper between each pleat

Pleats are yet another way to control fullness and can be used on all kinds of material. They are prepared in a very similar manner to tucking, but a little more time and patience is needed for the accurate marking and tacking required, which is the secret of perfect pleating. In general, the amount of fabric required is three times the finished width.

On the wrong side of the fabric, using tailor's chalk, draw a series of alternate broken and solid vertical lines across the area to be pleated. Take great care to keep the lines straight and an equal distance apart. It will save time if the pleats are made from the wrong side of the fabric, otherwise the pleat markings will have to be transferred to the right side of the fabric with tacking stitches.

With the right sides of the material together, match up the solid line to the broken line of each pleat. Pin the top, bottom and centre of each pleat to hold it straight and then place pins at 2.5cm (2in) intervals along the pleat. Beginning at the lower edge, tack by hand along the chalk mark to the top with even tacking stitches, removing the pins as you tack. Tacking on the wrong side will also prevent the fabric from being marked when the pleats are pressed.

There are several kinds of pleats but probably the most useful for children's clothes are either knife pleats or soft unpressed pleats for pretty skirts ; and either box pleats or pressed pleats for school uniforms. With knife pleats, the pleats are arranged so that the top edge of one pleat meets the under edge of the next one, giving a concertina effect, and the pleats go from right to

edge of the pleat with tailor's chalk and then flatten out the fabric so that the marking is in the centre on top of the tacking. For pressed pleats, work from the wrong side of the fabric and press the inside foldline of each pleat before it is turned to one side. Place the pleat in the right direction and pin the foldline to the skirt at the upper edge. Tack into position with even tacking stitches 1.3cm ($\frac{1}{2}$in) below the cut edge. Turn to the right side of the fabric and press each pleat on the outside edge. It is a good idea to place a strip of brown paper between the pleats when pressing to prevent the crease marking the adjoining pleat.

A pleated skirt in wool, wool-blends, or their synthetic counterparts, makes a warm and pretty addition to a little girl's winter wardrobe. Plain and checked fabrics are equally attractive and, of course, tartan for a kilt. Hem the lower edge before pleating the fabric. Decide on the size of the pleats allowing three times the width for each pleat. Pleat up the fabric to fit the child's waist comfortably and join to a self-fabric waistband. In a kilt, the fabric will have a plain wrap-over in front and a wide piece of fabric should extend underneath to form the underwrap. The waistband should fasten at the edge of the underwrap and at the edge of the wrapover, the side fastening with a kilt pin.

left around the waist. For unpressed pleats work from the wrong side of the fabric. Match up the chalk markings and tack. Pin the fold edge of each pleat to the skirt with pins going vertically and tack into place with even tacking stitches 1.3cm ($\frac{1}{2}$in) below the cut edge. From the wrong side, box pleats resemble two knife pleats facing each other, one turned towards the right and the other towards the left. The quickest and easiest way to make these pleats is to tack a pleat twice the width of the finished pleat. Mark the

Collars

Collars can be very useful for children's clothes, providing a pretty finishing touch to a basic dress, a new look to a shirt or dress handed down from an elder brother or sister and, as children are quickly bored with clothes, a collar adding a different look can give a new lease of life to an outfit which still has plenty of wear left in it. Collars on little boys' shirts and young girls' blouses tend to wear out faster than the main part of the garment. These can be easily replaced, which saves buying a new shirt or blouse. A dainty lace edging around the collar and embroidery on the points looks most attractive. This can turn a girl's simple blouse into a pretty party outfit and makes a perfect pageboy's shirt for a boy. Collars require very little fabric and can be made from left-over pieces of self-fabric from the original garment or remnants of a compatible contrasting material.

Peter Pan Collar

A Peter Pan collar is commonly seen on children's clothes and is one of the easiest to make. It is useful, too, as it can be attached so that the edges meet either at the back or front of the dress or blouse. This collar lies very flat and the neck edge of the collar is the same shape as the neck edge of the garment. The secret of applying this type of collar successfully is to match up these shapes exactly. Carefully fold the garment in half and pin the neck edge to keep the shape in place. Tack and remove the pins. Place a piece of paper on a flat, hard working surface

and position the back fold of the outfit level with the edge of the paper. Secure with pins, one at the neck edge and the other 7.5cm (3in) below. Smooth out the garment and pin down the front of the outfit in the same way. With a sharp pencil draw the outline of the neck edge and about 10cm (4in) down the centre front fold. Remove the garment and decide on the desired depth of the collar. This will really depend on the size of the child as too large a collar will swamp a small child and look ridiculous. Conversely, too small a collar on a plump child is unflattering. Mark the width with a series of dots measured from the neck curve. When joined up, they will form a curve parallel to the neckline. In order to prevent a point occurring at the centre back, draw the beginning of the curve at ninety degrees to the edge of the paper. To form the front edge of the collar mark a point 1.3cm ($\frac{1}{2}$in) beyond the centre front on the outer edge of the collar. Join this point with the centre front on the inside edge. Mark the centre back of the collar with tailor's chalk or tacking thread to avoid confusion with the centre front once the pattern piece has been cut out.

Measure from the centre back of the pattern piece to the end of the shape in a straight line to ascertain the amount of fabric required. If you are short of fabric the under collar can be made from a compatible contrasting fabric or from lining material. Fold the fabric on the crosswise grain and pin the centre back edge to the fold. Cut out once or twice according to whether the under collar is to be cut from the same fabric or not, allowing sufficient for a seam allowance around the edges. Mark the

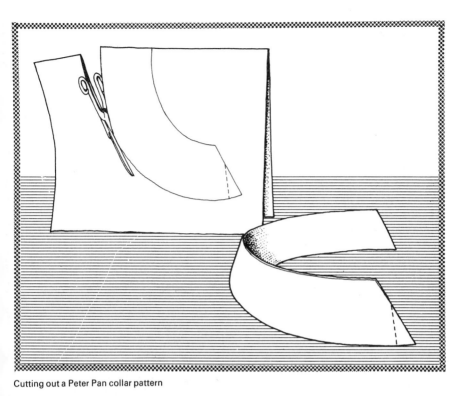

Cutting out a Peter Pan collar pattern

centre front and the centre back of the collar. Cut a piece of interfacing the same size as the collar and pin to the wrong side of the under collar. Tack into place on the seamline and cut diagonally across the corners of the interfacing only 6mm ($\frac{1}{4}$in) inside the seam allowance. With right sides together sew the under and upper collars together leaving the neck edge open. Cut the interfacing close to the stitching-line and grade the seams leaving the widest amount of fabric on the upper collar. Cut the corners diagonally and clip the curves. Turn the collar through to the right side and press. Tack the neck edges together on the seamline.

On the right side of the garment, tack the collar into place with the under collar next to the outfit and matching centre front and centre back. Pin the facing or a bias strip of fabric over the collar, tack and remove the pins. Sew through all thicknesses on the seam. Remove the tacking stitches, grade the seam allowances and clip curves. Press the facing to the inside of the garment and slip stitch into place. If you would prefer the collar opening to the centre back instead of the centre front, the process is reversed and the centre front edge is placed to the edge of the paper when making the pattern piece and then to the fold edge of the fabric.

Collars

Two other sorts of collar often seen in children's clothes are the more tailored roll collar and the decorative mandarin collar.

Roll Collar

A roll collar gives a neat tailored look to a dress, blouse or shirt, but is much easier to apply than a proper shirt collar which is attached to a neckband first. The secret of making a collar roll or turn back correctly without the edges curling up is to cut the upper collar slightly bigger than the undercollar. The neck edge is the same but about 3mm ($\frac{1}{8}$in) should be added all around the outer edges of light and medium weight fabrics and about 6mm ($\frac{1}{4}$in) to thicker fabrics. The interfacing is sewn to the wrong side of the under collar and the two collar pieces are then joined together as described for a Peter Pan collar. However, when the collar is turned through to the right side, roll the edge of the upper collar to the underside when pressing so that the seamline does not show. With the top collar facing upwards, shape the collar before attaching it to the neckine by rolling the upper collar over the edge of your hand and pinning along the line on which the collar turns back just above the seamline. Tack the neck edges together and you will find the top collar will lie back just short of the edge of the under collar. Pin to the right side of the garment with the under collar next to the outfit. Tack the facing over the top and sew through all thicknesses. Grade the seam allowances and clip the curves.

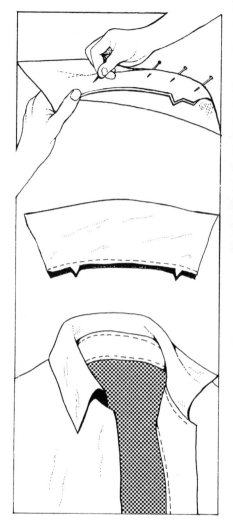

Press the seam towards the facing and understitch, finishing about 5cm (2in) from the edges, to prevent the facing being pulled out. Turn the facing to the inside of the garment, press and catch stitch to the garment seams, being careful not to catch in the outer fabric so that the stitches show through to the right side.

Mandarin Collar

A mandarin collar is cut on the straight grain of the fabric in one rectangular piece twice the finished width of the collar and attached to the curved neckline with a shaped facing. Mark the centre or foldline of the collar and cut a piece of interfacing half the size of the collar fabric. Join the interfacing to the wrong side of half the collar section, tacking it on the seamline and slip stitching it to the centre foldline. Cut the corners of the interfacing 6mm ($\frac{1}{4}$in) inside the seam allowance. Fold the collar in half lengthwise and machine the short side seams. Cut the interfacing close to the stitching-line, grade the seam allowances and cut the corners diagonally. Turn the collar through to the right side and press. Tack the neck edges together on the seamline. However, if curved corners are desired rather than square ones, the collar has to be constructed in two parts and the under and upper collars joined as previously described. Pin the collar to the neck edge of the garment and tack into place on the seamline. Pin and tack the facing over the top of the collar, right sides together and sew through all thicknesses. Cut the interfacing close to the stitching-line, grade the seam allowances and clip curves. It will be necessary to understitch the facing and collar seams together to prevent the facing rolling back towards the collar. Press the facing to the inside and slip stitch it to the shoulder seams.

Mandarin collar

(*Opposite*) To make a roll collar : roll the upper collar back from seamline and pin along seamline ; tack raw edges together ; attach collar to garment

Simple Pockets

Pockets are most essential for children's clothes. Of course, they are useful for the necessities of life such as hankies, pocket money or bus fares, and sweets, but children are like squirrels when it comes to collecting things during the day and what better place to hide them than in a pocket. You can make pockets out of left-over fabric from the garment or you can have patch pockets which look very attractive made in contrasting materials. Embroidery motifs and appliqué give a very pretty finishing touch to pockets.

Pockets are quite easy to make. Decide on the size required and allow 2.5cm (1in) at the top and about a 1cm ($\frac{3}{8}$in) seam around the other edges. Neaten the raw edges either by hand or with a machine zig-zag stitch and turn down the top edge on the 2.5cm (1in) hem allowed to the outside of the pocket. Starting at the folded edge stitch on the 1cm ($\frac{3}{8}$in) seamline around the pocket. Cut the corners at the top diagonally and clip the curves if making a rounded pocket. Turn the top hem to the inside and turn in on the stitching-line. Mitre the corners on a square pocket. Tack the seams and press. Pin the pocket to the garment. Tack and remove the pins. Sew into position close to the edge of the pocket, remove the tacking stitches and press. Curved pockets are probably best for children as they tend to collect dust less quickly than the corners of square ones.

If a pocket is going to be in constant use rather than just being decorative, it is a good idea to line it as this will help to preserve its shape. Cut the lining the same size as the pocket up to the bottom of the hem flap plus a 1.3cm ($\frac{1}{2}$in) seam allowance. With right sides together, pin the upper edges of the lining and the pocket together. Stitch along the seam allowance leaving a 2.5cm (1in) opening in the centre so that the pocket can be turned through to the right side. Press the seam towards the lining. With right sides together, fold the pocket on the hemline marking and pin. Stitch the lining and the hem allowance to the pocket around the outer edges. Grade the seam allowances and cut the corners diagonally. Turn the pocket to the right side, carefully pulling out the corners with a pin. Slip stitch the opening and press the pocket. Pin the pocket to the garment. Tack into place and remove the pins. Sew the pockets close to the edge by machine or slip stitch by hand. Remove the tacking stitches and press.

A little boy may prefer to have a pocket in the side seam of his trousers. This is quite easy to do during construction ; the pocket should be inserted before the side seam is sewn up. First decide on the depth of the pocket opening and the width required. For a small child about 12.5cm (5in) deep would be sufficient. With a paper and pencil draw a vertical line 12.5cm (5in) long and another line 9cm (3$\frac{1}{2}$in) long at right angles to this. Mark a spot 2.5cm (1in) below the bottom of the vertical line. Draw a curved line joining the top and bottom point slightly slanting so that the bottom of the pocket extends below the bottom of the opening. Cut out two pocket

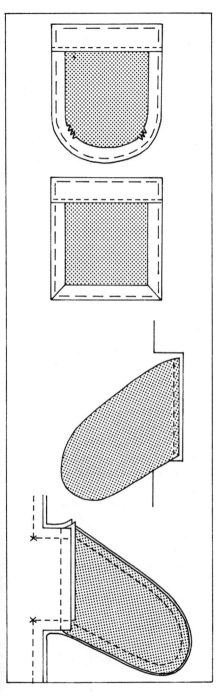

shapes either from self-fabric, if you have any to spare, or from lining material. Extend the seam allowances on the trousers by 2cm ($\frac{3}{4}$in) continuing 1.5cm ($\frac{5}{8}$in) above and below where the pocket is to be inserted. On the original seamline, mark 1.5cm ($\frac{5}{8}$in) in from the top and bottom edges of the extension either with tailor's chalk or tacking stitches. On the wrong side of the fabric sew one pocket to one seam extension and the other pocket to the other extension. Press both seams towards the pocket. The side seams of the trousers and the pockets are sewn together at the same time. Begin from the top of the trouser leg and, when you reach the 1.5cm ($\frac{5}{8}$in) mark at the top of the pocket opening in the seamline, release the tension, if sewing by machine, and swivel the fabric around so that you are ready to start sewing up the pocket. Replace the foot and sew around the outside of the two pocket shapes. When you reach the bottom 1.5cm ($\frac{5}{8}$in) mark, once again release the tension and swivel the fabric around. Replace the foot and continue to sew the rest of the side seam.

(*From the top*) Round pocket seen from the wrong side ; patch pocket seen from the wrong side with edges turned in, ready to apply to garment ; inserting a pocket into a side seam

Simple Skirts

A simple gathered skirt is a pretty and practical addition to a little girl's wardrobe, as it can be worn with many different T-shirts, blouses and sweaters, thus providing several outfits from one basic garment. It is easy to make, too, as the only part where fitting is required is around the waist. Choose a plain fabric or one with an overall design so that there is no need to worry about matching the seam. Also choose a soft material which will gather easily, such as a lightweight cotton, cotton blend, lightweight wool, a wool blend, and the synthetic counterparts.

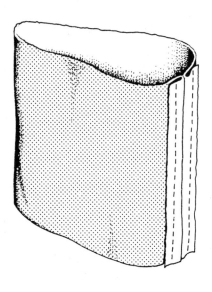

The amount of material required is approximately one and a half times the waist measurement or twice the amount if a really full skirt is desired. Test on a sample piece of fabric first to see how much fullness is required as a thin child will benefit from the extra width afforded by a very full skirt and a chubbier child will be better off with less gathers.

There are three quick and easy ways of making the skirt. It can be either made all in one with an elastic casing at the top ; gathered into a self-fabric waistband ; or, if you are short of fabric, gathered on to decorative elastic. In all cases allow as large a hem as the fullness will allow without looking bulky, so that this can be let down as the child grows. Again this can be tested first on a sample piece of material.

When an elastic casing is used to control the fullness, measure the finished length required plus the hem allowance and 2.2cm ($\frac{7}{8}$in) at the top for the casing. Turn under 6mm ($\frac{1}{4}$in) to the wrong side of the fabric at the top edge and press. With right sides together, join the side seam taking a 1.5cm ($\frac{5}{8}$in) seam allowance. Press the seam open and neaten the raw edges. Turn under 1.5cm ($\frac{5}{8}$in) at the top edge and stitch very close to the foldline. Stitch again close to the bottom edge leaving a 2.5cm (1in) gap through which to insert the elastic. Cut a length of 1.3cm ($\frac{1}{2}$in) wide elastic so that it fits comfortably around the waist plus an extra 1.5cm ($\frac{1}{2}$in). Attach a safety pin to one end of the elastic and thread it through the casing. Overlap the ends of the elastic by 6mm ($\frac{1}{4}$in) on each end and sew together securely. Hem the remainder of the opening in the casing. Turn up the hem.

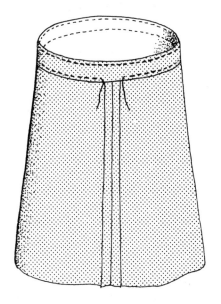 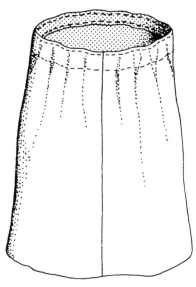

When joining a gathered skirt to a
waistband of decorative elastic or one
of self-fabric, again measure the
finished length of the skirt plus the hem
and a 1.5cm ($\frac{5}{8}$in) seam allowance at
the top edge. Gather up the fabric to
the required width with two rows of
gathering stitches, one on the 1.5cm
($\frac{5}{8}$in) seamline and the other 6mm ($\frac{1}{4}$in)
above this in the seam allowance,
leaving 1.5cm ($\frac{5}{8}$in) seam allowance at
each side of the gathers. Adjust the
gathers evenly. With right sides
together join the two sides taking
a 1.5cm ($\frac{5}{8}$in) seam and finishing
11.5cm ($4\frac{5}{8}$in) below the top edge.
Tack up the remainder of the seam and
press open the seam. Insert a 10cm
(4in) zip with the zip head ending
1.5cm ($\frac{5}{8}$in) below the top of the skirt.
Remove the tacking threads. Join the
skirt to the waistband.

Making a simple gathered skirt
(*From left to right*) join side seam; leave a gap in
lower stitching of waistband to insert elastic;
finished skirt

Skirts and Waistbands

If you wish to use decorative elastic for the waistband, first cut a length of the elastic so that it fits comfortably around the waist, plus an extra 2cm ($\frac{3}{4}$in). Turn in 3mm ($\frac{1}{8}$in) at either end of the elastic to neaten the raw edges. Lap the elastic over the gathered skirt fabric just covering the bottom row of gathers. Pin and tack into position with the left side parallel to the left side of the zip opening and the right-hand end extending by 1.3cm ($\frac{1}{2}$in). Machine on the seamline through the bottom row of gathers, catching in the elastic. Sew snaps or hooks and eyes under the overlap on the elastic to hold the waistband in place. Turn up the hem.

To make a self-fabric waistband, cut a length of material so that it fits comfortably around the waist plus 4.5cm ($1\frac{3}{4}$in) by twice the width of the finished waistband plus 3.2cm ($1\frac{1}{4}$in). Cut out the interfacing, making it the same length as the fabric but half as wide. Pin the interfacing to the wrong side of half the waistband. Tack along the long and short sides 1.5cm ($\frac{5}{8}$in) in from the edge and stitch to the centre of the waistband with loose hemming stitches. Cut across the corners of the interfacing diagonally 6mm ($\frac{1}{4}$in) inside the stitching-line. Turn up 1.5cm ($\frac{5}{8}$in) to the wrong side of the other long edge and press. With right sides together, pin the interfaced side of the waistband to the skirt extending the left-hand side by 1.5cm ($\frac{5}{8}$in) and the right-hand side by 2.8cm ($1\frac{1}{8}$in). Stitch into place taking

a 1.5cm ($\frac{5}{8}$in) seam allowance machining through the bottom row of gathers. Trim the interfacing close to the stitching line and grade the seam allowances. Press the seam towards the waistband. Fold the waistband in half with the right sides together and sew the short sides together taking a 1.5cm ($\frac{5}{8}$in) seam. Clip the corners diagonally and grade the seam allowance. Turn the waistband through to the right side and pull out the corners gently with a pin. Hem into place along the 1.5cm ($\frac{5}{8}$in) seamline and press. Sew hooks and eyes or snaps under the overlap to close the waistband. Turn up the hem.

For a smart tailored look, choose an A-line skirt. This is also a more flattering line for a plump child than a gathered skirt whose fullness is more beneficial to a thin child. It is easy to make if you choose one with two side seams. Shaping is usually given by waist darts and the skirt fastens with a zip in the side seam. The skirt can be attached to a fabric waistband in the same way as a gathered skirt, or the waistline edge can be finished easily by using a grosgrain ribbon facing. Use 1.5cm ($\frac{5}{8}$in) wide ribbon and cut a piece long enough to fit your child's waist comfortably plus a 1.5cm ($\frac{5}{8}$in) extension beyond the front edge and 1.3cm ($\frac{1}{2}$in) beyond the back edge of the zip. With right sides up, pin the grosgrain ribbon to the waist seamline, extending beyond the edges as described and edge stitch to the waistline. Cut the skirt fabric to 6mm ($\frac{1}{4}$in) from the stitching-line. Turn in the edges of the ribbon and hem stitch to the tapes of the zip. Turn up the hem.

EVERYDAY HOME REPAIRS

Mike Smith

The Tools

For any kind of maintenance work about the house you are going to need a selection of tools. How many you require and what type of tool is often a difficult question—there are hundreds to choose from and with such a selection it is easy to buy tools that you will hardly ever use. But, of course, when you do need them they are often indispensable. I have selected a basic kit which should cover most emergencies about the house:

Hammer

Hammers are the most common tools in use and there are several different types: peine, ball peine and claw. These are available in different head weights. I would suggest a claw hammer of 566g (20oz) weight as this will not only put nails in, but also pull them out should you bend one, thus doing two jobs for the price of one.

Maintenance

Keep the face of the hammer clean and free from glue, paint and grease (*see* 'Nails' for the reasons why, p 270).

Saw

When choosing a saw look for one with a handle which does not cramp the hand, and make sure that it balances well. Some saws have a 90° × 45° angle formed in the handle which acts as a square for setting out the timber to be cut and saves money on buying a separate square. Seven teeth per 25mm (1in) is a good saw to begin with. If you choose a hard point, that is, with the teeth specially hardened at

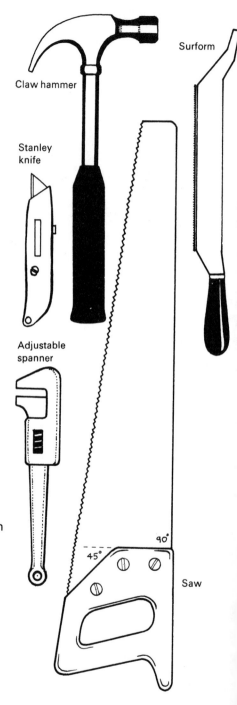

Claw hammer

Surform

Stanley knife

Adjustable spanner

Saw

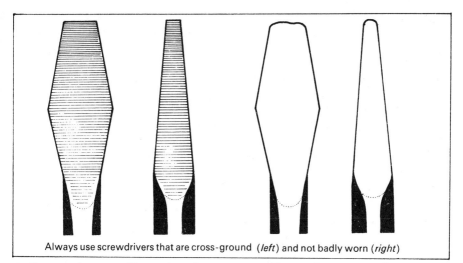

Always use screwdrivers that are cross-ground (*left*) and not badly worn (*right*)

the factory, the saw will stay sharp for a long time ; however this type of saw cannot be resharpened like a conventional one. With care and if not used every day it will last a very long time.

If you use a conventional saw it is a very skilful job to set and sharpen it, but there are now devices on the market to make this job easier for the amateur. You will have to decide which type to buy, but do remember that a blunt saw or a saw without enough set on will not cut square or true. You will have to use much more pressure to make it work and thus increase the risk of it slipping and giving you a cut hand.

Maintenance

Lightly oil after use.

Screwdriver

When selecting a screwdriver look first at the handle to make sure it affords a good purchase and is comfortable in the hand. The blade should be cross ground for maximum strength. Choose three different sizes, small, medium and large. These will manage most of your maintenance jobs and the selection can be added to later.

Maintenance

Keep the ends of the screwdriver ground flat. Unless you have a grindstone this will have to be done at your local garage. Badly worn screwdrivers soil the end of the screw and make it very difficult to drive in.

Note Screwdrivers should never be used for lifting floorboards, removing skirting boards, cutting holes in cement or for general prising.

The three tools just described are the essentials. Useful additions are : a surform ; an adjustable spanner ; a Stanley knife ; and an electric or hand drill. Remember when buying always to choose good quality tools, and never be tempted to save money by buying cheap, inferior ones. Look after them with care and they will last a lifetime.

Materials

Timber

To do any job around the house you will need materials of some sort whether it be nails, screws, timber or whatever. Let us turn first to the developments in timber.

Wood comes in all sizes and shapes, in both soft and hardwood. DIY shops, builders' merchants and timber importers are the source of supply.

Sawn timber generally comes in the size stated, ie 25×25mm (1×1in) but if the wood is planed (abbreviated PAR—'planed all round') then it will finish approximately 22×22mm ($\frac{7}{8} \times \frac{7}{8}$in). It is as well to allow for these differences if you are working on a project.

Softwood is the wood most commonly available. Select your own lengths, and look for straight, dry and true timber, avoiding dead knots, shakes, twists and splits. Most timber

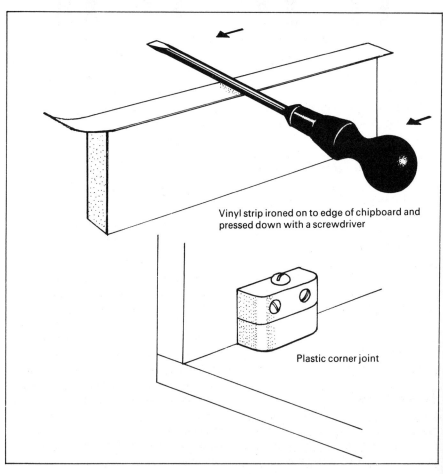

Vinyl strip ironed on to edge of chipboard and pressed down with a screwdriver

Plastic corner joint

merchants will cut timber off to the length required so measure the job in hand before you set off to buy the timber.

Plywood consists of a number of layers of thin veneer glued together, giving immense strength and used for a wide variety of working jobs. The standard sizes are as follows : 3mm, 4mm, 6mm and 12mm ($\frac{1}{8}$in, $\frac{1}{6}$in, $\frac{1}{4}$in and $\frac{1}{2}$in).

Blockboard is similar to plywood, having thin veneers of plywood stuck to a core made from strips of softwood and as the sizes are generally thicker than plywood, 18mm and 25mm ($\frac{3}{4}$in and 1in), it is ideal for use in large areas.

Chipboard is manufactured from small chippings of wood, hence the name. The chippings are bonded with adhesive and then pressed to the required thickness. This material is ideal for roof cladding, though some other uses include furniture that is to be covered with fabric, doors and vertical partitions. Do not use it for shelves as chipboard will sag under its own weight. Standard sizes are 12mm and 18mm ($\frac{1}{2}$in and $\frac{3}{4}$in).

A recent development in chipboard is to cover the face of it with either a wood veneer, melamine or with a vinyl face. This type of material is often used by kitchen-unit manufacturers. Known as 'faced boards' these have meant big gains for the DIY person, due to the vast number of sizes available. Several different wood veneers are available, oak, mahogany, teak, etc, which can be polished to match any existing furniture. Matching edging-strips of wood and vinyl are also available.

These strips are easy to fix : you simply use a domestic iron as the edging strips are coated on the back with a hot melt glue. Place the cut strip on the edge to be covered then, using a piece of brown paper to protect the face of the wood or vinyl, just rub the iron along the strip until the glue melts and sticks to the edge of the board. Next, press the strip down with a screwdriver to compress the edges, then wait to allow the glue to harden. After one hour rub the edges flush with a fine grade sandpaper.

Cutting these boards calls for a sharp saw and always score a line with a knife on both sides of the board as this will stop the veneer tearing as you cut, and will also leave a clean edge for sticking on the edging strip. One disadvantage with this type of board is that unless well supported it is unsuitable for shelves due to the chipboard core. Chipboard is most suitable for building any type of furniture and requires little or no skill since you only need the ability to cut the board to the required length and to use a domestic iron. Simple plastic corner-blocks will make a firm secure joint. Standard lengths are : 1.8m (6ft) and 2.4m (8ft) ; standard widths are : 150mm (6in), 225mm (9in), 300mm (12in), 375mm (15in), 450mm (18in), 525mm (21in), 600mm (24in), 675mm (27in) and 750mm (30in).

Hardboard is used for all manner of things : cladding for partitions, backs of cupboards, levelling old floorboards, pelmets, etc. When using hardboard make sure that there are enough supports, as this material tends to sag in the same manner as chipboard.

Materials

Nails

There are many different sorts of nail, but I shall deal only with those most widely used about the home. Before discussing them in detail, it is worth making the point that nails will bend if not driven in properly, and this can be avoided by always making sure that the face of the hammer is clean. New hammers are coated with sealer to prevent rust while in storage before being sold, and so the first job with a new hammer is to rub the face on a piece of fine sandpaper to remove this film of lacquer.

When using glue or any substitute that will adhere to the face of the hammer, the same procedure applies—always clean it off.

The smallest nail in general use is the panel pin. This is available in sizes ranging from less than 12mm ($\frac{1}{2}$in) to 50mm (2in) and is used for thin sheet material such as hardboard and plywood. Up to about 12mm ($\frac{1}{2}$in) panel pins are ideally suited for framing pictures since they have a very small head and are unlikely to split the wood. Some lengths are available with a diamond head (see drawing), and once driven home these need no punching in to hide this head as with the conventional panel pin.

Oval nails are perhaps the most common and are used in all types of work. Sizes vary from 22mm ($\frac{7}{8}$in) to 65mm ($2\frac{3}{4}$in). Their main job is for joinery work, as their oval profile is easier to hide than round-headed nails.

When nailing two pieces of wood together you should dovetail the nails as shown in the drawing, which will give the joint extra strength. When driving nails into wood, it will often split, especially when working near the end of a piece of timber. To prevent this happening, flatten the pointed end of the nail either with a file or by putting the head onto a brick or any hard surface and tapping the point flat. This stops the nail acting like a wedge, forcing the fibres of the wood apart or splitting it. The flattened end will cut through the wood knot and spread the wood fibres so that there is less chance of the wood splitting. Any nail can have the point flattened and will act in the same way. Round-headed nails are generally used for rougher work about the house and garden.

Screws

Sizes of screw are given by the length and size of the head. Common sizes are 6, 8 and 10 by whatever length you require. There are different types of head, with either a simple slot, Phillips or pozidrive designs—these have cross- or star-shaped finishes with four or eight turning points as opposed to the two of a slotted head. With a pozidrive there is less chance of the screwdriver slipping out and marking the wood.

For each size screw head you should use the correct size screwdriver, and one that is correctly ground. When screwing two pieces of wood together you must first drill a hole to clear the shank of the screw and, if using a countersunk screw, the wood must also be countersunk before inserting the screw so that the screw head finishes flush with the face of the wood. A pilot

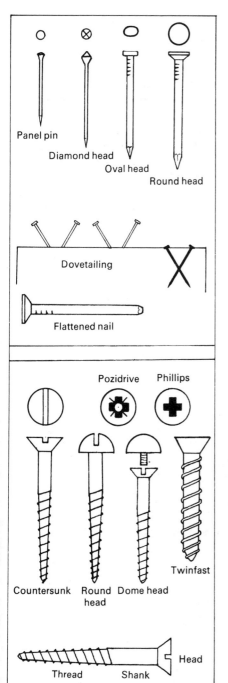

Panel pin

Diamond head

Oval head

Round head

Dovetailing

Flattened nail

Pozidrive   Phillips

Countersunk   Round   Dome head
head

Twinfast

Head

Thread   Shank

hole should be made for easy entry.

When screwing into hardboard, rub the threaded part of the screw on a piece of soap or a candle. This will lubricate the screw so that it enters more easily and the head is less likely to be twisted off. This can often happen when using brass screws since they do not have the strength of their steel counterparts. However, they do not rust or discolour surrounding wood. One can also get zinc-plated screws, which withstand wet conditions inside or out and can look quite decorative.

A useful new addition to the screw family is the 'Twinfast' by GKN. This has two threads compared to one on the normal screw, and it has a parallel shank which makes it ideal for chipboard and other particle boards because it gives a very firm grip.

One other decorative screw in common use is the dome-headed screw, generally used for fixing mirrors. After the screw has been turned in, the threaded dome is screwed into the screw head giving a decorative finish and hiding the screw head at the same time. One point to remember when screwing a mirror to a wall is never to overtighten the screws, or the mirror may break.

So much for putting in screws, but what about removing a stubborn one? First remove any paint from the slot by scraping or tapping out with a bradawl. When this is completely clear put in a screwdriver of the correct size— one that fits the full width of the slot— and give the end of the screwdriver a tap with the hammer, while turning it at the same time. Once the screw has started to move, turn the screwdriver by hand to remove the screw.

Filling Holes

Holes in any type of surface look unsightly and hold dust and dirt so it is worth filling them as soon as possible. The method to be used varies according to the type of surface.

Wood

Wood tends to bruise easily and is often subject to man-made holes or defects in the natural timber. New wood, which has been bruised by a hammer dent, can usually be made good by putting a drop of water on the damaged area. This raises the grain and can be sandpapered smooth later. If the bruise or a shallow dent cannot be smoothed out by this method it will have to be filled with a fine grade filler. These are readily available in DIY shops and should be applied according to the manufacturer's instructions. Once the filler has dried the area should be rubbed smooth using fine sandpaper and a sanding block (Fig 1). Small holes, scratches and other defects are treated in the same manner.

This method is suitable only for surfaces which are going to be painted. If the wood is to be left natural you should add a dye to the filler to match the existing wood. The colour will lighten as the moisture dries out so experiment on an old piece of wood first to achieve the correct colour match. Alternatively, you could use

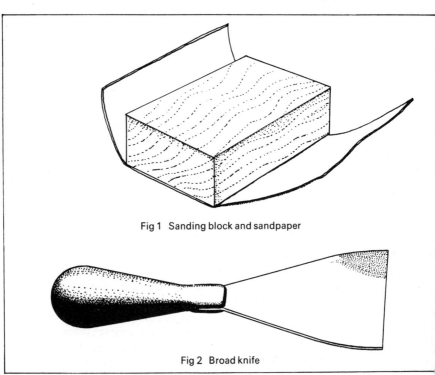

Fig 1 Sanding block and sandpaper

Fig 2 Broad knife

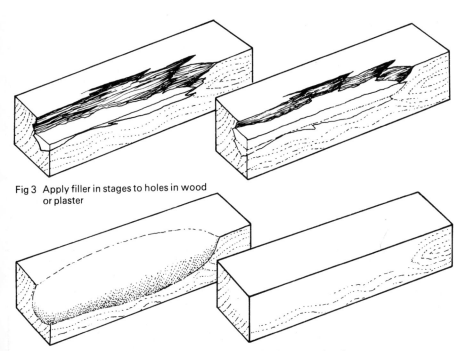

Fig 3 Apply filler in stages to holes in wood or plaster

Fig 4 Apply last layer of filler too thickly and smooth down to correct level

ready-made coloured fillers, but the disadvantage is that you are likely to finish up with three-quarters of the tin over, so it is worth experimenting with your own colours.

Many people use putty for filling holes in wood, but there is the problem that as the oil dries out the putty tends to shrink, leaving neat little depressions showing along the paintwork.

Plaster

Holes and defects, including cracks, in plaster can usually be filled with a cellulose filler. Cracks can be filled by using a broad knife (Fig 2), while larger holes will have to be built up in layers (Fig 3), waiting for each filling to dry before applying the next coat.

If you don't do this a depression will be left as the filler dries. You should also make the last coat a little too thick, leaving enough filler to smooth down to the level of the existing plaster (Fig 4).

When you are filling in holes on surfaces which are likely to be vibrated or shaken, such as doors, windows and frames, mix in a drop of PVA white woodworking adhesive with the filler as this will help the filler to hold better and be less liable to crack and fall out. When using a powder filler such as Polyfilla on any surface that is due to be painted, always apply two undercoats before putting on gloss paint. If you don't do this, you will get a matt finish to the gloss which shows the outline of the filled area.

Paint Preparation

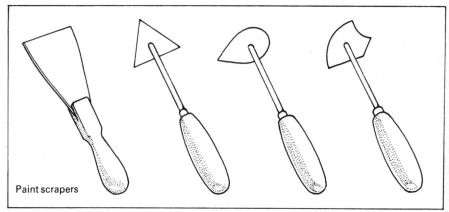

Paint scrapers

A great deal has been written about the techniques of painting, but it is often forgotten that even the most expert technique or expensive paint will be wasted if the object to be painted has not been properly prepared. So let us look at how to prepare some surfaces ready for painting.

New Wood

All the knots in the wood should be sealed with a proprietary brand of knotting sealer. This stops the resin in the knots from weeping out when the final coat of paint has been applied. You should then apply a good quality primer which is usually pink, white or yellow in colour. When this has dried rub down the surface with M2 grit sandpaper and fill any defects, such as nail holes, with putty or cellulose filler. The undercoats come next, and these should be of the correct colour for the final coats—this is usually specified on the tin containing the final colour. If the correct undercoat colour is not used this will affect the chosen colour, causing light or dark shading according to the undercoat used. Each undercoat, when dry, must be rubbed down before the next coat is applied. The final finish on the top coat is worth that little bit of extra labour.

Finally, apply the finishing coat, brushing well in the same direction to avoid drips and runs. If you are painting outside, wait for a fine, dry day, otherwise the gloss finishing-coat may bloom and dry dull.

Old Paintwork

Old paintwork will need particularly good rubbing down to remove any runs before you paint over it. It is best to use wet and dry emery paper, making sure that all flaking paint is removed and the edges are rubbed smooth. Do all the rubbing down first and dust off after completion. Two coats of undercoat will generally be required, especially if the finishing coat is a light colour.

It is sometimes necessary to remove old paintwork either by stripping or by burning. Burning is usually quicker, and ready-to-use gas lamps, which can be bought from a 'Do-It-Yourself'

274

shop, are better than the old paraffin types. With gas you have a greater control over the heat output. Play the flame continuously backwards and forwards across the wood to prevent scorching. The idea is to remove the paint without burning the wood. *Do not* attempt to burn paint from facia and soffit boards, or near thatched roofs or asbestos, and take great care when working close to glass windows. Chemical strippers are useful substitutes where heat cannot be applied, but be sure to follow exactly the manufacturer's instructions. After stripping with either heat or a commercial stripper, rub down the surface thoroughly and then proceed as for new wood.

Paint Application

Paint manufacturers have introduced new developments such as matt vinyl, sheen, gel, non-drip and a host of other names. Do not be confused by these words. There are two basic differences in finishing paints : they are either standard liquid paints or gel paints.

The gel or 'thixotropical' paints are perhaps the easiest to apply as they are less liable to drip or run off the brush and consequently avoid tears and sags once applied to a flat surface. When using liquid paints you must apply them evenly onto the surface, otherwise the paint will run leaving ugly tear marks. Since this does not happen when using gel paints they are much more easily applied than the liquid type.

Should you need to strain paint you will find it easiest to place a stocking over the can to be strained and to pour through the stocking into a clean empty can. This method is much cleaner and easier than the traditional one of tying a stocking over the clean can and then pouring the paint.

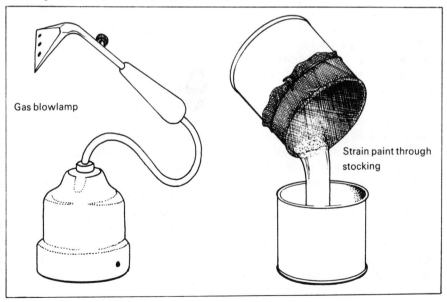

Gas blowlamp

Strain paint through stocking

Wallpaper

Much has been written about the art of wallpapering, but recent developments by manufacturers have meant a number of changes in technique. In addition to the old-style papers, which had to be pasted before hanging, there are now ready-pasted wallpapers which you just dip into a trough of water, and vinyl papers where one pastes the walls rather than the back of the paper. Despite these changes which have made things a lot easier, you will not get a pleasing end result if you do not set about the job in the right manner.

Choosing the best place to start is sometimes the most difficult decision. This will vary from room to room, so here are a few rule of thumb guides. Try to start from the lightest part of the room, near a window for instance. If you are going to use a large-patterned wallpaper start over a chimney-breast or a main focal point of the room, and set out the paper from the centre of the chosen spot in order to achieve an equal pattern on either side (Fig 1). When cutting the wallpaper to length you may find that you will waste less paper if you use two rolls side by side ; this is especially so when using large-patterned wallpapers. Always try to finish the wallpaper in the darkest part of the room.

Another important point is to make sure the wallpaper is upright. The easiest way of doing this is to mark an upright line with either a level or a plumb-bob (Fig 2). A plumb-bob can easily be made by tying a nut or any weight to the end of a piece of string ; when this is suspended it will automatically give an upright line. Do not try to wrap wallpaper around internal or external angles. Cut the paper 10mm ($\frac{3}{8}$in) oversize and just overlap the remaining piece (Figs 3, 4). If you are hanging vinyl wallpaper use either Copydex or Solvite overlap paste as ordinary wallpaper paste will not adhere to vinyl.

Sizing

It must be stressed that the walls should be fully prepared before you attempt to apply wallpaper. Holes, cracks and any other defects to the plaster must be made good. The wall will then need to be sized (sealed) so that the wallpaper when pasted will slide into position. If the walls are not

Fig 2   Home-made plumb-bob

sized and you attempt to put the wallpaper straight on, because the plaster is porous it will suck the paste from the wallpaper, making it impossible to move the paper into position.

Sizing the room can be done by diluting wallpaper paste or by buying a proprietary size and mixing it according to the manufacturer's instructions. When this is applied to the walls it will form a seal so that as you begin to hang the wallpaper it will slide easily into position.

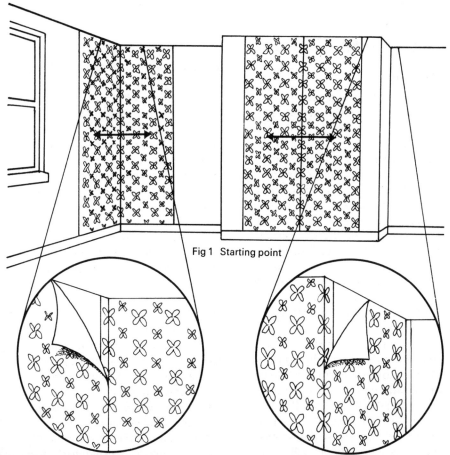

Fig 1 Starting point

Fig 3 Internal angle : overlap 10mm

Fig 4 External angle : overlap 10mm

Removing Wallpaper

When removing wallpaper you will need to use water to make the job easier. Therefore take care when working close to any open electricity sockets—it is advisable to turn off the electricity before you begin.

Wallpaper should first be soaked with water. When this has penetrated through the paper it can be removed easily with a broad knife.

Washable wallpapers need to be scratched before water is applied ; use a coarse grade of sandpaper to break the

surface of the paper. Washable wallpapers are the most difficult of all papers to remove, so extra time should be allowed for the water to soak through and penetrate.

If washable wallpapers are the most difficult to remove, Vinyl wallpapers are the easiest. Starting at one corner, lift the film of vinyl and pull off each piece which will leave the backing paper still stuck to the wall. This may be left on to act as a lining paper, or removed with water in the conventional way.

Fixing into Masonry

Drilling

Drilling into brick and plaster often seems a difficult task, but there are a number of tips which can make it much easier. The first essential is to have either a hand or electric drill; the other important tool is the drill bit itself, which must be specifically designed for masonry. This has a very hard tip on the end, making it easier to drill into bricks, plaster, concrete and stone. It is important to ensure that the drill size is correct for the size of screw being used. A number 10 is the most common one in use.

After fixing the drill bit into the chuck of the drill, put the tip onto the point where the hole is going to be and turn it slowly so that it goes through the plaster into the brick. After a start has been made, you can increase the speed, but pull the drill out at intervals to clear any brick dust. Always drill 5mm ($\frac{1}{4}$in) deeper than the length of the screw, this allows a small clearance for debris when inserting the plug. If you are using an electric drill the same procedure applies; use the slow speed if you have a two-speed drill, and once the hole is started use a pump action —pushing the drill in and withdrawing it at intervals—to remove the brick dust from the hole. Some electric drills have a hammer action which allows the drill bit to cut more rapidly, but care must be taken when starting the hole as the drill bit tends to jump and skid until entry is made.

It is possible to drill into brick without using a drill bit. Take two 60mm ($2\frac{1}{2}$in) oval nails and cut the heads off with a hack-saw. Put them into the drill chuck, and drill into the brick. The nails will twist together forming a spiral, and a number of holes can be made with them before they need to be replaced. Nails are especially useful when drilling into building blocks since these are softer than bricks. You may find that some old plasters containing lime are much softer than modern types. If this is the case stick a piece of sellotape over the point where the hole is to be drilled to stop the plaster crumbling away as you drill.

Inserting a Plug

Before putting a screw into masonry you must insert a plug for the screw to bite into. Individual plastic plugs are the best and most readily available. They come in different sizes for different screws, and the most useful ones are the universal types that will fit three or four different screw sizes. After selecting the size required, push it into the hole and tap it home so that the plug is approximately 3mm ($\frac{1}{8}$in) below the surface of the plaster. This is to ensure that when the screw is driven in, expanding the plug, the plaster around the edge of the hole does not crumble away.

One point to remember is that when fixing cupboards or shelves to the wall always use screws long enough to carry their weight when they are full! Screws fixed only into the plaster will not hold securely enough.

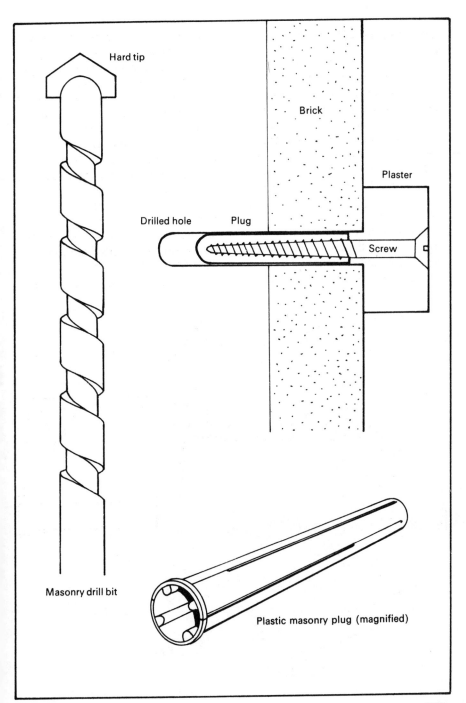

Hard tip

Brick

Plaster

Drilled hole   Plug

Screw

Masonry drill bit

Plastic masonry plug (magnified)

Fixing a Shelf

It is often necessary to put up shelves, particularly when you have just moved into a new house or flat—there just never seems to be enough shelf space. How often have your shelves sagged or fallen down, either because the wrong material was used or because the screws were too short ? As with every sort of home maintenance or repair, it is never worth doing a cheap or quick job.

There are now many shelving systems available in which you screw a pair of slotted uprights to the wall and clip on the shelf brackets. This type of shelving is very easy to use but do remember to put enough screws into the upright to secure the shelves well into the wall. One tends to forget just how much books weigh, and if the uprights are not securely fixed the whole lot will tumble down.

Fitting shelves into a recess is not difficult since you do not have to put up any side pieces to take the supports for the shelves to rest on (Fig 1). If the shelf is to take heavy loads such as books then you should fit a bearer along the back as well as the ends. The bearer can be of timber sized about 75 × 50mm (3 × 2in) or you may wish to use aluminium angle (Fig 2). The

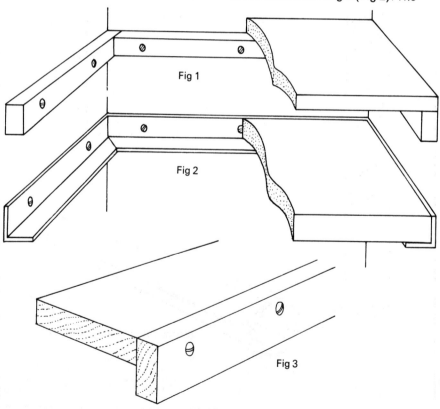

Fig 1

Fig 2

Fig 3

latter makes a neat unobtrusive job. The shelf should be of solid timber, such as Parana pine. Avoid particle boards since they tend to sag. On longer lengths the shelves can be strengthened by screwing a strip of solid timber along the front edge (Fig 3). This has the additional advantage of giving a neater looking shelf as it will cover the ends of the bearers.

To fit a shelf into a recess it must obviously be cut to fit precisely. One good way to do this is as follows: first of all measure and cut the shelf 25mm (1in) longer than required and then place it into the recess. With a compass opened to 12mm ($\frac{1}{2}$in) scratch a line on the shelf following the precise shape of the wall (Fig 4). Use a panel saw to cut along this line. Before you measure the other end, cut a thin lath to the exact size of the recess; this will prevent you from cutting the shelf too short or leaving it long if your measurements are inaccurate. Then, with one end of the lath flush with the cut end of the shelf, make a pencil mark at the uncut end at the opposite end of the lath (Fig 5). Put the shelf back into the recess, set the compass to the pencil line and scratch the shape of the wall onto the shelf. When this is cut the shelf will fit like a glove.

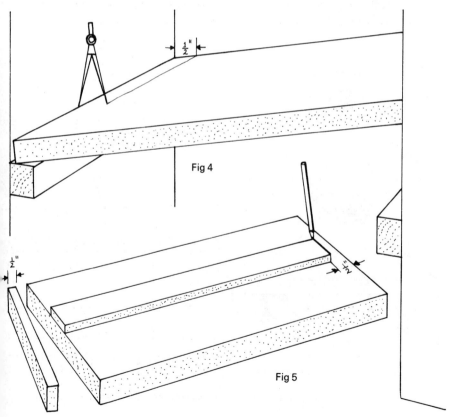

Fig 4

Fig 5

Floorboards

Creaking Floorboards

How many times have you tried to creep home at the dead of night only to be detected on the last step by the infernal creaking stair or floorboard ? Well, never again, because there are cures for horrific creaks !

There are several causes for these : staircases and floorboards are usually made of timber, and there will always be a shrinkage factor due to the timber drying out, thus opening joints in floorboards and sometimes breaking glued joints, as in a staircase. Even when the timber has finished drying out there will always be a certain amount of movement due to the humidity in the air. Have you noticed how a door which sticks in winter will shut quite freely in the summer ? This type of movement occurs year in year out.

Another reason for movement, creaks and groans is that heating pipes may be fixed too close to the underside of the floorboards. This has two effects : firstly, the continual heating and cooling of a domestic heating system adds to the movement of the wood ; secondly, if the pipes actually touch the underside of the floorboard, it will expand as the pipes heat and contract as they cool, thus causing creaks. The cure for this is to lift the floorboard and cut away the wood where the pipe actually touches it,

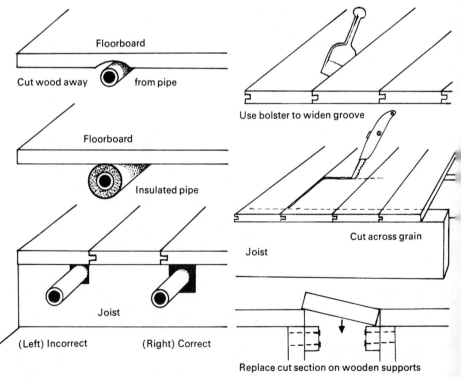

Floorboard

Cut wood away from pipe

Floorboard

Insulated pipe

Joist

(Left) Incorrect   (Right) Correct

Use bolster to widen groove

Cut across grain

Joist

Replace cut section on wooden supports

taking care not to cut through to the face of the board. You should also inspect the notched cut-out in the joist to make sure that the pipe is not touching the sides of the notch. If so, fit a piece of heat-resistant rubber to form an expansion area. You may have to cut the notch wider to do this, but do not cut away more than is absolutely necessary as this will weaken the joist. When the offending pipes have been checked and put right, nail down the boards. Once again you should take care, as a nail in the wrong position may result in a burst pipe.

Floorboards are usually nailed down with the nails punched just below the surface. To eliminate creaks, go over each board and check that all the nails are hammered home and punched in. If not, go over the whole floor punching in these nails. (This will result in dust rising from the joints so cover any furniture you have in the room with dust sheets.) If you add any nails to the floorboard beware of what could be underneath, eg wires and pipes. It is worth remembering that screws will have greater holding power than nails.

A very good tip to stop noisy floorboards is to sprinkle talcum powder liberally into the joints of the floor. This acts as a lubricant and it is an amazingly easy way of eliminating noisy floorboards.

Removing a Floorboard

Removing a floorboard is a job that often needs to be done when renovating a house, when you want to add an extra power point, or put in a water pipe. Very often you can see split boards where someone has shoved a tyre lever or something similar into the joint without thinking, and then just heaved it.

There is a better method, which is not only easier but cheaper, since you won't have the expense of buying a new piece of timber to replace the board taken out. You will need a metal bolster and a Stanley knife with a wood sawblade fixed in the handle. Most floorboards are tongue and groove so place the bolster in the groove and hit it with a hammer until you break through the tongue. This gap will enable you to insert the sawblade. Take care as there may be wires or pipes under the board and it is advisable to switch off the electricity at the meter. If you do come across a pipe when sawing, stop immediately.

Cut along the tongue until you reach the joist, then gently and gradually turn the saw, cutting at the same time so that you cut across the grain along the side of the joist. Cut 20mm ($\frac{3}{4}$in) into the next board, so as to sever the tongue to allow the board to be lifted out easily.

Repeat the cut across the end grain at the side of the next joist. Three sides of the board are now cut, so sliding the bolster into the cut tongue, gently pop out the board. Of course, when you replace the board it will drop through as there are no supports ; to prevent this nail two pieces of 50 × 25mm (2 × 1in) wood which are 50mm (2in) wider than the width of the floorboard to the joist. The cut board will now be supported and can be nailed back after the wire or pipes have been run.

The Staircase

A staircase is a major contributor to creaks and squeaks. It is usually made up of three main parts : the strings, which are the two side pieces, and the treads and risers, which are supported by them (see diagram). In time, as the timber shrinks, there may be movement, and when pressure is put on the tread a creaking noise can often be heard. To stop this you must be able to get at the underside of the staircase, which is not always the easiest of jobs since the cupboard which is usually found under the stairs often houses electricity meters, gas meters and all sorts of household junk.

Once the area is cleared you will probably have to remove either a piece of hardboard or plasterboard that will be nailed to the two edges of the strings. Take care as this will need to be replaced when the job is finished. Gently prise the board away, starting from one edge and working down, releasing the nails as you go. When this has been removed and the underside of the staircase exposed, use a vacuum cleaner to remove all dust and debris. This will make for cleaner working conditions, and stop you having to work with dust and dirt falling around you.

You will now see that the treads and risers are held in position by wedges ; check to see if any are loose or missing. If so, remove the loose ones, one at a time, and apply PVA woodworking adhesive to both sides of the wedge. Then replace them and knock them home with a hammer, using a piece of scrap wood to avoid bruising the timber. Knock the tread into the string and do the same with the riser.

Working on one tread and riser at a time, the next operation is to check the angle blocks, which should be fixed between the top of the tread and the riser. If they are loose, remove them, put on some woodworking adhesive, and hold them in position with a small nail until the adhesive dries. Make sure that the nail does not stick through either the tread or the riser. If there are no blocks on the staircase, cut some out from scrap wood and fix them as already described. The last job to do before nailing back the piece which has been removed is to punch in the nails that hold the bottom of the riser to the back of the tread.

Modernizing the Staircase

Modernizing an old staircase is a job well within the scope of most people. The most popular way of doing this is to board in the banisters, and this is best done using plywood rather than hardboard, which tends to buckle easily. This form of modernization incorporates the stair rails, but you may wish to have a more open aspect by removing the rails and fitting in a new wide rail to the top part of the handrail.

The only point to watch here is to make sure you do not cover up or destroy a nice piece of existing wood. If your staircase is of a particularly nice wood you can, of course, strip off any old paint, thus allowing the natural beauty of the wood to show. Many staircases look very attractive when treated in this manner.

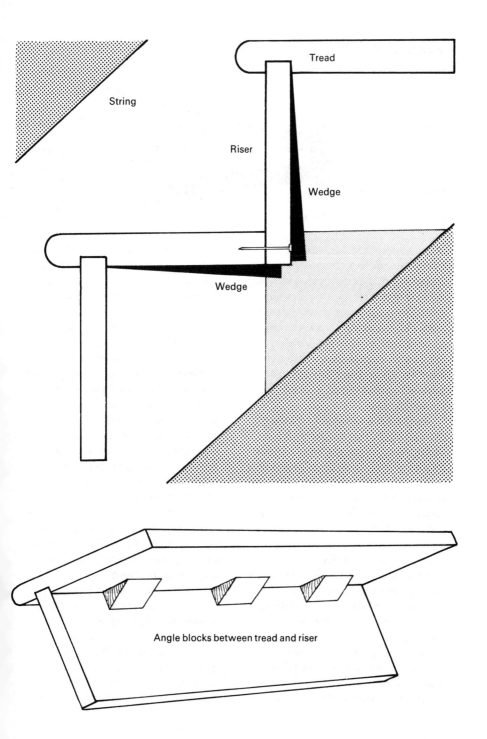

String

Tread

Riser

Wedge

Wedge

Angle blocks between tread and riser

Fixing a Plug

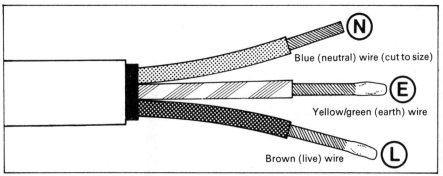

Blue (neutral) wire (cut to size)

Yellow/green (earth) wire

Brown (live) wire

All appliances such as washing machines, vacuum cleaners and food mixers need to be connected to a plug. All new installations are now square-pin 13 amp, although if your house is fairly old you may still have round-pin 15 amp fixtures. However, any appliance needs to be wired to a plug whether it is a square-pin or a round-pin and this must be done in the correct manner.

There are many different makes of plug on the market and they vary considerably in price. Choose a good quality plug (a name brand) and make sure that it is suitable for your purpose; for example an electric fire or fan heater must have a plug that will take the amount of wattage stated on the appliance. Do check this carefully with your local supplier.

After purchasing the plug look at the wires on the appliance; you will normally find three : yellow and green stripe (*earth*) brown (*live*) and blue (*neutral*). Quite often these wires will have soldered ends and in most cases they are longer than required. First they must be trimmed to the correct length, and it does not matter if you

cut off the soldered ends. Cut the wires so that the outer casing covering the three coloured wires is inside the plug and held in the clamp provided. Then secure each wire in turn as in the diagram, making sure that it is held tight. Loose wires can lead to arcing which will cause heat and eventually fire.

The most important wire is the earth —green and yellow stripes—which must be connected to the correct terminal. The live wire (brown) is connected to the fuse side of the plug ; you may find that you have to remove the fuse to do this. The neutral (blue) is connected to the remaining terminal.

Check the screws for tightness and clamp the outer casing to the inside of the plug. After checking that all screws are right, make sure that you have fitted the correct fuse—13 amp for washing machines, vacuum cleaners, or fan heaters, 3 amp for lighting. Check the fuse rating for each individual piece of electrical equipment when you buy it. It is wise to keep some spare fuses handy for any failure or emergency. The final thing is to replace the top of the plug.

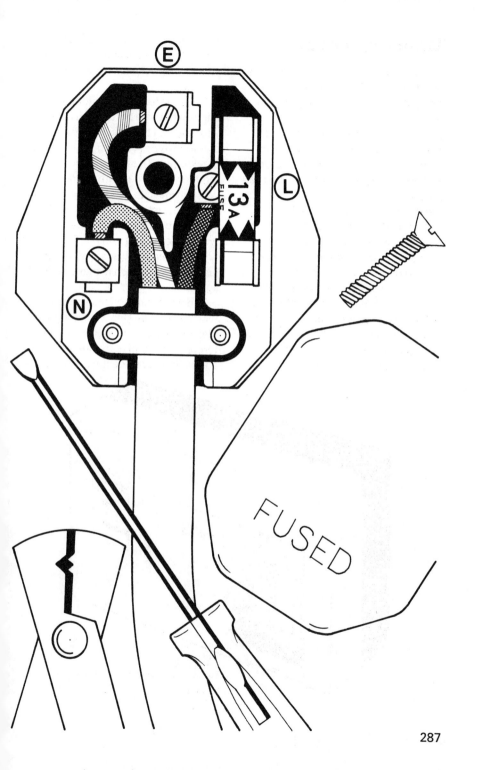

E

L

N

13A
FUSE

FUSED

Mending a Fuse

Suddenly the whole house is plunged into darkness. The television goes off, the lights go out. Your first thought probably is that there has been a power cut ; but all the other houses have their lights on, so a blown fuse must be the answer. There may then follow some minutes' confusion as you struggle to find a torch, or a candle, and the necessary items needed to repair the fuse that has blown.

Well, that little scene has probably happened to everyone at some time, so be warned and be prepared. Electrical fuses are like a safety valve : if a circuit is overloaded then the fuse will break and not the appliance. It is wise to make sure you know what to do while it is still light, so that you are prepared for any failure in a domestic

fuse system. First you need to know where the fuse board is : under the stairs is a popular place, or in the garage.

Once the fuse board is located, check what type of fuse you have ; you may find that you have the cartridge-type fuse (Fig 1) or contact breaker (Fig 2), neither of which requires fuse wire. With cartridge fuses you only need to keep spare fuses of the correct rating, which is usually stamped on the plastic holder. Keep two of each type as spares. The contact breaker needs no fuses : if it has blown just press the button to make contact again.

The most common fuse is the type which uses wire (Fig 3). It is a good idea to keep an insulated screwdriver, torch, candle and fuse wire of the correct rating beside the fuse box. If a

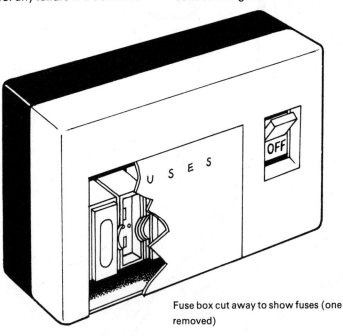

Fuse box cut away to show fuses (one removed)

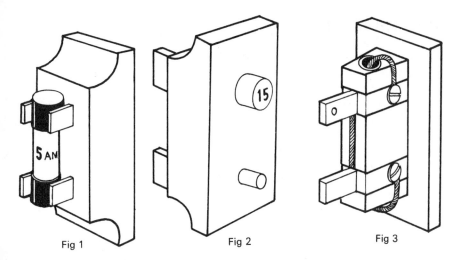

Fig 1   Fig 2   Fig 3

wire-type fuse blows, first turn off the electricity at the fuse box—there is usually a large switch marked 'on' and 'off'. Remove the fuse cover and then the blown fuse by gripping the top and bottom and easing it until it comes free. Release the old fuse wire by undoing the two screws. Thread new wire, wrapping it around the screw heads, and tighten them up (a little vaseline on the contacts will help ease entry). Replace the fuse and fuse cover, and switch on. Make sure you replace the screwdriver and other tools.

Important—never use a fuse wire of a higher rating, and always turn off the electricity before removing a fuse. If the fuse continues to blow, call in a qualified electrician.

Repairing an Electric Kettle

Another very simple household repair you can easily do yourself is renewing the element of an electric kettle. If the kettle has just stopped working, first of all check that the over-ride switch

has not tripped ; this switch is found at the socket end of the kettle. Push the plug firmly into the kettle ; if the plug does not engage properly, reconnect the trip switch by pushing it in firmly. If the plug pushes in easily then the element in the kettle is probably at fault, but before taking the kettle to pieces check that the fuse at the mains plug has not blown.

Once you are sure that the fuse is not at fault, unplug the kettle from the main supply. Hold the kettle firmly and with your free hand unscrew the plug socket, and when this has been unscrewed make a note of how it is assembled : remembering this will help you to put back the new element in exactly the same way. You will notice that there are two washers, one inside and one outside, which make the waterproof joint. After removing the old element, replace the new one in exactly the same manner. Before plugging into the mains, check for any leaks.

Windows (1)

Windows which will not shut or which will not open are everyday problems. One of the major difficulties with wooden windows is that they are affected by the weather and the amount of humidity in the air. Another common reason for windows which stick is too much paint which has been applied over the years. Successive coats build up and then eventually jam. So let us look at prevention of and cures for some of the most common faults in the different kinds of window.

Wooden Windows

With wooden windows, it makes no difference whether they are double-glazed or not, the treatment is similar. Normally wood windows come ready primed (see Paint Preparation). They will need two undercoats and one gloss coat. When painting do make sure that the paint does not build up on the edges. Always brush the edges of windows well with the paint brush.

Old wooden windows with excessive paint on them will need the paint

Avoid build-up of paint on edges

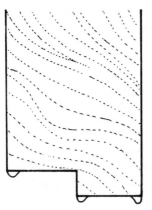

Excessive paint

removed down to the bare wood (see Old Paintwork). Once the paint has been removed check that the window operates satisfactorily—some of the wood may have to be shaved off to make it fit properly. Use a surform for this, remembering that in winter the window will have expanded slightly due to humidity, so do not shave off too much wood. Check that the hinges and catches are operating properly—if not, remove and soak them in penetrating oil, cleaning them thoroughly before fixing back to the frame and window.

Metal Windows

Metal windows bring their own type of problems. Paint can be removed from them only by using a paint stripper. If movement has taken place due to settlement of a house the only way to shave them down is with a metal file. One is available to fit the surform but since metal windows are dipped and galvanized this operation will, of course, remove this protective coat, and you should apply a proprietary rust inhibitor to all exposed metal parts. Read the manufacturer's instructions before buying and make absolutely sure that the rust preventer can be painted over. Maintenance of metal windows includes removing any rust spots with a file and wire brush, after which rust preventer should be applied. When this has been completed treat all metal work with metal primer paint, and then continue the normal painting procedure as with wood windows. Aluminium and plastic are being used increasingly for windows. These need little maintenance, except an occasional wash down with warm soapy water, and never need painting.

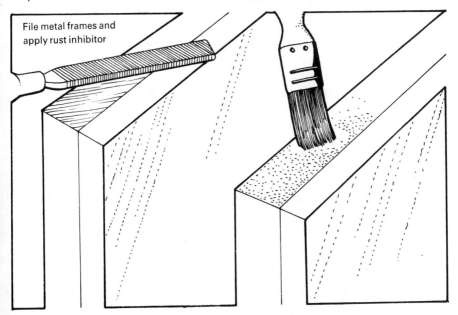

File metal frames and apply rust inhibitor

Windows (2)

Sash Cords

Sash windows suffer from the same problems as casement windows, as they are also made of wood and are still fitted in thousands of houses. The one additional maintenance job with this type of window is to check the cords by which the windows are counterbalanced. Over the years these will need replacing. The easiest way to do this is to start by gently prising the stop bead away from the frame using a flat chisel. Lever from the back of the stop bead so that you avoid bruising the paint and wood on the face edge, and remove the stop bead on the opposite side in the same way.

If the two sash cords are broken remove the sash from the frame or, if you cannot do this easily, cut the cord and gently lower the sash weight into the cavity. Even if you only need to replace one cord it may be worth replacing all four; the reason will become obvious when—after you have carefully replaced one cord—another one breaks a few weeks later and you have to repeat the work all over again.

Remove the broken cord ends from the sash (Fig 1). Then remove the parting bead (Fig 2), using the same procedure as for the stop bead. This will expose the pocket through which the weights can be removed, and this is also prised out. Then remove the sash weights and the broken piece of cord. The two pieces of cord can be put together to give you the length of new cord; otherwise you should measure from the bottom of the sash to the bottom of the cord groove and

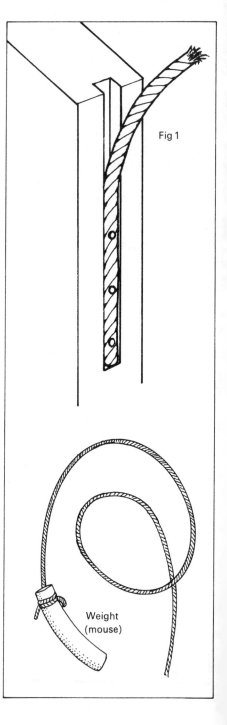

Fig 1

Weight (mouse)

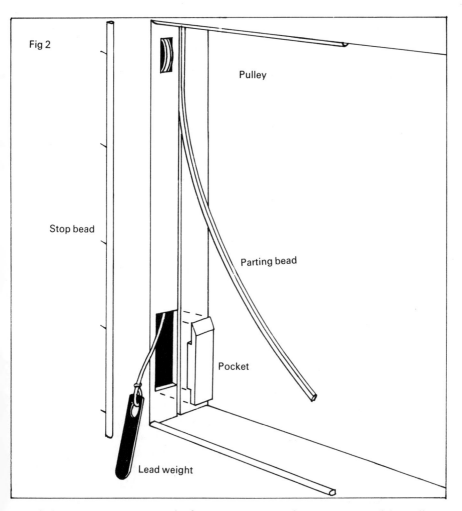

Fig 2

Pulley

Stop bead

Parting bead

Pocket

Lead weight

mark that measurement onto the frame with a pencil, taking care to ensure that the cord is not too long—so that the sash will not open fully—or too short—so that you cannot close the sash.

Then, using a 'mouse' (a weighted piece of string) thread this over the pulley, lower it into the pocket and tie it to some good quality sash cord. Pull this up over the pulley, remove the string, and tie on the sash weight. Then pull the weight up and down by hand to ensure free movement of the pulley, making sure you pull it right up to the top of the sash. When you have cut the cord to the right length replace the pocket and parting bead.

Fix the cord to the frame with a 25mm (1in) round-headed nail then cut the cord at the pencil mark which you made earlier. Fix the cord into the groove on the sash using nails or staples, and replace the stop bead to complete the job.

Replacing a Glass Pane

Almost every home suffers a broken pane of glass at some time ; replacing the glass in a wood or metal window creates no great problem and you should follow the same procedure in both cases. However, if you have aluminium or double-glazed windows, these are best left to experts to repair.

Either measure the broken pane from rebate to rebate (Fig 1), and take off about 3–4mm ($\frac{1}{8}$in) so that the pane will fit in neatly, or cut a piece of newspaper or cardboard to make a pattern. Take the measurements or the pattern to a glass merchant who will cut the glass to the correct size. It is important to give him the exact thickness of the glass you require, particularly if you are replacing glass in a rise and fall sash window. Take a piece of the broken glass with you so that the glass merchant knows what thickness and weight to give you, as this type of window relies on counterbalanced weights, and different weights of glass will affect the operation of the window.

With the glass cut to size, break out the remaining pieces of old glass, taking extreme care. Clean out all the old putty with a chisel, leaving no high spots, and remove any small nails. Once this has been done, prime the rebate with wood primer or, if you are working on a metal window, use metal primer. Metal windows have spring clips instead of nails, which should be removed and put somewhere safe as you will need them for replacing the glass.

Before you put in any putty, check the glass for size by placing the pane into the rebates. If it is correct, place a bed of putty all around the rebates. The putty should be soft and easy to work ; if it is too sticky add a small amount of powdered Polyfilla. This will stiffen it and stop it sticking to your fingers. Do not use old putty with lumps in or you may break the glass when bedding it in. Put the glass into the rebate and press gently against the putty with a rag. Any putty that squeezes out round the edges can be trimmed off later. Using 15mm ($\frac{1}{2}$in) panel pins fix one on each side of the glass, and tap them home with a small hammer, sliding this down the glass (Fig 2). This will secure the glass until the putty sets. On metal windows use putty made especially for metal windows (not linseed oil putty) and secure the glass with the spring clips removed earlier.

Now, using your thumb, press a thin roll of putty on top of the glass along the rebate all around the window, and then smooth this to a neat angle using a putty knife. It makes it easier to get a smooth finish if you dip the putty knife into some water, and you can erase any bumps with a soft dry paint brush. All that you have to do now is leave the putty to set for approximately fourteen days, and then paint it the required colours.

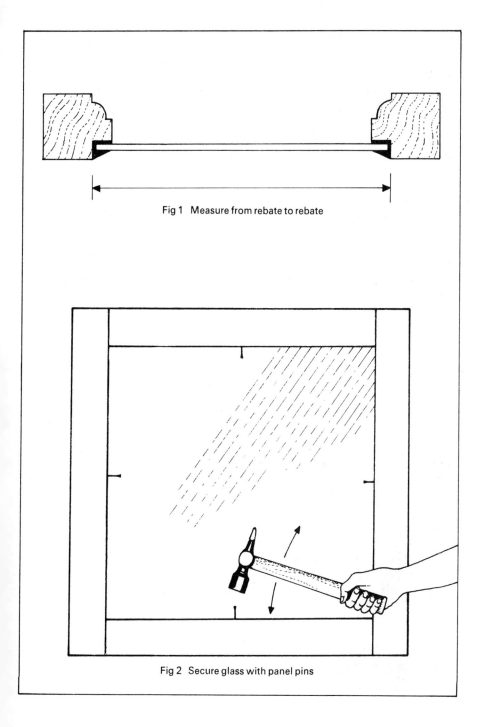

Fig 1   Measure from rebate to rebate

Fig 2   Secure glass with panel pins

Cutting Glass

Instruments

Most people when asked if they can cut a piece of glass shudder at the very thought of a hardened steel wheel scoring across glass, but I shall try to dispel any worries you may have about glass cutting.

First you need a glass cutter. There are several types available; the most common in general use is a hardened steel wheel that leaves a scratch line as it revolves over the glass. A more expensive version of this is a tungsten wheel which has a very much longer life due to the extra hardness of the wheel. This type of wheel, however,

does not leave such a clean scratch line as the hardened steel wheel.

There are, of course, diamond cutters, which have a small industrial diamond inserted into a handle (to give leverage) and to enable the user to score the glass. Contrary to most people's belief the diamond cutter is the most difficult cutter to use and only practice will enable the user to cut glass successfully.

For the purpose of this book we will use the hardened steel wheel cutter. The wheel of the cutter must always be able to revolve, so a light oil is used to lubricate it. A piece of sponge in a jar, impregnated with a light oil, will serve as a dip for the glass cutter (Fig 1), and should be used after every scribe. It is

Fig 1 Using a glass cutter

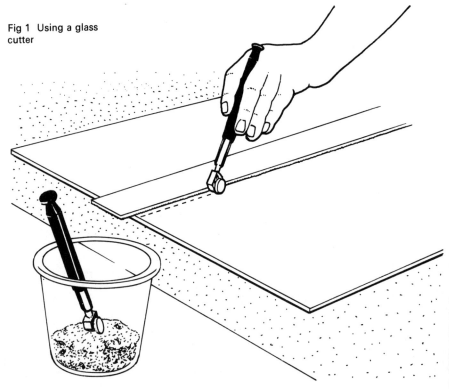

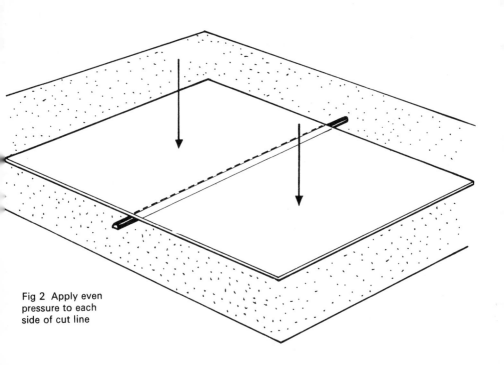

Fig 2 Apply even
pressure to each
side of cut line

a good idea to store the glass cutter in the jar. Failure to keep the wheel lubricated will blunt it rapidly due to small glass particles clogging the wheel, and more pressure will be needed to scribe the line, resulting in an uneven line. Also, excessive pressure will probably break the glass.

Cutting

The glass to be cut should be laid onto a firm, flat surface, ie a kitchen table. Lay newspaper over the surface to cushion it—an alternative idea is to place a piece of carpet or carpet underlay over the table. Lay the piece of glass onto the flat surface and measure the glass to the required size. Glass can be marked with either a felt pen or a chinagraph pencil. A straight edge is required and this can be made

from an offcut of hardboard. Always place the rough side of the hardboard to the glass as this will help to stop the straight edge from slipping and sliding on the glass.

Place the straight edge to the lines and score lightly along the straight edge. (Never score over the same line twice as this will blunt the glass cutter quicker than anything. Practise on a scrap of old glass until you have the knack of applying the correct pressure.) Remove the straight edge and then slip a 5mm ($\frac{1}{4}$in) dowel under the glass, centred on the scored line (Fig 2). Applying even pressure to both sides of the glass with your fingers, press down, and the glass will break along the scored line. When cutting obscure glass always score on the smoothest side of the glass.

Doors

Doors usually require little or no maintenance except perhaps for painting. This is quite remarkable really when you consider that a door does more work than any other part of the house, opening and closing all day. Normally a spot of oil on the hinges is all that is needed.

Trimming

One problem which does sometimes occur is when you have some new carpet laid and find that the door will not go over the top. It needs to be taken off its hinges and the bottom trimmed. Obviously you will need to know the thickness of the carpet to do this so collect a sample from your supplier—not forgetting any underlay that will be going with it. Cut a scrap of wood the thickness of the carpet plus 3mm ($\frac{1}{8}$in)—this will give enough clearance and not drag across the pile of the carpet. With the door closed, draw a line along the bottom of the door, using the block of wood as a rule (Fig 1). After each door has been marked, open the door and wedge it underneath for support while you unscrew the hinges, starting with the lower ones. Remember to clean the slots to remove any existing paint.

When all the screws have been removed, gently tap with the palm of the hand to break the paint joint at the hinges (Fig 2). If you just pull the door away there is a good chance that the paint will chip and even that the wood may split which will look very unsightly when the door is replaced. Lay the door on a flat surface, like a

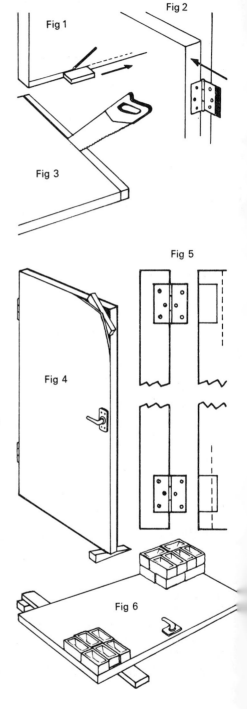

Fig 1

Fig 2

Fig 3

Fig 4

Fig 5

Fig 6

kitchen table, and with a straight edge score the wood with a Stanley knife along the marked line. Do this round the door on both sides. (Sometimes the piece to be cut off is not completely straight so remember to allow for this on the other side.) This will stop the paint chipping or the veneer splitting when you cut. Using a panel-saw cut along the scored line, keeping just on the waste side (Fig 3). Then smooth the edges with sandpaper and rehang the door using the wedge for support.

Warped Doors

Badly fitted doors or doors which have warped will cause all sorts of problems.

Warping will cause doors to jam ; the locks will not fit into their keeps and this also makes entry for any intruder that much easier.

It is not a simple job to refit doors that are twisted and warped ; therefore prevention is the best cure. There are various ways to avoid warping : always paint or lacquer the door as soon as it is hung—not forgetting the top of the door—and be sure to paint the bottom edge before hanging the door. This is particularly important on any outside door. Doors which are waiting to be hung should be stored flat to avoid any warping before hanging, and if you are fixing laminate to a door always laminate both sides ; if this is not done warping will almost certainly occur.

But what if you have a door which is already warped—how can you put it back into shape ? Unfortunately the success rate is low, though you can try these methods : wedge the door as shown (Fig 4), leaving it for as long as

possible—for instance while you are away on holiday. Another method is to try 'throwing the hinges', by letting in one hinge more deeply and pushing out the other (Fig 5), so that the door can shut even though it is still twisted.

An unpainted wood door which has warped can be liberally sprinkled with water on both sides and then laid across battens and weighted with bricks to try and counteract the warping (Fig 6), then left for a few days to dry. This should remove the twist. The wood will need to be rubbed down with sandpaper as the water will raise the grain, and it should be painted as soon as possible.

Lubrication of Wood

Anything made of wood, such as drawers, doors and windows, is liable to expand or contract because of changes in humidity, and if you plane off any of the wood to ease it, you may find that when it shrinks again draughty windows or loose drawers may occur. However, it is easy and very quick to overcome these problems. Runners and the sides of a drawer can be rubbed with either soap or a candle ; never use linseed oil, which tends to go sticky and makes the drawer jam worse than before, or engine oil, as this will stain the wood and collect dust.

Washing-up liquid has many uses other than simply washing dishes. A spot of liquid on a hinge will instantly stop any squeak and the hinge may be wiped afterwards so that you don't have the mark or greasy stain which often occurs with conventional oils. But don't use this liquid on locks.

Burst Pipes

Should you be so unlucky as to have a burst pipe there are several things you must do very quickly, if you are at home at the time, although invariably pipes seem to burst when you are out of the house or away on holiday.

Proper insulation will safeguard against this disaster, but should a burst occur the first job is to turn off the water supply. Usually, the cold stop tap will be found under the sink, and the hot in the airing cupboard, but it is worth making sure that you know where they are in your own home. Also check that the taps can be turned, for they can get very stiff, and a regular check is obviously essential—just imagine water pouring through the ceiling with you unable to turn the tap off!

If there is a leak or burst pipe in the hot water system, you should immediately turn off the immersion heater or shut off the boiler, to prevent any further expansion of hot water. Turn off the main stop cock to the hot water, usually found in the airing cupboard, and open all the hot water taps in the house to let the surplus water drain away. Once the water has been cleared from the affected area, work can begin.

Replacing a small section of pipe is quite difficult so I suggest that you use a proprietary flexible copper connector, which makes the job of connecting two pieces of pipe relatively easy. There is nothing worse than having a catastrophe and not being able to do anything about it because you lack the necessary equipment, so it is advisable to buy one of these and keep it for such an emergency, just as you would an electrical fuse. These connectors come complete with instructions, and after you have cut out the split section of pipe, they take no more than five minutes to connect.

After the new piece of pipe has been installed, turn all the taps off before turning on the water supply. When the main valve has been turned on, release any air trapped in the pipes by undoing all the taps until the water runs evenly. Check for leaks and if all is well turn the immersion heater on again, and reset the boiler.

If the leak is on the cold water system, turn off the main stop cock, which is usually under the kitchen sink. Turn on all cold taps to release any trapped water and when the water ceases to run proceed with the repair in exactly the same way as already described.

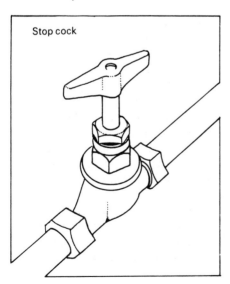

Stop cock

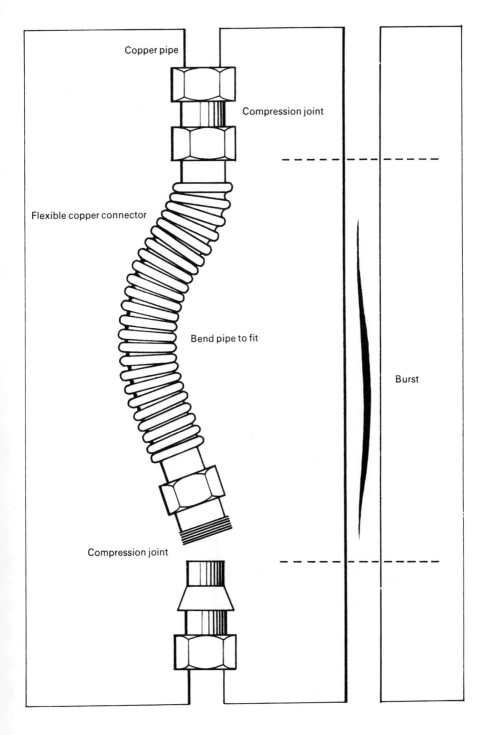

Copper pipe

Compression joint

Flexible copper connector

Bend pipe to fit

Burst

Compression joint

Unblocking a Pipe

We must all have suffered at one time from a blocked pipe either in the sink, waste pipe or any of the other pipes which run in the average house. Let us look at ways we can avoid blockages in the first place ; then at how to remove an obstruction should one occur. The most frequent problem area is the kitchen sink—just think how much debris goes down the waste pipe. Remember that prevention is always better than cure, so do not force potato peelings, carrots, or tea leaves down the sink—put them on the compost heap.

If a blockage does occur you will need the following : a rubber plunger, a length of fencing wire—about 3mm ($\frac{1}{8}$in) in diameter—and a pair of pipe grips. The rubber plunger is ideal for dealing with slight blockages. Fill the sink with 25mm (1in) of water and

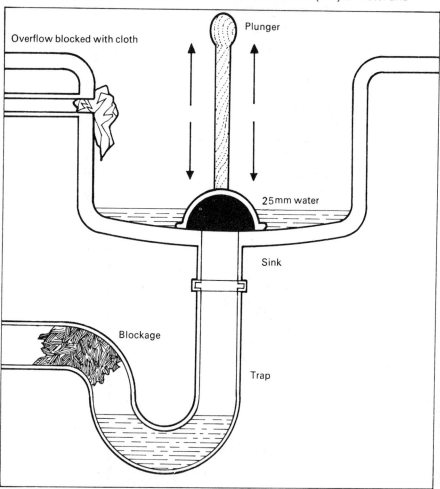

Overflow blocked with cloth

Plunger

25mm water

Sink

Blockage

Trap

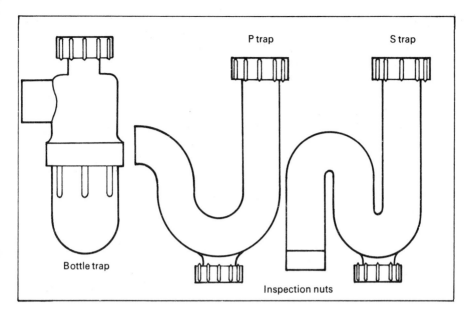

P trap

S trap

Bottle trap

Inspection nuts

block the overflow with a dish cloth. This will need to be held firmly in place because air and water will try to escape via the overflow as you apply pressure with the plunger. If the overflow is uncovered a smelly and soggy result will occur. With the dish cloth held in place, position the rubber plunger over the waste outlet and press sharply down, forcing air at pressure into the outlet. Several pumps with the plunger will normally clear minor obstructions.

If this fails you will have to look under the sink for the trap, which acts as an airlock to stop unpleasant smells coming up the pipe from the drain. There are many different types of traps and the most common are shown in the diagrams. All will have an inspection nut that can be removed with a pair of pliers. Place a bucket underneath and then remove the nut to see if the blockage is in the trap. If it is, remove

it through the inspection nut. Failing this take off the whole trap assembly and dismantle all the components. Remove any debris and clean all the parts thoroughly before reassembling.

If the blockage is in the actual pipe leading to the drain the trap must be removed and fencing wire put down the pipe. Bend the first 10mm ($\frac{1}{2}$in) of wire so that it can be used as a hook. This method will usually remove any obstruction lodged in the pipe. Once the pipe is clear and the trap screwed back in place flush the pipe through with clean water.

It is worthwhile remembering that the overflow of any sink or basin will block up over a period of time, and then if you leave a tap running there will be a minor disaster. From time to time use a thin gauge wire to clear any soap residue, hair or other obstruction and flush through, using an old plastic bottle full of clean water.

303

Tap Washers

Drips can be very annoying, not only because of the constant noise but because they cause stains on sanitary ware which can be impossible to remove if left for any length of time. It is not the most difficult job in the world to renew a tap washer though one might think so when one sees the number of houses which have dripping taps. In some areas local water authorities will replace tap washers free of charge, so it is worth ringing them first to find out. If not, then you will probably have to do it yourself. Most taps, whether in bath, basin or sink, need the same treatment, although bath taps usually have a larger washer.

Before beginning any work, always

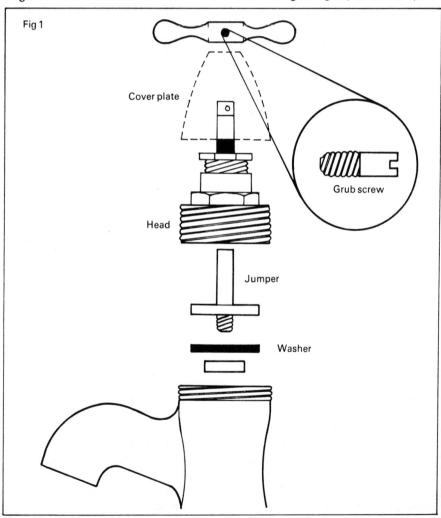

Fig 1

Cover plate

Grub screw

Head

Jumper

Washer

make sure that the water has been turned off (the cold supply stop tap is usually under the kitchen sink and the hot domestic supply in the airing cupboard). Once this has been done, turn on the taps to allow water which is still in the pipes to drain off. Open any other tap on the same supply—either hot or cold—to release air and allow the water to drain properly. Put in the plug firmly to avoid losing any small parts down the waste pipe.

Find the grub screw that holds the turning part of the tap ; this is usually in the side (Fig 1) or, on more modern taps, under a cover plate located on the top (Fig 2). Tap or prise the head off and unscrew the domed cover plate to expose the head. You may need a pair of pliers to remove the cover ; if so place a piece of rag around it to protect the chrome. The handles of some taps now act as the cover for the head, so that once the handle is removed the head is exposed.

Using a spanner remove the head, which will expose the jumper and the washer. Pull out the jumper, unscrew the washer and replace it with a new one. Check that there is no grit on the seating in the tap bottom. Should the sealer be worn then a reseating tool is required. This can be hired or bought quite cheaply. Now put the whole assembly back together again and apply Vaseline to the threaded and moving parts.

Once this is done, turn off any taps you had opened before turning on the water supply again. Once the water is turned back on, open the taps to release any air from the pipes.

One sort of tap we have not dealt with yet is the super tap (Fig 3). It is not necessary to turn off the water when replacing a washer on this tap. Loosen the locking nut above the tap nozzle, and turn the tap on. Water will run out but gradually stop. Once the flow has stopped continue to unscrew, and when the nut is undone tap gently, and the washer, jumper and anti-splash device will be released. Renew the washer and reassemble.

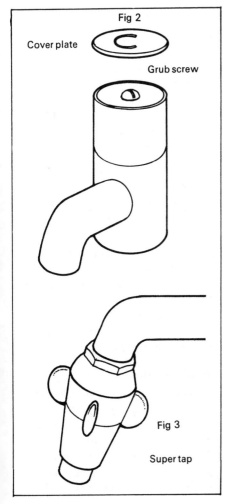

Fig 2
Cover plate
Grub screw

Fig 3
Super tap

Heating and Insulation

Thermostats

Setting water temperature and room temperature is usually done with thermostats. Their function is to switch on the boiler or immersion heater automatically when the temperature drops below the selected level.

If your hot water is heated by an immersion heater the thermostat will be found under the top cover. Before removing this cover turn off the electricity supply. Then undo the retaining screw to give access to the thermostat (Fig 1). You will see an arrow and calibrated lines with the temperature marked on them, either in centigrade or fahrenheit. Select the temperature required by turning the arrow with a small screwdriver. Then reassemble the cover plate and switch on the electricity.

Heating boilers will have a water temperature control on the boiler. The position and design of these vary according to the type of model but they all function in the same way. There will probably be a locking screw to be undone in order to alter the temperature of the water. After selecting the required temperature tighten the screw.

Room temperatures are selected either from one centrally sited thermostat, usually in the hall, or from individual thermostats in each room. When the temperature drops below the setting, the boiler will ignite to bring the temperature back up to the level required. The setting of wall thermostats is just as easy as any other type, by turning a knob to the desired

room temperature (Fig 2). Wall-mounted thermostats are connected by cables to the boiler so when the temperature drops a micro switch makes the contact to start the boiler or appliance connected to it. There are also types that fit directly to a radiator and when the air temperature drops below the setting they automatically open a valve and let hot water flow through to the radiator (Fig 3).

Maintenance

Central heating systems usually have the water circulated by a pump which frequently cannot be dismantled for maintenance. If a squeak does start in a central heating pump, then locate the central heating header water tank—which is usually in the loft space—remove the lid and give a squirt of washing-up liquid. Make sure not to overdo this—an egg-cupful should be adequate—and don't forget to replace the lid. Next you will have to drain off about two gallons of water from one of the downstairs radiators or any radiator that has a drain cock. This allows the liquid in the header tank to circulate into the heating system and as the liquid reaches the pump so the squeak will disappear. Do not forget to turn off the radiator drain cock after releasing the water.

Roof Insulation

By insulating the roof area not only will you save money over a period of time, but you will benefit by having a warmer house. There are several different types of insulating material. The most common are fibre-glass rolls that come in several different thicknesses—

25mm (1in), 50mm (2in) and 75mm (3in) being the most common (Fig 4). Remember the greater the thickness the better the insulation value.

The other common type of insulation is Vermiculite granules which come in large bags. To lay this you simply pour the granules from the bag and spread them between the joists, levelling off at the desired thickness with a shaped piece of wood (Fig 5). To lay the glass-fibre you need to roll the fibre between the joists. Use a pair of gloves for fibre-glass and tie them at the wrist to avoid any irritation to the skin.

Insulation of Pipes

Water pipes, both hot and cold, need to be insulated against freezing weather and heat loss. The most vulnerable place for pipes to freeze is in the roof area. It is false security to insulate a loft and not the surrounding pipes, since there is no warm air seeping through to keep water pipes from freezing.

There are several types of insulation for pipes. If the pipes are already fixed use either the bandage type (Fig 6) or the split tube (Fig 7). The bandage is made either from thick felt material or fibre-glass rolls, while the split tube will be either of foam or rubber. The foam lengths are easily slid on to the pipe and held in place by sticking the edges together or binding with wire or sellotape. Any outside pipes and even pipes running down the inside of garage walls need to be insulated. If you have an outside tap, you should not only insulate the pipe, but make a box to fit over the tap or the whole of the exposed pipe (Fig 8). Fill the inside with fibre-glass.

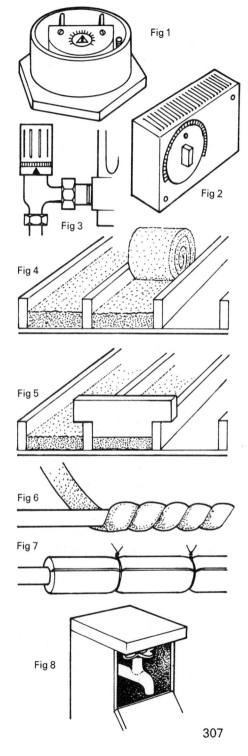

Fig 1

Fig 2

Fig 3

Fig 4

Fig 5

Fig 6

Fig 7

Fig 8

307

Repairing a Chair

A wobbly chair is neither the most comfortable thing to sit in, nor is it safe to use for standing on. Chairs are usually abused by people rocking back on them; this puts great stress and strain on the legs and joints, so that in time the glue holding the legs and rails may break, causing the chair to wobble. If left unchecked the chair will eventually fall apart, and it is obviously advisable to take steps to prevent this.

The chair must be taken apart before beginning any repairs; use a hammer and a block of wood to push out the joints (Fig 1). Number all the pieces as you take them off, as this will make reassembly much easier. Once the chair has been dismantled clean all traces of adhesive from the joints with a scraper or knife. Then reassemble the chair using your numbered guide, putting fresh wood glue on each joint as you do so. Tap each piece home using either a mallet or a hammer with a block of wood.

If any of the joints are loose they can be tightened in this way: cut a slot no deeper than the shoulder line (Fig 2); then cut a wedge 5mm ($\frac{1}{4}$in) shorter than the length of the saw cut. Apply adhesive to the two parts and start the wedges into the saw cut (Fig 3); then hammer home, making sure the expansion does not occur with the grain as this may split the wood (Fig 4).

If a rail has split, take it out and drill two screw holes on one side (Fig 5). Apply adhesive to the split edge and marry the two pieces together. Hold them together with a clamp or vice whilst you insert the screws, and once

the screws are driven in wipe any surplus adhesive from the wood and leave to dry before assembling.

Fixing a Mirror

Fixing a mirror to a wall is not difficult as long as you follow a few simple rules. After deciding on its position, mark a line on the wall to indicate the position of the bottom of the mirror,

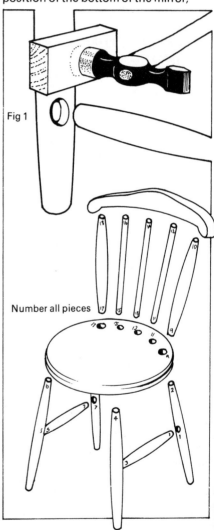

Fig 1

Number all pieces

making sure that it is level. Holding the mirror to the line, mark the position of the holes with a bradawl. Then remove the mirror to a safe place and drill the holes to the required depth (see Fixing into Masonry). Using domeheaded screws (see Screws) place these through the holes in the mirror, and put a rubber washer on to the screws, against the back of the mirror (see Fig 6).

Position the mirror and screws on the wall, locating the plastic wall plugs by turning the screws in by hand. When all the screws have been located, tighten them up with a screwdriver. The art of screwing mirrors to a wall is for the screws to just hold the glass firm ; tighten them too much and the mirror will break.

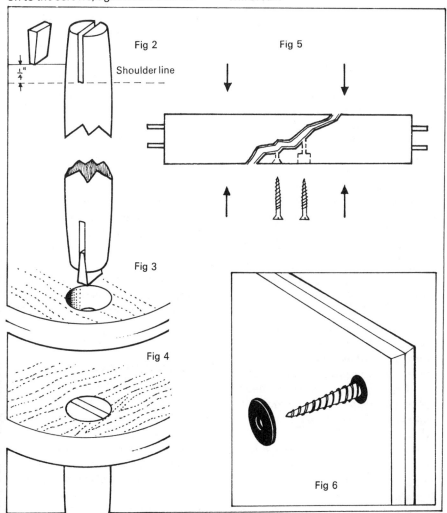

Fig 2

Shoulder line

Fig 5

Fig 3

Fig 4

Fig 6

Woodworm and Household Pests

Every home opens its doors to visitors. Friends and relations come and go but there are also many visitors both welcome and unwelcome, who do not need to have the door opened to let them in. Wasps, moths, flies, ants, earwigs, silverfish, spiders, mice and bats are but a few of these. Most of the unpleasant ones can be removed by proprietary brands of sprays and baits but the most feared bug, grub or insect is probably the woodworm. Detected by the small round holes or fine powder which it leaves, this little grub will eat away timber at a frighteningly fast rate. Therefore, precautions must be taken as soon as you detect it.

If the wood affected is a piece of furniture then the cure is fairly simple. Take the offending piece of furniture out of doors and remove enough of the upholstery, drawers or doors to let you get at the affected area. It is fairly easy to treat this by painting the surface with a proprietary worm killer, applying several coats and letting the liquid soak into the wood ; alternatively, if there are only a few small holes, use a can with a thin spout to inject each hole. Several types of worm killer are available in cans with the necessary spout. You will find that as you squirt the fluid into one hole it will reappear from another, but make sure that each hole is treated separately.

Apart from liquids there are various types of worm killer and wood preservative in paste form. The paste is smeared onto the surface of the wood and then left to soak in. This may take several days, depending on the hardness of the wood. The advantage of paste is that it is easy to apply and the penetration is very good. Wood that has been treated with any worm killer should be left for several weeks before painting or polishing, and the worm holes should be filled before this is done. Keep a regular check to make sure that the grubs are dead ; should any new holes or dust appear the treatment must be undertaken again.

Unfortunately the roof area is a good target for woodworm so if you find that your loft or attic is infested you have a major problem. If the attack is not too severe then you may wish to tackle the job yourself. The loft must first be cleared of anything you may have stored there and boards laid out over the joists so that you can move around easily without putting your feet through the ceiling. Large affected areas are treated by sprays which can be hired from your local hire-shop.

You will need some protective clothing, the minimum being goggles and face mask. The spray canister is pumped up to the necessary pressure and then you should start at one end of the roof and work your way to the other end, making sure that you spray all the roof and ceiling timbers.

Important Points

Remember to keep the loft trapdoor shut ; beware of spraying near any electric lights and switches ; and make sure that you cover any water tanks in the roof area. If you feel there is extensive woodworm, call in experts on woodworm control as prolonged attacks will weaken the roof timbers and some rafters may have to be replaced.

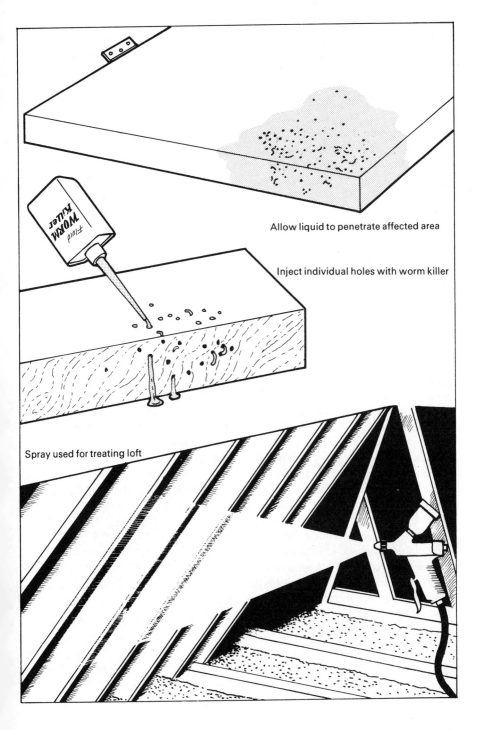

Allow liquid to penetrate affected area

Inject individual holes with worm killer

Spray used for treating loft

The Fireplace

Removing a Fireplace

In many older houses there is frequently an abundance of fireplaces, even in the bedrooms, and it is often an advantage to remove the fireplace to make room for fitted wardrobes ; or you may perhaps want to redesign a fireplace in the living area.

Whatever idea you have in mind, removing the existing fire surround is not a difficult job, but it is rather dirty, with the years of soot and debris which have accumulated in the chimney. Before you begin, clear the room of all furniture and seal any doors with sticky tape to stop the dust filtering through.

Most tiled fireplaces are held back to the wall with fixing lugs and these must be exposed. Chip away 25mm (1 in) of plaster all around the fireplace ; this will stop any large lumps of plaster falling off as the fireplace is levered away from the wall, and also expose the fixing lugs. Remove the screws from the fixing lugs and then, using an iron bar, lever the fireplace away from the wall. When this has been removed, clear out all the fire back and rubble ; this may have to be broken up with a hammer and iron chisel. The hearth is usually bedded on a weak mortar mix and will lift off quite easily with the iron bar. After all the rubble has been cleared it is advisable to sweep the chimney to remove any accumulation of soot, if this has not already been done.

If the fireplace is to be boarded over then you will have to either cap off the chimney or fit a ventilator where the fireplace was. Capping the chimney is the better way as this will prevent rainwater from dropping down the chimney, but it does mean climbing up to the chimney to do the job.

Building a Fireplace

Should you decide to build your own fireplace you would be well advised to look at what some of the fireplace manufacturers are offering, because there are many kits available in stone, brick and slate. Many of these firms will build you a fireplace to your own design and measurements and will advise you if necessary on any problems that arise.

Fireplace kits generally come numbered and with full instructions so it really is quite simple, in fact, almost like painting by numbers. A word of warning !—a stone fireplace is very heavy, so if your design overhangs the width of the chimney breast then the floor beneath the stone work will need to be supported if it is a wooden suspended floor ; on solid concrete or asphalt floors, there is no such problem.

When selecting or designing your fireplace remember you could incorporate a shelf for the television, stereo, aquarium or even a small cupboard, and the fireplace can thus become a main feature of the house.

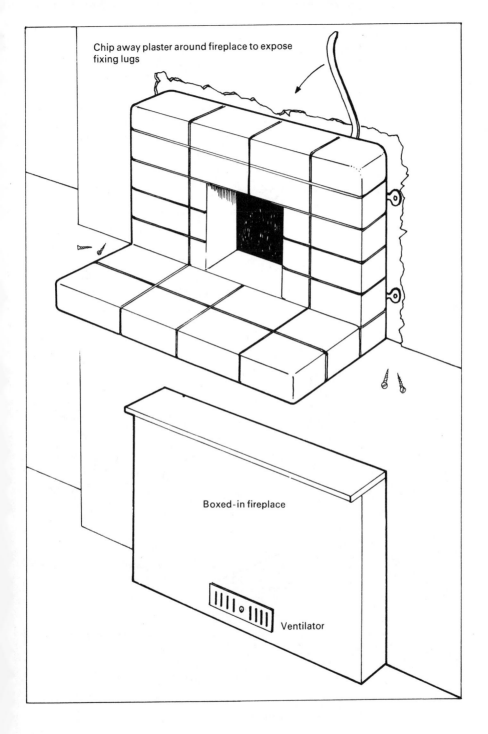

Chip away plaster around fireplace to expose fixing lugs

Boxed-in fireplace

Ventilator

Replacing a Tile

Cracked, chipped or broken tiles are both unsightly and unhygienic, and it is quite easy to replace them when you know how. First you must remove any grout from around the edges of the tile, using an old kitchen knife, to clean all debris from around the edges. Then use a small iron chisel to break the tile from the centre outwards. Do not try to lever the tile from the edges, as this will only break the surrounding tiles, but chip out small pieces at a time.

When all the tile has been removed, clean off any adhesive remaining on the wall and make sure there are no bumps or high spots. If you don't get rid of these, the new tile will not bed in level with the existing tiles. Make sure the replacement tile fits into the opening, and if it is a fraction too large,

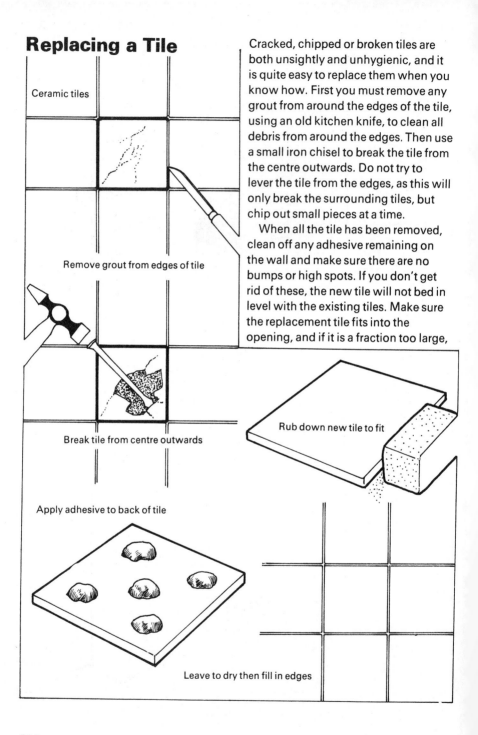

Ceramic tiles

Remove grout from edges of tile

Break tile from centre outwards

Rub down new tile to fit

Apply adhesive to back of tile

Leave to dry then fill in edges

rub down the edges on a piece of yorkstone or something similar. Once it fits, apply the correct adhesive to the back of the tile and push into position so that it is flush with the surrounding tiles. Leave it to dry for four to five hours, and once it is set fill in the edges with grouting powder mixed with water.

One problem when repairing tiles in this way is that the replacement may be a different shade from the others, so when you are putting up tiles in a kitchen or bathroom always keep a few spare for such emergencies, then if you have to replace a tile at any time you can be sure that the colour will be exactly the same.

A similar procedure is followed for replacing a lino tile which has worn badly. Once again, remember not to damage the edges of the surrounding floor tiles, and prise the tile up with an old kitchen knife. If the tile is difficult to lift then apply heat with a fan heater onto its surface. This will soften the adhesive enough to make its removal easier. Once all the pieces of tile are removed scrape the adhesive from the floor, making absolutely sure there are no high points as these will show through the new tile once it is laid. Trim the new tile to fit with a Stanley knife and spread onto the floor. Then press down the tile, working from one side towards the other so as not to trap any air. Remove any of the adhesive which has squeezed through and try not to walk on the tile until the adhesive has dried.

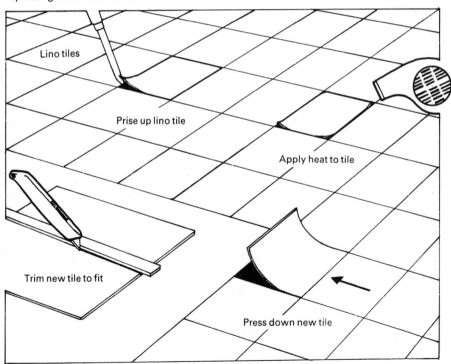

Lino tiles

Prise up lino tile

Apply heat to tile

Trim new tile to fit

Press down new tile

Floor Levelling

Wood Floors

If you are about to lay lino, cork or vinyl tiles onto a wood floor the surface must be even and level otherwise any defects will show through, such as warped floorboards, or nails that have risen above the boards due to wear. Therefore the floor should be levelled. Any protruding nails need to be punched below the surface, then the floorboards need to be sanded level using a large floor sander available on hire from most good hire shops. Only when the floor is absolutely level and flat should tiles be laid. Any wide joints between the floorboards should also be filled with papier mâché and sanded flat and dry. It is as well to remember when using a professional sander to sand across the boards at an angle of 45° to the grain (Fig 1) otherwise, if used at right angles to the boards, the sander will merely ride over the bumps.

An alternative method of levelling a wood floor is to lay sheets of hardboard and nail these to the floorboards.

Fig 1 Sand floor at 45° angle to grain of floorboards

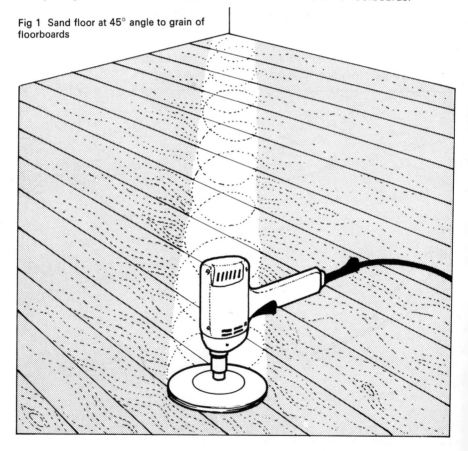

Stagger the joints (Fig 2) between the sheets and nail down. Starting from the centre of the sheet nail at 200mm (8in) intervals and 100mm (4in) intervals around the edges.

Cement or Tiled Floors

Cement or tiled floors are perhaps more difficult to level as you cannot nail hardboard to them; consequently different techniques have to be used. First you must inspect the floor for any sign of damp—if you lay tiles onto a damp floor the tiles will eventually lift. A simple check is to warm a piece of flat metal on a cooker or with a blowlamp. When warm, place the metal onto the floor and leave until it cools. If the floor is damp the piece of metal will have beads of moisture underneath it and there will be a damp patch on the floor. Use this method on several parts of the floor to ascertain the extent of damp area.

There are several ways to tackle this kind of damp; one of the most successful is to apply two coats of Synthaprufe. This should be applied also to the wall up to the damp course. When the Synthaprufe has dried apply a proprietary floor-levelling compound such as Arduit Z8 or F9. These compounds are self-levelling so very little trowel work is required. The Arduite F9 when mixed with the correct amount of water can be spread with a soft broom and left to level itself; as these materials harden they provide a very smooth and level surface. Non-porous floors, ie quarry tiles, that need to be levelled will require Ardex neoprene primer before applying the levelling compounds.

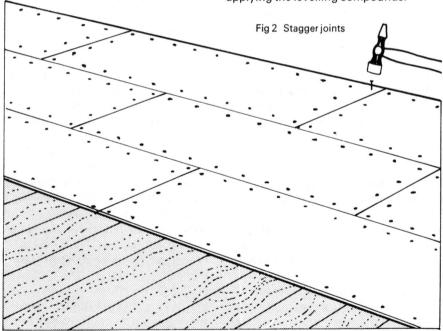

Fig 2 Stagger joints

Laying Floor Tiles

If you are about to lay floor tiles it is necessary to spend some time considering where to start. Against the longest wall seems the most obvious place to begin but do not be misguided. Buildings are very rarely square, so if you use this as a starting point invariably the tiles will run out of true line. Always stack the tiles loosely in a warm room for a day or so before you start work. This will make the tiles more supple and easier to work with.

So where do you start? First lay out some tiles on the floor; butt the edges together and mark each joint onto a rod, eg a piece of lath. This will act as a guide when setting out the floor. Using the rod as a guide, mark a line near the centre of the room. Allowance must be made for trimming the edge tiles. Check the other side of the room with the rod to make sure that you avoid having to cut a narrow strip of tile that is not only unsightly but difficult to fix. When the best starting position is found mark both ends of the room and join marks with a tape or chalk line. Do exactly the same for the other two walls. Where the two lines cross will be the starting points.

Some tiles are self-adhesive and need only the paper backs removed before sticking down. If your tiles need adhesive then spread about 1 sq m (about 1 sq yd) of adhesive at a time, being careful not to obscure the chalk lines. Place the first tile true to the chalk lines, then proceed to lay the other tiles, taking care not to squeeze any adhesive onto the face of the tiles.

Do not slide the tiles into place as this will squeeze the adhesive out of the joints. They need to be placed down so that the two edges butt up against the last tile. Roll down any edges that are not flat with a small wooden roller. Any adhesive on the face of the tile should be removed immediately, following the manufacturer's instructions as to what solvent should be used.

After sticking down the first square metre, apply the adhesive to the next area and so on until you are two tiles from the edge of the walls. It is better now to allow the area just laid time to dry as cutting in the tiles around the edge calls for working on the tiles so there is a chance that you may move them by working on the tiles whilst still wet. Also make sure that all excess adhesive is cleared from the finishing edge of the tiles otherwise, when you come to lay the last two tiles, you will be unable to press them level because of the hardened adhesive.

When the tiles have dried sufficiently to work on you can proceed to fill in the margin. This is done by butting one tile against the last centre one laid. Lay another tile on top, but this one should be butted against the skirting board. With a Stanley knife score the tile underneath, break the tile on this line and trim the edge clean. Place the cut tile and the full tile into position, remembering to put the cut edge to the skirting. The two tiles should now fit like a glove. Continue fitting the tiles into the margin in this manner. When cutting the tile to fit around a doorway the tile should finish half-way under the door when the door is closed.

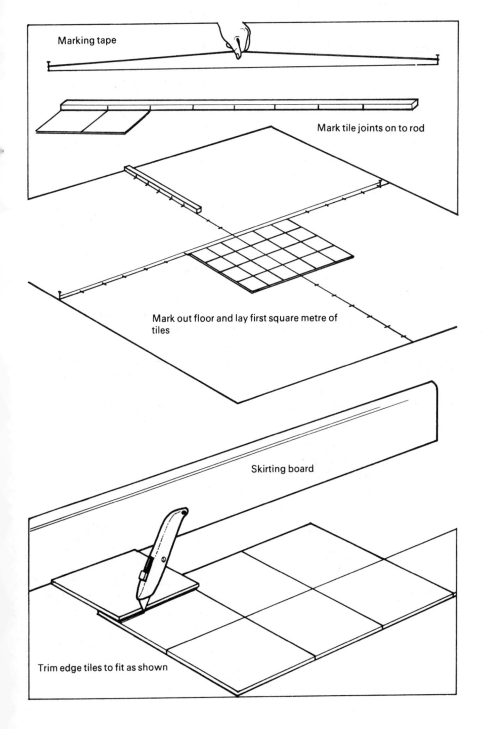

Marking tape

Mark tile joints on to rod

Mark out floor and lay first square metre of tiles

Skirting board

Trim edge tiles to fit as shown

Cement and Sand

Cement and sand are part of the heavy brigade in home maintenance ; nevertheless these materials will be needed for certain maintenance jobs in and around the home. There are several useful tips about using cement that will make life that much easier. First of all, let us look at the materials themselves.

Cement

This comes in 50kg (one hundred-weight) bags which are very heavy, so if you need only small amounts try to buy a split bag ; this may be messy but it is cheaper. Most builders' merchants have a split bag or a bin in which the cement is kept and sold in small lots. There are also several different types of cement—some for brickwork, some for concrete, fast-setting and of course coloured.

Sand

This also comes in different grades, soft for brickwork and plaster and rough for floors. This latter should always be used for floors as it gives strength to the cement so that the floor does not wear and cause the surface to dust up.

Mixing the cement and sand together is a job that must be done thoroughly. Turn the required mix over three times dry and three times wet to ensure they are completely mixed. Quantities of sand and cement vary according to what you are using them for. Three parts sand to one part cement is a good guide if mixing by hand, but if you are using a cement mixer four parts sand and one part cement will be just as strong since the cement mixer will blend the sand and cement quicker and more efficiently than by hand.

Water content is also important,

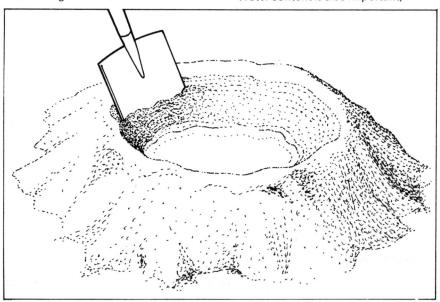

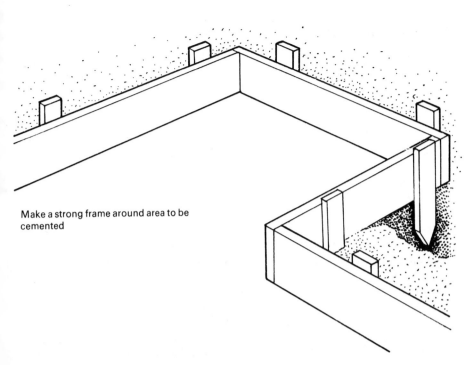

Make a strong frame around area to be cemented

since the mix needs to be of a good, thick, creamy consistency when you are laying bricks. One way of achieving this is to add washing-up liquid to a mix to make the sand and cement creamy and easier to work. A thimbleful for every gallon of water is adequate. If you are using sand and cement for a floor, the mix should be nearly dry. When you pick up a handful of the mix, it should just hold together if it is the right consistency. If the mix is too wet the cement will float to the top as you are trowelling the floor, and this will cause weak mix under the surface and the floor may eventually break up.

Cement and sand for small jobs around the house can be bought in pre-mixed bags containing the correct amount of sand and cement in grades for bricks, plaster, floors, etc.

Ready-mixed Concrete

Another source of supply for cement and sand is to buy ready-mixed concrete, which can be delivered to your home. The dealer will insist on a minimum delivery of cubic metres, so check this first with your local supplier whose address can be found in the yellow pages. Check also that the delivery lorry has access to your property. Ready-mixed concrete has a lot of advantages over mixing concrete by hand and you can be sure that the mixture is of the correct consistency. There is, as in all good things, one problem and that is that ready-mixed concrete sets in about one hour, depending on the weather, so do have at hand a willing band of helpers with shovels to help you spread it.

Pointing Brickwork

Repointing brickwork is almost certainly the most laborious job in house maintenance. Of course, not every house needs to be repointed, but it is very often necessary on older properties, and Building Societies, when they offer a mortgage, often stipulate that certain areas of the brickwork must be repointed. These are often the walls most exposed to extremes of weather, and the worst of all is frequently the chimney, probably the most exposed of all the brickwork. It is common to find the cement falling out of the brick joints here and if not attended to the chimney will eventually fall down. If your chimney does need repointing you will need some form of scaffolding to do the job safely. This can be hired, but you may feel that this job needs professionals, as not everyone likes venturing out onto a roof.

If the area to be repointed is fairly large then do hire a tower frame, as this will make working much easier and safer (Fig 1). Tools which you will need are shown in Fig 2. The first job is to rake out all the loose mortar, working on 1 square metre (approx 10 sq ft) at a time. Use an iron chisel and cut out the old mortar to a depth of 15mm ($\frac{1}{2}$in). Clean out the vertical joints first, then the horizontal ones, and use the head of a soft brush to remove any cement dust from the joints. When 1 sq m (approx 10 sq ft) has been finished, start the next but remember never to reach out too far from the scaffolding. When the whole wall has been cut out and brushed down, clean away all the old debris and place a board against the bottom of the wall. This will catch any cement droppings and thus avoid making any marks and stains on paving slabs or paths. When mixing the new mortar you should try to get the mixture as near as possible in texture to the old. This, of course, is difficult to tell precisely, so as a guide, mix one measure of lime, and one of cement to five of soft sand. Do not mix up too much at a time and don't forget to add a small squeeze of washing-up liquid.

The procedure for pointing is to fill the vertical joints first then the horizontal. There are several ways of filling the joints, and you will find which suits you best. You can either load the hawk and then scoop a small amount along the trowel and push it into the joints (Fig 3) or use a piece of hose-pipe, and do the same, rubbing well into the joints (Fig 4). Another method is to hold the hawk against the lower edge of the joint and push the mortar off it into the cracks (Fig 5).

After the mortar has set, rub the joints with a piece of bent round iron or a piece of hose-pipe so as to indent the mortar, and finally brush off any waste from the joints and brickwork with a soft broom. Before you start repointing a wall you should dampen it by flicking water onto the brickwork and joints with an old brush. This is to prevent the brickwork absorbing the moisture from the new mortar.

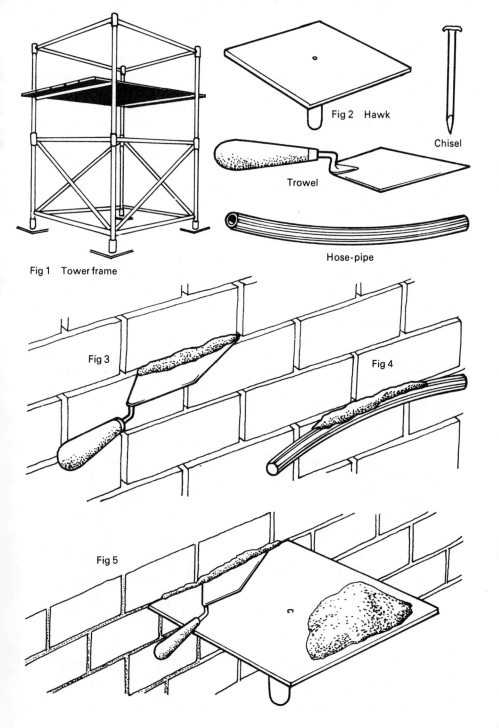

Fig 2   Hawk

Chisel

Trowel

Hose-pipe

Fig 1   Tower frame

Fig 3

Fig 4

Fig 5

323

Gutters

Dripping gutters are one of the big nuisances about the home. Have you noticed how they can wash away the earth from plants, and cause rust marks on paving slabs? To make any repairs to gutters or drain pipes you will obviously need a ladder. If you don't own one, they are inexpensive to hire. When working on a gutter you will find that a 'stand off' will be a great asset (Fig 1). This device will keep the ladder away from the gutter, making the work involved easier and much safer. It is also very simple to fit as it hooks over two of the rungs of the ladder and is held in place by a spring hook attached to the rung below.

Gutters made of iron will tend to rust over the years, especially where there is no paint, and often at the back where they are attached to the facia. Joints that are made with red lead tend to harden and allow water to seep through. To replace a section of worn guttering, undo the two nuts that hold the joints together. If they are rusted in cut them off with a small hacksaw. Then tap the joints apart with a hammer, taking care not to break the guttering. Lift the worn section out and lower it to the ground. The two remaining ends of the gutter should then be cleaned with a wire brush, and all moisture dried from them. The new piece of gutter should be painted at the back with Bitumastic paint to protect the area where, when the gutter is fixed, you are unable to paint. When joining the two ends it is sensible to use a waterproof sealant. Apply this to the overlapping ends of the two sections and bolt them together using 6 × 25mm ($\frac{1}{4}$ × 1in) bolts. As these are tightened up so the sealant makes a waterproof joint. Paint the inside of the gutter with Bitumastic paint, and the outside to match the existing paintwork.

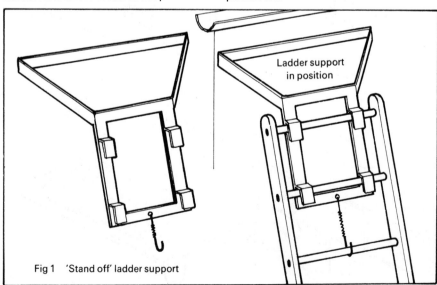

Ladder support in position

Fig 1   'Stand off' ladder support

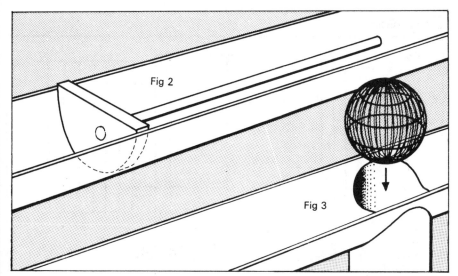

Fig 2

Fig 3

Down pipes usually suffer at the back because you cannot reach them with a paint brush. If they have rusted through they will also have to be renewed, so start at the top by removing the screws and lowering the whole pipe. Replacing it is just as easy since there are no joints to make. Simply place one end into the socket and fix it back to the wall, remembering to paint with Bitumastic in the inaccessible side. If trees overhang your house you will have to clear any leaves and debris from the gutters every year. A scraper (Fig 2) will make this job simpler and easier, but remember never to over-reach when standing on a ladder.

It is a good idea to place a galvanized wire balloon into the drainpipe outlet to stop the leaves blocking it (Fig 3). If you have a lot of guttering to be renewed, you would be well advised to think of replacing it with the plastic type since this needs no maintenance or painting, except for cleaning and the occasional wash with soapy water.

Ladders and Safety

Whether you own your own ladder or hire one the procedures to be followed for safety on ladders are the same. Too many people fall off ladders, so do take care. Never over-reach from a ladder— you should come down and move the ladder along. Always place the ladder on firm even ground and never wedge the ladder on bricks or similar objects. The safest method is to always have someone standing on the bottom to stop the ladder sliding.

Use good footwear on ladders— soft-soled shoes like plimsolls will make your feet tire very quickly, so wear a pair of hard-soled shoes. Also, tuck your trousers into your socks ; this will prevent you from treading on the bottom of your trousers as you climb or descend the ladder.

Never leave a ladder lying around ; always hang it away and padlock it safely, as a ladder is an ideal piece of equipment for any would-be burglar.

Fences

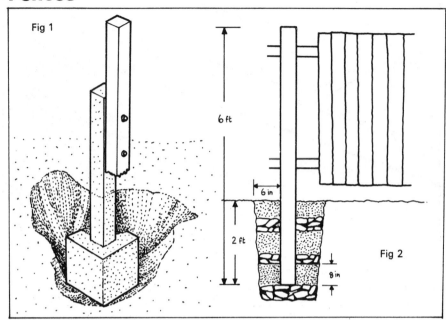

Fig 1

6 ft

6 in

2 ft

Fig 2

8 in

Fences seem always to be falling over and their slats or boards falling off. The main problem is usually that the wooden posts tend to rot through ; this need not happen if they have been treated correctly at the beginning, but this is often neglected.

If you do find that you need to replace rotten posts, the whole section of fence will have to be taken down in order to give access to them, so that stumps can be dug out. The best method for replacing the posts is to substitute the bottom half with a concrete spur (Fig 1) ; this should be driven into the ground and then either set into concrete or have the earth rammed in hard around it. The broken upper part of the wooden post can then be used by bolting it to the concrete spur, after first trimming off any rotten wood, and then dipping the

post in creosote. The fence is then rebuilt on the posts. The advantage of this method is that it will outlast any wooden post set into the ground.

If you are replacing with wood then place it in an old bath or some similar large receptacle and soak the bottom half of each post in creosote or any other wood preservative. You can buy timber already preserved at most good timber merchants.

After the posts have been soaked in preservative dig a hole : do not dig the hole too big. Allow 150mm (6in) on all sides of the post. A 2m (6ft) post should be sunk into the ground to a depth of 600mm (2ft). Drop in some small rubble and flatten this down firmly with a length of wood. Place the post into the hole and ram in 200mm (8in) of earth until the post is held firmly. Continue in this manner until the hole is filled, checking at each stage that the post is upright (Fig 2).

If the posts are to support a very heavy fence in an exposed position then you will be advised to use concrete instead of earth. Ram earth down the first 200mm (8in) of the post ; this will support the post in an upright position while you pour in the concrete. Always finish the concrete 100mm (4in) below the ground level so that earth may be filled in the top and do check that the post is upright before the concrete sets. If you are completely renewing your fencing, then it is always better to use concrete posts. I agree they are not so good to look at and easy to handle but their life is far longer than wood.

The cladding of fences can be made of many different sorts of wood, but one problem is that after several years the slats tend to come loose. It is a simple job to nail back the boards that have become loose, but you should make sure the bottoms do not touch the ground as this will draw up moisture from the earth and in time will rot the boards. If this has happened then you should cut the bottom off about 150mm (6in) above the ground and replace it with a gravel board (Fig 3). One way of getting a nice straight line to cut along, is to use a string covered with chalk (Fig 4). One final thing to remember about fences is to give them a coat of creosote every now and then to prevent decay.

Fig 3

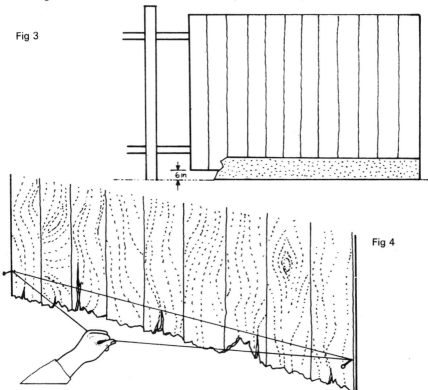

Fig 4